D0006137

E. F. Healey

June 1996

THE CATHOLIC CHURCH AT THE END OF AN AGE

WHAT IS THE SPIRIT SAYING?

RALPH MARTIN

THE CATHOLIC CHURCH AT THE END OF AN AGE

What Is the Spirit Saying?

IGNATIUS PRESS   SAN FRANCISCO

Cover by Roxanne Mei Lum

© 1994 Ignatius Press, San Francisco
All rights reserved
ISBN 0–89870–524–X
Library of Congress catalogue number 94–76954
Printed in the United States of America

"...and I, when I am lifted up from the earth, will draw all men to myself."

—John 12:32

CONTENTS

INTRODUCTION

We are passing through a difficult transition time. In both the world and the Church, old orders are crumbling and the outcome is neither clear nor assured. Indeed, it is uncertain if the "new world order" will even come to pass or, if it does, be an improvement on the old.

And the same with the Church. The new paths that Vatican Council II launched the Catholic Church on have proven to be much more difficult to travel than imagined, and the hoped-for destination is taking much longer to reach than anticipated. In fact, if the statistical measurements are considered, in some ways the destruction of the old is still much clearer than the birth of the new.

In the midst of this time of transition I believe the voice of the Spirit can be heard, clear and insistent, giving guidance to the Church and genuine hope to the world. The Spirit who spoke through Vatican II continues to speak, lead, guide, and encourage. We indeed have not been left orphans.

I certainly don't presume to know all of what the Spirit is saying, nor do I claim to hear or articulate perfectly that which I do hear. I depend on the discernment, input, and correction of others and know that God seldom shares all of his counsel with his creatures. But I do believe I am hearing something that is genuinely the voice of the Spirit and that I am not the only one hearing it. That is one of the reasons that I am writing.

I believe that many are receiving insight from the Lord: into his word and purposes, into our history as a Church, into our situation in the world today, and most especially insight into what he is leading us to today. Some are able to articulate what they are sensing and hearing, but many are not. As usual I am writing for the many who are hearing and sensing similar things but need someone to give voice to what the Spirit is putting into their hearts also.

The time is ripe, I believe, as we near the close of the twentieth century, indeed, of the second millennium "in the year of the Lord", and approach the possibility of the dawn of a new millennium, to gather together some of the voices through whom the Spirit is speaking and attempt to articulate what is being said.

For that reason I will be relying on citations from the writings of others, from the Scriptures and other documents, more than I have in most of my previous books. I am hearing and seeing something that is being spoken not just to me, and I want you to see and hear that too.

I believe that if we consider some of the facts of our situation as a Church and the growth of Christianity in the world today, both the good and the bad, and listen to a number of the voices that I believe God is raising up to give us insight and direction, we will indeed hear something important of what the Spirit is saying to the Church today. What could be more important than that?

I would like to ask for your patience in actually reading the citations from others and the Scripture passages and other documents cited. The argument of the book is not independent of them. They are not merely illustrations; they are an essential part of the argument. I believe some of the citations you will read are alone "worth the price of admission", so important are the insights they contain. One of the purposes of this book is to draw together "documentation" from many different sources that together provide striking testimony to what the Spirit is saying.

Also, while I write as a Catholic and primarily focus on what the Spirit might be saying to the Catholic Church, I believe that much of what I deal with will also be of real interest and relevance to brothers and sisters in other Christian bodies. We are truly "in this together".

May all of our hearts and minds be increasingly attentive to the whisperings of God so we may clearly hear the urgent things that the Spirit is saying to the Church at the end of one age and the beginning of another.

And do them.

Ralph Martin
Ann Arbor, Michigan

September 14, 1994
Triumph of the Cross

PART ONE

The Big Picture

Chapter One

An Incredible Century

As we draw to the end of the twentieth century and consider what we will face in the fast-approaching new century, it is worthwhile to reflect on what some of the main features of this century have been.

One very striking feature is the astounding advancement in human knowledge and technology. Many of us have witnessed the advent of television, powerful telecommunications technologies, space exploration, jet travel, stealth airplanes, nuclear power, ever more powerful computers, the discovery of antibiotics and powerful disease fighters, microsurgery techniques, organ transplantation, and numerous other advances in many different fields of knowledge. There has been a veritable accelerating explosion of knowledge and technology. It has become commonplace to hear that the overwhelming majority of human knowledge from the beginning of time has been amassed in this century.

Father Marie-Dominique Philippe, O.P., founder of a new religious order in France, which now has a branch in Laredo, Texas, thinks that this very acceleration is itself one of the signs of the times that we need to see as significant. "We are heading towards the end of time. Now the more we approach the end of time, the more quickly we proceed—this is what's extraordinary. There is, as it were, a very significant acceleration in time; there's an acceleration in time just as there's an acceleration in speed. And we go faster and faster. We must be very attentive to this to understand what is happening in today's world."[1]

The benefits of all this knowledge have been many. Most of us depend on and make use of many of these developments almost daily. There would not be many votes for doing away with indoor plumbing, central heating in cold climates, air conditioning in warm climates, modern medicines, or communication possibilities. However, more than a few of us feel uneasy that a price is being paid as an international, homogenized, often pagan culture is increasingly dominating the "global village". Brand names of international conglomerates; pop stars in music, sport, and film; the quest for Western affluence and often along with it the absence of Western moral values increasingly dominate the worldwide television culture.

This century has also seen some significant social and political advances accompany the technological developments. A growing respect for the dignity of every man has surfaced that has expressed itself in a greater understanding of the evil of racism and unjust discrimination. A concern for the rights of minorities, of workers, of women and children, and of the handicapped is increasingly being expressed. A rudimentary international cooperation has developed in this century, expressed in the United Nations, the World Court, and other international institutions that attempt to provide an alternative to settling disputes through war. While all of these nontechnological advances are fragile, imperfectly realized, and often the scene of ideological conflict, they nevertheless qualify in most people's eyes as genuine advances.

In fact, John Paul II sees some of these very advances in the social, technical, and political spheres as divinely directed developments to prepare for the preaching of the gospel: "In fact, both in the non-Christian world and in the traditionally Christian world, people are gradually drawing closer to gospel ideals and values, a development which the Church seeks to encourage. Today in fact there is a new consensus among peoples about these values: the

---

[1] Fr. Marie-Dominique Philippe, O.P., *Follow the Lamb* . . . (Laredo, Tex.: Congregation of St. John, 1991), p. 210.

rejection of violence and war; respect for the human person and for human rights; the desire for freedom, justice and brotherhood; the surmounting of different forms of racism and nationalism; the affirmation of the dignity and role of women."[2] It is also quite remarkable to recognize the striking move away from a totally materialistic and mechanistic view of the universe taking place in modern science. More and more our picture of the universe and its origins, of man and his nature, derived from modern science is looking consonant with the view of the universe and man revealed to us by God.

The distinguished scientist Sir John Eccles puts it like this:

> However, now in the 20th century the revolution in physics and cosmology has transformed the story because in quantum physics the conscious observer has become essential as a participator in the scientific measurements; and the origin of the universe in a unique cosmic explosion, the Big Bang, about 12 thousand million years ago alters the concepts of space and time and ushers in the wonderful story of contingencies that leads from our solar system to planet Earth, to the origin of life, to biological evolution and so to human persons. From being an insignificant creature on a modest planet circling around an ordinary star in an immense galaxy of 100 thousand million other stars, man has now become exalted as a participator in a great cosmic drama, there being even the concept of the Anthropic Principle, that the whole cosmic happening from the Big Bang onwards was designed in order that conscious observers could exist at some place and time in the expanding Universe . . . in which mind and mental events have a status matching that of the material world.[3]

Amazing studies in physics and astronomy have determined that the universe is expanding at precisely the right rate for there to be human life, as if it were designed for human life to be possible: "The properties of matter, then, on the smallest scale and

---

[2] John Paul II, Encyclical *Redemptoris Missio* (*Mission of the Redeemer*), 86.

[3] Robert M. Augros and George N. Stanciu, *The New Story of Science: Mind and the Universe* (Chicago: Gateway Editions, 1985), p. vi.

on the scale of the whole universe appear uniquely suited to life. Not only are there many instances but in each case a slight increase or decrease in the parameter would render life impossible. . . . The more I examine the universe and study the details of its architecture, the more evidence I find that the universe in some sense must have known we were coming . . . the origin of the universe, the structure of the universe, and the beauty of the universe, all lead to the same conclusion—God is."[4]

But there has been a very dark side to this century that perhaps casts the dominant shadow. A succession of devastating wars shows no signs of letting up. By one measure, up until World War I there had been about nine hundred major wars in the history of civilization. In World War I more than seven times as many people were killed as in all previous wars combined.[5] And this most bloody of centuries was just beginning and was to expand to include literally hundreds of wars and atrocities, both large and small. World War I gave way to World War II, and then it was Korea and Vietnam, Cambodia and Afghanistan, Ethiopia and Angola, Lebanon and Iraq, Kurdistan and Armenia, Nicaragua and El Salvador, Burundi, Bosnia, Angola and Rwanda, and the list goes on. According to Zbigniew Brzezinski, national security advisor in the Carter administration, about eighty-seven million people have died in this century in wars alone.[6]

The initial euphoria that followed the collapse of the Soviet Union has now given way to the horror of "ethnic cleansing" unfolding in its wake. Systematic ethnic hatred, violence, and rape continue to erupt in many places throughout the world and bring in their wake another avalanche of human suffering and inhumanity. Added to the tens of millions who have already been killed, maimed, psychologically scarred, displaced, uprooted, orphaned, and widowed in this century's wars, the toll in human death and

---

[4] Ibid., pp. 65–69, 82. See also, idem, *The New Biology: Discovering the Wisdom in Nature* (Boston: New Science Library, 1988).

[5] Christopher Potter, "Poets' Friendship Portrayed", *Ann Arbor News*, March 21, 1993, p. E5.

[6] Jakub J. Grygiel, "Faith as a Political Strategy", *Catholic World Report*, August–September 1993, p. 54.

destruction is very great indeed. "For nation [*ethnos*] will rise against nation [*ethnos*], and kingdom against kingdom, and there will be famines and earthquakes in various places: all this is but the beginning of the sufferings. . . . Immediately after the tribulations of those days the sun will be darkened, and the moon will not give its light, and the stars will fall from heaven, and the powers of the heavens will be shaken" (Mt 24:7–8, 29).

Twice in this century messianic political movements arose that in attempting to create a social and political paradise on earth enslaved, coerced, and murdered millions in an effort to implement their plans.

Out of the ruins of czarist Russia arose Soviet communism, whose attempts to build a kingdom of justice and peace on earth and forge a new Soviet man left dead in its wake perhaps sixty million as well as hundreds of millions who have suffered the death or the deformation of their personalities and character.

In the heart of "enlightened" Europe nazism arose and with its compelling "spiritual" force mesmerized millions of supporters, including some of the "best and the brightest" in the universities and medical profession, who provided the rationalization for the "ethnic cleansing" of the Jews and the devastation of World War II. Many in the churches actively supported the Nazis or silently ignored the injustice and atrocities.

During this period, many Christians within the dominant Protestant churches in Germany had adopted Hitler's National Socialism as part of their creed. Known as "German Christians", their spokesman, Herman Gruner, made it clear what they stood for:

"The time is fulfilled for the German people in Hitler. It is because of Hitler that Christ, God the helper and redeemer, has become effective among us. Therefore National Socialism is positive Christianity in action. . . . Hitler is the way of the Spirit and the will of God for the German people to enter the Church of Christ."

By September 1933, the conflict was out in the open. In the "Brown Synod" that month (so called because many of the clergy wore brown Nazi uniforms and gave the Nazi salute), the church adopted the "Aryan Clause", which denied the pulpit to ordained ministers of Jewish blood.[7]

Nearer to our own time I have read many similar statements by both Catholic and Protestant clergymen in relationship to the Sandinista revolution in Nicaragua, equating the revolution with the coming of the kingdom of God. The temptation we have to identify the kingdom of God with political and social ideology is strong indeed.

As we near the end of this technologically advanced century, we are facing also a worldwide environmental problem. As decades of economic pursuits without regard for environmental consequences are tallied up, we see vast numbers of the world's lakes and streams seriously damaged by industrial pollution so that fish from them are not safe to eat. In my own state of Michigan all eleven thousand inland waterways are so polluted with mercury that no larger fish can be safely eaten from them. The devastation of many of the lakes and rivers of the former Soviet Union is even worse.

As great as the environmental pollution is, the moral pollution of the most privileged Western nations is greater still. One foundation in the United States, commenting on the results of their two-year study, claims that "a hole in the moral ozone" has opened up in the lives of a whole generation of American youth.[8] In Britain 30 percent of all children born are now illegitimate, and the numbers are still rising. Rising rates of crime and drug abuse are noticeable in every European country.[9] In the United States more than one in five Americans, or fifty-six million people, are infected with a sexually transmitted viral disease, infections that can be controlled but not cured. These numbers are expected to grow.[10]

[7] Geoffrey B. Kelly, "The Life and Death of a Modern Martyr", *Christian History* 10, no. 4:11.

[8] Garry Abrams, "Study Finds Weak Ethics in Young", *Ann Arbor News*, November 12, 1992, p. A15.

[9] Joanna Bogle, "Europe's Social Problems Growing as Year 2000 Approaches", *Wanderer*, April 22, 1993, p. 3.

[10] Felicity Barringer, "Report Finds One in Five Infected by Viruses Spread Sexually", *New York Times*, April 1, 1993, p. 1.

Doctors from the United States, Western Europe, Asia, and Latin America are also reporting that they are treating far more children below the age of fourteen for sexually transmitted diseases than they did ten years ago. In part this is because children are being pressed into prostitution for "special clients" as the fear of sexually transmitted diseases increases.[11] In some countries of Africa one-quarter to one-third of all adults in urban areas are believed to be infected with the AIDS virus. In Uganda life expectancy in twenty-five years will be thirty-two years—down from fifty-nine years before AIDS was discovered. In sixteen countries—thirteen African nations plus Brazil, Haiti, and Thailand—AIDS will slow population growth rates so dramatically that there will be 121 million fewer people than previously forecast.

In Asia the AIDS virus is now also rapidly spreading: "AIDS came relatively late to most of Asia, but it is now spreading so rapidly—and so randomly—that scientists are convinced that AIDS will kill more people on this continent than on any other.... Conservative estimates suggest that by the end of the decade, the AIDS virus will infect more than one million Asians each year, more than in the rest of the world combined.... AIDS has begun to reach even the most remote corners of Asia. It can now be found in tiny Nepalese villages nestled in the Himalayas, just as it is found in the gaudy neon-lit brothels of Bangkok and Seoul."[12]

Add to this the growing number of divorces, abortions, and the increase of crimes of all sorts, and the human wreckage of this century becomes unbelievable.

Each year in the United States alone, approximately 1,600,000 abortions are performed. No more than 1 percent involve cases of rape or incest. No more than 7 percent even *claim* to be done in response to threats to the mother's psychological or physical health. That leaves 92 percent of the abortions—1,472,000—performed

[11] Marlise Simons, "The Sex Market: Scourge on the World's Children", *New York Times,* April 9, 1993, p. A3.

[12] "AIDS Finally Arrives in Asia, But It Strikes with a Vengeance", *Ann Arbor News,* November 8, 1992, p. A7.

for social, economic, or personal reasons. Three out of four women having an abortion say a child would interfere with work, school, or other responsibilities.[13] The United States surpasses all other Western nations in the number of abortions per thousand women of childbearing age.[14] Forty-five percent of minors who obtain an abortion do so without parental knowledge.[15] Virtually one-fourth of all pregnancies end in induced abortions.[16]

The number of abortions that have been performed in the United States since 1973, the year the Supreme Court legalized abortion in all fifty states, is now more than thirty million,[17] more than twenty times the combined number of Americans who died in the Civil War, both world wars, and the Vietnam War.

The disregard for human life manifest in abortion is spilling over into other areas as well:

> Violence is raging like a virus through American culture. . . . More than 3,000 studies over the past 30 years offer evidence that violent programming does have a measurable effect on young minds. Some studies suggest that a steady diet of violent entertainment, whether it's fist-flying cartoon heroes, a tabloid TV show's grisly profile of a serial killer, or the brutal eroticism of music videos, leads vulnerable minds to view the world as a dangerous place, where the only way to survive is to be on the attack. . . . A single day's viewing of 18 hours worth of cable and network programming in 1992 contained 1,846 violent acts, from serious assaults, gunfire, and brandished weapons to punches and slaps, according to the Washington-based Center for Media and Public Affairs. . . . The typical American child spends 27 hours a week watching the tube. . . . In a landmark, 22 year study, University of Michigan psychologist Leonard Eron . . . [concluded] that those who consistently viewed violent fare were more likely as adults to be aggressive when drunk, to use

---

[13] Rachel Benson Gold, *Abortion and Women's Health* (New York and Washington, D.C.: Alan Guttmacher Institute, 1990), pp. 11, 19, 20.

[14] Christopher Tietze and Stanley K. Henshaw, *Induced Abortion: A World Review*, 6th ed. (New York: Alan Guttmacher Institute, 1986).

[15] Alan Guttmacher Institute, *Facts in Brief* (1989).

[16] Gold, p. 11, reports a total of 6,355,000 pregnancies and 1,600,000 abortions.

[17] Alan Guttmacher Institute, *Facts in Brief* (1989).

violence against family members, and, in some cases, to be convicted of violent crimes.[18]

Similar studies have been done on the proliferation of explicit sex on television and in the movies, and a regular analysis of the plots and characters on prime-time television, provided regularly by the *Journal of the American Family Association,* is truly amazing.[19]

Even secular critics are beginning to perceive that the direction in which we are rapidly going is truly appalling. A review in our local newspaper of a popular Fox network program, *Martin,* about a man named Martin and his girlfriend, Gina, brings this out clearly:

> When Gina wore a body hugging open-backed dress to a party, Martin's biological urges soared to 10 on the Richter Scale. Bumping, grinding and pawing, he was all over her in public— his body pumping like a piston, his tongue thrusting lewdly— acting generally like an animal: "I'm telling you, baby, I got's to have it!"
>
> Driven totally by his sexual hunger to the point of panic, he was absolutely relentless: "Baby, baby", he gasped at one point, "we'll only be gone five minutes. They won't even notice."
>
> Finally after Gina gave in, they ditched the party and had their "quickie". Afterward, when Martin was challenged by Gina and a friend to distinguish between love and sex and was unable to do it, he agreed to a test. To prove that love was more important to him, he and Gina would "go without sex for two weeks".
>
> *Two weeks?* Was it humanly possible? It was time for further lowjinks.
>
> After a commercial break, cut to an overhead shot of Martin and Gina lying side by side in bed a week later, creeping out of their skins while attempting to ignore their imploding sexual frustrations. When Gina discovered Martin was wearing an ice pack on his groin, he insisted that he'd "pulled a thigh muscle"

---

[18] Joan Connell, "TV = Televised Violence?" *Ann Arbor News,* June 20, 1993, p. 1.

[19] Subscriptions to this publication are available by writing to AFA Journal, P.O. Drawer 2440, Tupelo, MS 38803.

and limped from the room . . . they were unable to hold out for the two weeks.[20]

The program in question was cleared by Fox's standards and practices department for airing at eight o'clock on Sunday evening, making it available for young kids to watch during prime family viewing time.

At the root of these distressing developments is the rejection of God and absolute truths and values that has become increasingly characteristic of our culture. According to one 1991 poll, 67 percent of American people believe there is no such thing as absolute truth,[21] and this view is still being actively promulgated in virtually every major university. The distinguished historian and friend of presidents Arthur Schlesinger expressed what many in academia and centers of culture and entertainment also think: "It is this belief in absolutes . . . that is the great enemy today of the life of the mind. The mystic prophets of the absolute cannot save us. Sustained by our history and traditions, we must save ourselves at whatever risk of heresy or blasphemy."[22]

Recently a theologian from a mainstream Protestant seminary expressed some "second thoughts" on the choices we have made in our culture: "I've come to a new appreciation of the wisdom and mercy embodied in the divine instruction given us in the Scriptures. . . . Disregard of God's laws has resulted in a drug war that we are not winning, in burgeoning crime that has made city neighborhoods uninhabitable, in teenage pregnancies and 'children having children', in rampant abortions, swelling welfare rolls, sexually transmitted diseases, self-indulgent neglect of community good, and countless ruined lives. We chose our own way and . . . brought on ourselves the way of death."[23]

---

[20] Howard Rosenberg, "Martin Plays into Ugliest Stereotypes", *Los Angeles Times,* syndicated in *Ann Arbor News,* December 16, 1993, p. D10.

[21] Cited in Charles Colson, *The Body* (Dallas: Word Publishing, 1992), p. 171.

[22] Ibid., pp. 170–171.

[23] Elizabeth Achtemaier, cited in *Fellowship of Catholic Scholars Newsletter,* June 1992, p. 30.

The economic cost of all this, a burden all of us bear, is staggering. The turning away from God is costing all of us immense pain, not to mention billions and billions of dollars. Even secular observers of the current situation are beginning to point this out: "An associate professor of medicine said medical costs are out of control because morality is out of control. Franklin Payne of the family medicine department in the Medical College of Georgia said, 'Health without morality is impossible. An effective approach to medicine without morality is impossible.' As an example, he said that without a transformation of public health policy in the United States, the spread of diseases such as AIDS was inevitable."[24]

The situation of the Christian churches and movements in this century has, as usual, been mixed. They have experienced devastating setbacks, as well as some wonderful advances.

For the first time in world history an organized atheistic movement arose that succeeded in dominating the lives of almost two billion people while eliminating most visible signs of the Church, her institutions, and her activities. The campaign to eliminate God from the consciousness of humanity was unrelenting for more than seventy years and still holds sway over more than a billion Chinese. While the campaign was not universally successful, it did manage to eliminate the open proclamation of the gospel and the teaching of the Faith in such a way that hundreds of millions have grown up without faith in or knowledge of Christ. Many Christians were killed, imprisoned, tortured, persecuted, discriminated against, and marginalized because of their faithfulness to Jesus.

Almost paradoxically, in the Christian West (North America, South America, Australia, New Zealand, and Europe), where the Church had full freedom and substantial societal respect and even government support, there has been a massive turning away from the Church and from Christ. The mainline Protestant denominations led the way in allowing a sceptical scholarly treatment of the Scripture to erode the faith and confidence of many millions in the truthfulness and reliability of God's word, with a subsequent

---

[24] "Morality Out of Control", *Ann Arbor News,* December 25, 1993, p. E4.

decline in church attendance, financial giving, and adherence to traditional Christian belief and morality.

Some of the same internal confusion and scepticism has also greatly affected the Catholic Church in recent decades. In the early 1980s I wrote a book analyzing how widespread and destructive this undermining of faith, morality, and mission was within the Catholic Church.[25] While some significant positive advances have happened since the early 1980s, there is still a very substantial "crisis of truth" plaguing many Catholic institutions, and the tragic stories of how Catholic students studying at Catholic institutions have their faith and morality undermined in the classroom continue to abound.

Just recently the Detroit-area Jesuit University hit the news as the head of the religious studies department declared that Mary was not a virgin before she married Joseph, that she may have been raped, and that Jesus was "illegitimate". She admits she is a threat to the Christian Tradition with her radical feminist ideology and, when challenged, says, "If they tried to get rid of me, they know I'd sue them." Officials of the university were incredibly wishy-washy in their response.[26]

A recent graduate of another Catholic university summed up his experience like this: "Virtually all of my professors had assaulted whatever fragile sense of objective truth and absolute morality I had gleaned from 12 years of religious education. Yet they were adamantly asserting that no one could ever adamantly assert anything, particularly if the assertion was being made by someone with magisterial authority and the guidance of the Holy Spirit. We were being commanded to exchange the treasured 2,000 year old tradition of Catholic moral teaching for a twenty-year-old trail of conflicting opinions from men and women who had, by and large, lost their faith in Christ and His Church. Yet these were the people to whom I and thousands of my peers, the

[25] An analysis of this problem is contained in my previous book, *A Crisis of Truth: The Attack on Faith, Morality, and Mission in the Catholic Church* (Ann Arbor, Mich.: Servant, 1982).

[26] David Crum, "Bible Scholar Seeks to Uproot Tradition on Women", *Detroit Free Press,* February 14, 1993, p. 1F.

future leaders of the Catholic church in this country, were being entrusted."[27]

The Bishop of South Bend–Fort Wayne, Indiana, recently had to correct publicly the seriously faulty theology of a pamphlet distributed at the dedication of the renovated chapel at St. Mary's College in South Bend: *"What is obviously missing?* There is no mention in this presentation of those words which are at the center of our teaching on the Holy Eucharist. God is never mentioned, nor is there any mention of sacrifice, redemption, sin, mystery, salvation, Paschal Mystery, death and resurrection. The words memorial, Body and Blood of Christ, grace and sin, Holy Spirit, are never used. The word Jesus Christ is used once, but in an incorrect manner."[28]

One American priest who has worked for many years in the Vatican and now holds a responsible position at an American seminary gave a very frank assessment of the situation of many Catholic universities today: "The vast majority of them are just fake Catholic universities. They're not really Catholic universities. I know they were bought by lemonade sales and cake sales run by selfless nuns and priests in the past. But since the 1960's and 1970's they were sold off, and billions and billions of dollars of Church property was alienated. I'm sure for public relations purposes most bishops would say, 'Sure, they are Catholic universities', but of course that's all bull, because they don't want to get beat up in public."

When asked why the bishops are not doing anything, he responded: "I think both the Holy See and many right-thinking bishops are scratching their heads and wondering what realistically can be done. I think that they're overly distracted by other huge problems in their local churches: lecher priests; financial stuff; wacko nuns; personnel problems. You fight the problems you have with the soldiers you've got . . . the problems are truly intractable, and I don't know what to do about them, and if you

[27] Michael J. Mazza, "Learning the Hard Way: A Catechist's Education", *Fidelity,* September 1993, p. 27.

[28] Bishop John M. D'Arcy, "The Eucharist: A Response", *Fellowship of Catholic Scholars Newsletter* 16, no. 4 (September 1993): 32–38.

made me the bishop of South Bend tomorrow, I couldn't promise you we'd have a resolution in two days. I think there are a lot of good bishops out there who simply don't know what to do. And I don't blame them because I don't know what to do either."[29]

Another development in the decade since I've written *A Crisis of Truth* is the widespread proliferation of pantheistic New Age spirituality through many Catholic institutions. A number of bishops have written pastoral letters on the subject, and the Pope himself has spoken about it publicly in his meetings with American bishops. Usually, by the time something gets to this point, it is widespread indeed! "Many of you have written Pastoral Letters on the problems presented by pseudo-religious movements and sects, including the so-called 'New Age Movement'. New Age ideas sometimes find their way into preaching, catechesis, workshops and retreats, and thus influence even practicing Catholics, who perhaps are unaware of the incompatibility of those ideas with the Church's faith ... overturning the true concept of sin and the need for redemption through Christ."[30]

This is a typically diplomatic way of saying we have huge problems with the infiltration of New Age spirituality into the Catholic Church.

Cardinal Ratzinger speaks of the Church today facing a time of judgment: "The truth is that the faith, today more than ever, faces a time of judgment, and that even within the Church herself there are painful divisions, as the Lord predicted."[31]

This is reminiscent of the words of Pope Paul VI to Jean Guitton in 1977: "There is great distress at this time in the world for the Church and the thing being questioned is the faith.

---

[29] Msgr. Thomas Herron, cited in E. Michael Jones, "Odium Theologicum: Slouching toward Secularism with Their Pants around Their Ankles", *Fidelity*, November 1992, pp. 31–32.

[30] Pope John Paul II, "Be Courageous Shepherds Who Preach Whole Mystery of Christ", *L'Osservatore Romano* (English ed.), June 2, 1993, p. 3.

[31] Cardinal Joseph Ratzinger, "The Realization of Vatican II", *Catholic World Report*, October 1993, p. 56.

I find myself repeating that obscure phrase of Jesus' in the Gospel of St. Luke: 'When the Son of man comes, will he still find the faith on earth?' "[32]

While perhaps at a peak of institutional strength in the mid to late 1960s, the years since have seen a steady and substantial decline in church attendance; number of active priests, nuns, and seminarians; and number of Catholic schools and hospitals.

While internal weakness and confusion about the fundamentals of the Faith have substantially contributed to the decline of both mainline Protestant and Catholic institutions and continue to do so, there have also been radical shifts in the culture as a whole that have greatly impacted the churches. Starting perhaps in the mid to late 1960s, there has been a progressive secularization of the cultures of most of the traditionally Christian countries. It is certainly not coincidental that this process of secularization occurred during what may have been the peak of prosperity and affluence for these countries. While not a necessary result, relative affluence often has a spiritually deadening effect.

As Father Benedict Groeschel, one of the founding friars of the new Franciscans of the Renewal, has said:

> Unfortunately, when Christianity becomes too comfortable, when it gets bedded down in a kind of pious materialism, when it forgets the powerful confrontation that one finds when Jesus preaches the Good News, it loses its sense of ongoing repentance. Devout Christians may, at such a time, occupy themselves neurotically with picking out their little faults while the rest of Christianity, unmoved by the thought of repentance, blissfully accepts that everyone is saved, that we are all going to heaven in a toboggan and that there is no possibility of eternal loss. At such times, one can expect a severe decline in religious life and other institutions of the Church. Christianity is based on repentance and on the awareness that we must struggle to take hold of the kingdom of God in our daily lives. When Christianity does not do this, it begins to become anemic and may even die away

[32] Cited in: Joseph Ratzinger, "The Anguish of an Absence", 30 *Days*, no. 3 (1994): 37.

in some parts of Christendom. This has happened many times in the history of the Church. Is it happening now?"[33]

But while the internal problems of the churches and the spiritually deadening effects of the relative prosperity of recent decades have been important factors, there is also another. Organized pressure groups or "change agents" have explicitly and consciously worked to displace the Christian worldview and value system as the dominant moral force and influence in our societies. Holding views very much at variance with the population as a whole, they have worked to implement their agenda through their dominant positions within the media and communications and entertainment industries and through the courts. Various studies have shown how the beliefs of a small minority in key positions in the media, very much at variance with the population as a whole, have dominated the entertainment and information that we often receive.

But whatever the exact constellation of causes, the fact is that something like a massive falling away from Christian faith and morality has occurred in most of the traditionally Christian countries in the course of this century and in an accelerating manner in the past thirty years. As we shall see when we examine all this in greater detail in subsequent chapters, the scope of this falling away has been so great that the biblical description of the great apostasy comes to mind.

All this is not to say that there have not been wonderful bright spots for the Church in this century. The missionary work of both Protestant and Catholic missionaries, particularly in the first half of this century, was widespread and effective. The achievement of the Catholic school system, particularly in North America, up until recently was extraordinary. The heroic witness and faithfulness of many through persecution and even martyrdom, even to this day, is extraordinary. The efforts of the Catholic Church in the Second Vatican Council to renew herself through a return to her roots in the Bible and in the early centuries of the Church, to

[33] Fr. Benedict J. Groeschel, C.F.R., *The Reform of Renewal* (San Francisco: Ignatius Press, 1990), p. 45.

reengage effectively with the modern world, and to turn a hand of friendship to the other Christian churches in the ecumenical movement are efforts that will eventually have a fuller fruitfulness than has yet been seen. Another real bright spot has been the rapid growth of the worldwide Pentecostal movement, born on the very first day of the twentieth century and at the moment the most rapidly growing element of worldwide Christianity. We will look at this development more in depth and attempt to discern what the Spirit might be saying through this in a later chapter.

Before such a vast panorama as the twentieth century, are there any spiritual insights or clues that can help us to understand the big picture of what has been happening in a way that would cast light on the path that the Church as a body and we ourselves as individuals should set out on as we approach the end of this century and the beginning of the next? I believe there are.

One of these is accounts of the vision that Pope Leo XIII is reported to have had shortly before the beginning of this century. The story has come down to us through various confidants of the Pope, primarily cardinals who were close to him.[34] While differing in exact details, the main lines are clear. While concluding a liturgical celebration in the last part of the nineteenth century in the Vatican, Leo XIII suddenly stopped and looked transfixed. He later recounted to his close collaborators what he had experienced. He had been allowed by the Lord to overhear a conversation between Satan and the Lord. The conversation was reminiscent of the conversation that Satan and the Lord had regarding the testing of Job in the Book of Job. Satan declared that if he had enough time and enough power he would be able to destroy the Church. God gave permission to Satan to take the bulk of the twentieth century as a time in which he would be allowed specially to test and tempt the Church, but after that his power would be limited again. It was as a result of this vision that Leo XIII asked that a

[34] Stefano M. Paci, "Leo XIII's Diabolical Vision", 30 Days (December 1990): 52–53. See also John J. Nicola, Diabolical Possession and Exorcism (Rockford, Ill.: Tan Books, 1974), p. 151.

special prayer to St. Michael the Archangel be said after every Mass throughout the world. This was done until about the time of the Second Vatican Council. It was also Leo XIII who asked that prayer for an outpouring of the Holy Spirit upon the Church be prayed throughout the world on the first day of the twentieth century. On this very day, in Topeka, Kansas, the Pentecostal movement was born among a group of Protestants studying the Acts of the Apostles together in a farmhouse.

Another spiritual event that sheds considerable light on the history of the twentieth century is the apparitions of Mary in Fatima, Portugal, in 1917. At that time, as World War I was still raging, the Bolshevik revolution in Russia had not yet consolidated itself; there was considerable civil war and the possibility of outside intervention. Mary prophesied in her apparitions to the children that unless there was a widespread repentance in the world and a return to the Lord, there would be another and greater world war, and Russia would spread its errors throughout the world, but in the end Russia would be converted.

Have we seen in the sudden and unexpected collapse of communism the beginnings of the fulfillment of Mary's prophetic words? Have we seen in the fall of communism and the tremendous upsurge in the preaching of the gospel in the former Soviet empire the beginnings of the end of the unusual satanic hold that has gripped the world for so many years? Are we seeing in the purification and humbling of the Church that is going on, as sin is exposed and weakness is made apparent, the preparation for a new outpouring of the Holy Spirit that will equip a humbled, purified Church to proclaim the gospel in power? Are we seeing in the extreme consequences of rebellion against God, manifesting themselves throughout the world, God's merciful judgments, which are preparing the world to listen with new ears to the good news of Jesus Christ? Are we seeing in the initial reports of hundreds of thousands turning to Christ in the former Soviet empire and in the underground Church of China, or in the evangelical, Pentecostal upsurge in Latin America and Africa, signs of a new age of evangelization that both Protestant and Catholic leaders have proclaimed and prophesied? If we are, and I think this is likely the case, what can we as churches and individuals do to cooperate with what God is doing in this significant turning point, as we approach the end of this incredible century—but, more than that, the end of an age—and look to the dawn of the next?

Before we consider an answer to this question, let us first review in some detail the situation in which the Catholic Church finds herself today.

Chapter Two

The Situation of
the Catholic Church Today

Let us take a look now at some significant aspects of the situation of the Catholic Church in various parts of the world.

North America

In the years following the Second Vatican Council there has been a substantial weakening of faith, morality, and mission among North American Catholics. The sharply rising percentage of Catholics who have been divorced or legally separated is particularly striking. In roughly a ten-year period, from the early 1970s to the early 1980s, the proportion has risen from one in every seven Catholics ever married to one in every four. While the percentage of those ever married who have been divorced and separated in the general population rose by 50 percent in this period, the percentage of divorced and separated among Catholics rose by 90 percent. As a result, the percentage of the divorced and separated among Catholics ever married is higher today than was the percentage of the divorced and separated in U.S. society as a whole a decade previously.[1]

According to a poll taken for *Time* magazine in 1987, only 54 percent of Catholics in the United States attend Mass weekly,

[1] Joseph E. Davis and Kevin Perrotta, "Finally, Figures on Divorce among Christians", *Pastoral Renewal,* April 1984, pp. 120–22.

down from 75 percent in the 1960s; in larger archdioceses the attendance figure is even lower, for example, 25 percent in Chicago. More recent studies indicate that perhaps only 28 percent of Catholics attend Mass on any given Sunday.[2] In 1963 only 18 percent of U.S. Catholics disagreed with the Church's teaching on contraception. In 1987 70 percent disagreed with this teaching. In 1963 only 13 percent of U.S. Catholics felt that premarital sex was permissible. In 1974 52 percent felt it was permissible, and in 1987 71 percent felt it was permissible.[3]

In conjunction with the Pope's visit to Denver for the World Youth Day in 1993, more polls were done. The results were similar to 1987, but this time 49 percent of Catholics disagreed with the Church's teaching on homosexuality (that homosexual acts are immoral), and 87 percent now disagreed with the Church's teaching on family planning.[4]

Archbishop J. Francis Stafford, host of the World Youth Day as Archbishop of Denver, called such an "increasingly radical rejection of the teaching authority of the Pope . . . a great tragedy for the Church in the United States. It plays into the worst tendency of our culture, anarchical individualism."[5]

The difficulties with faith and morality are reflected in financial giving. "More than half of Roman Catholic households contributed less than $1 a week to the Sunday collection plate in 1991, according to a survey that seems to confirm Catholics' place on the bottom rung of givers. . . . Mormons gave 6.2 percent of their income . . . Baptists gave 2.9 percent . . . Lutherans contributed 1.3 percent . . . and Catholics gave 1.2 percent."[6]

"The Roman Catholic Church is in financial crisis—churches

[2] Peter Mullen, "Are Mass Stats Off?" *National Catholic Register,* October 10, 1993, p. 1.

[3] Richard N. Ostling, "John Paul's Feisty Flock", *Time,* September 7, 1987, pp. 46–51.

[4] "How U.S. Catholics View Their Church", *USA Today,* August 10, 1993, p. 6A.

[5] Archbishop J. Francis Stafford, "Praying with Peter", pastoral letter available from the Archdiocese of Denver.

[6] David Briggs, "Catholics on the Bottom Rung of Givers, Survey Says", *Ann Arbor News,* January 2, 1993, p. A10.

closing, archdioceses predicting financial doom—even as its members, once poor immigrants, have surpassed Protestants in average income.

"The generations that once built magnificent churches and a national network of schools and hospitals by sacrificing their labor and meager incomes have given way to a generation of relatively miserly givers."[7]

Enrollment in postcollege seminaries in the United States has dropped from 22,334 seminarians in 1968 to 9,560 in 1978, to 4,981 in 1988. The average age of the Catholic clergy in the United States has risen significantly, and deaths of elderly priests now outstrip ordinations. Worldwide, for the year 1990, the number of priests fell from 418,522 to 403,173.[8] The average age of the American nun has also risen sharply, overall numbers have decreased significantly, and new recruits have decreased to the point that many orders will no longer be viable in the near future.

One balanced observor of the American Catholic Church scene who served for many years as the American bishops' official spokesman described the situation like this: "After twenty-five years of institutional decline, the Catholic Church in the United States now may be entering an era of institutional collapse. Nearly every indicator of anything that can be measured and quantified suggests as much."[9]

According to a recent Gallup poll, only 30 percent of the Catholic faithful believe what the Church teaches on the presence of Jesus in the Eucharist.[10]

Father Benedict Groeschel, director of the spiritual life office of the Archdiocese of New York, thinks that this is "the darkest time in Catholic history and the history of the United States": "The collapse of religious life, the dearth of vocations, the lowering of ecclesiastical discipline, particularly vis-à-vis false teaching and

---

[7] David Briggs, "Catholic Church Giving Leaves Lot to Be Desired", *Ann Arbor News*, January 22, 1994, p. A10.

[8] *Annuario Pontificio*, 1992.

[9] Russell Shaw, "Conference in Defense of Western Civilization: Response to Rev. Richard John Neuhaus", October 6, 1992 (unpublished).

[10] Gianni Cardinale, "Clinton and Us", 30 *Days*, no. 12 (1992): 32.

moral teaching, the general confusion, the apostasy of the Catholic universities, the loss of the sense of the divinity of Christ, all these conspire to make this the most difficult time in Catholic history."[11]

Among Hispanic Catholics in the United States, who now constitute nearly a third of American Catholics, five million have left the Catholic Church in the last ten years to join evangelical or Pentecostal churches or other religious movements. In 1970 90 percent of American Hispanics identified themselves as Catholics. In the early 1990s only 70 percent so identified themselves.[12]

Evangelical and Pentecostal Protestants continue to find a strong response among Hispanics in North America. One leading Evangelical ministry, Robert Schuller's Crystal Cathedral in Southern California, has recently recruited a well-known Pentecostal Hispanic from Argentina, Juan Carlos Ortiz, to launch what has already become a successful outreach to Hispanics, most of whom are of Catholic tradition. This ministry is also already being telecast throughout Latin America as well as Hispanic markets in the United States: "An initial congregation of 25 doubled, then doubled again. Today, about 1,000 Hispanics from the Los Angeles area gather.... Most of the worshipers are from lower middle-class backgrounds, Ortiz said, and 96 percent of them are Roman Catholics."[13]

According to a survey of one researcher, the Catholic Church has become a primary supplier of the disenchanted, not only among Hispanic Catholics but also among all American Catholics, to conservative Protestantism. He estimates that 30 percent of today's thirty-five million evangelicals are first- or second-generation former Catholics.[14]

[11] Fr. Benedict Groeschel, "Dialogue", *National Catholic Register,* February 20, 1994, p. 10.

[12] Information from the *Yearbook of American and Canadian Churches* (Abingdon Press) cited in the *Wanderer,* April 7, 1994, p. 3.

[13] Mauro Pura, "Ortiz Expands Hispanic Outreach", *Charisma,* July 1993, p. 56.

[14] This information was provided by Mark Christensen to the author in a private letter.

The director of evangelism at a very prominent evangelical church in Illinois, Willow Creek Community Church, which attracts about fourteen thousand people during weekend services, estimates that more than half of those attending have some form of Catholicism in their background.[15]

The growth of non-Christian sects also draws heavily from disaffected Catholics. It is estimated that more than half of all Mormon converts in the United States are former Catholics. Of the ten countries boasting the largest number of Mormon centers, six of them (Mexico, Brazil, Chile, the Philippines, Peru, and Argentina) are in traditionally Catholic countries.[16] Another estimate is that in the post–Vatican II years the Catholic Church in the United States has lost twenty million members to the sects, the cults, and those who have just dropped out.[17]

All of this is reflective of serious problems within the household of faith. On the occasion of the fifth centenary of the evangelization of the Americas, the American bishops issued a pastoral letter in which they pointed out that only 2 percent of Catholics when polled say that they are personally involved in efforts of evangelization, and only one in three parishes has any evangelization program.[18]

In Canada a similar decline is evident. In 1992 only 18 percent of fifteen- to nineteen-year-olds attended church, compared to 23 percent in 1984. Also, 87 percent approved of premarital sex in 1992, compared to 80 percent in 1984.[19] The decline is both clear and far advanced.

Among Catholics in Canada the decline in faith and morality is also quite clear and quite far advanced. Only 39 percent attend church on even a monthly basis. Almost 91 percent approve of

---

[15] Rob Wilkins, "Finding the Way", *Moody,* November 1993, p. 23.

[16] *This Rock,* November 1992, p. 31.

[17] Peter Feuerherd, "On the Barricades!" *National Catholic Register,* May 16, 1993, p. 2.

[18] "Heritage and Hope: Evangelization in America", *Origins,* December 6, 1990, p. 422.

[19] "Church Attendance Drops", *Christianity Today,* December 14, 1992, p. 45.

artificial birth control, 82 percent condone premarital sex, 55 percent condone homosexual activity, and only 20 percent support the Church's teaching on abortion. One of the authors of the extensive study on which these statistics are based had this to say about the findings as they affected the Catholic Church: "If I were a bishop in the Roman Catholic Church, I'd be scared skinny."[20]

One notable exception to the trends of this study was that the conservative evangelical churches (Baptists, Pentecostals, Mennonites, etc.) in Canada were doing noticeably better than the Catholic and mainline Protestant churches.

Fifty-nine percent of these evangelicals attend church weekly (versus only 30 percent of Catholics). Seventy-five percent believe that homosexual behavior is morally wrong (compared to 40 percent of Roman Catholics). They are the only group of Christians in which the majority disapprove of premarital sex, and they are the strongest opponents of abortion; only 15 percent are "pro-choice". While only 29 percent of Catholics believe it is important to encourage non-Christians to become Christians, 67 percent of the evangelical church members do, and this is reflected in growth statistics. Only 6 percent of Catholics were not born that way, while 38 percent of the evangelicals were converts from a nonevangelical situation. One interesting fact is that among the Catholic Church's most faithful members, of the 39 percent who attend church weekly or monthly, 21 percent reported experiencing a profound conversion experience or awakening and considered themselves to be evangelicals; 31 percent of the most faithful Catholics considered themselves to be fundamentalist Christians.[21]

One especially sad note in the overall situation is the particularly steep decline of faith and morality in French-speaking Quebec, the only predominantly Catholic province of Canada. Once known throughout the world for its holiness, commitment, and inspiring bands of missionaries, it is even more devastated than the English-speaking Catholic areas. A recent article says it well:

---

[20] "Special Report: The Religion Poll", *Maclean's*, April 12, 1993, pp. 32–50. See especially pp. 34, 48, 49.

[21] Ibid., pp. 34, 36, 48, 49.

Once upon a time, to be French Canadian was to be a practicing Roman Catholic. No more. While 85% of Quebecers are baptized, most now attend church only for weddings and funerals. . . . Quebecers used to be among the most faithful churchgoers in the world. Now they're among the least. Attendance has dropped to an average 24 percent from 30 percent in the last five years alone.
At Notre-Dame de Grace's two Easter masses, the pews were only half-filled. There were many solitary elderly women, few men, even fewer children. . . . Quebec now has one of the lowest birth rates in the world. And as for nuns and priests in training, there are only 300 today, compared with 2,250 thirty years ago. . . . When the massive bells of Notre-Dame de Grace rang out the Resurrection twice on Easter Sunday, it seemed there were more people walking their dogs on its great sloped lawns than there were worshippers inside.[22]

Latin America

In Latin America the situation of the Catholic Church is even more dramatic. At a special meeting of the world's cardinals called by John Paul II in April 1991, Cardinal Obando of Nicaragua told the cardinals that a "Protestant explosion" has seen the number of non-Catholics in Latin America grow from four million in 1967 to thirty million in 1985.[23] By 1991 that figure was greater than forty million.[24] Fully 10 percent of Latin Americans are now Protestant. However, the number of actively practicing Catholics in Latin America (those with regular Mass attendance) is estimated to be only 15 percent.[25]
    A leading evangelical Protestant publication in the United

[22] Antonia Aerbisias, "Quebecers Owe a Lot to Neglected Church", *Toronto Star,* April 21, 1992, p. A17.
[23] Cardinal Obando, "Fourth Extraordinary Consistory: Regional Reports on Sects", *L'Osservatore Romano* (English ed.), April 15, 1991, pp. 7–8.
[24] Richard N. Ostling, "The Battle for Latin America's Soul", *Time,* January 21, 1991, p. 68.
[25] Joseph Davis, "The Protestant Challenge in Latin America", *America,* January 19, 1991, p. 37.

States devoted a cover story to the topic "Why Is Latin America Turning Protestant?": "A tidal wave of change is sweeping Latin America and transforming the face of an entire continent. Two recent books (David Martin's *Tongues of Fire* and David Stoll's *Is Latin America Turning Protestant?*) have created a stir by telling the story almost everyone else missed. While the press and religious establishment focused on the drama of liberation theology and its potential to bring the church back to the people, evangelical churches were proliferating at a staggering rate among the poor."[26] Pentecostals comprise about 75 percent of the evangelical population.[27]

If the growth factors for each country are averaged, the evangelical percentage of the Latin American population has tripled over the past twenty-five years to 10 percent of the population. If it triples again over the next twenty-five years, which it very well may do, evangelicals will be a third of the population by 2010.[28]

From 1960 to 1985, evangelicals have doubled their share of the population in Chile, Paraguay, Venezuela, Panama, and Haiti; tripled their share in Argentina, Nicaragua, and the Dominican Republic; quadrupled in Brazil and Puerto Rico; quintupled in El Salvador, Costa Rica, Peru, and Bolivia; and sextupled in Guatemala, Honduras, Ecuador, and Colombia. In light of these statistics, one observer of the situation claims that "Latin America is becoming Protestant more rapidly than Central Europe did in the sixteenth century."[29]

In Mexico local observers of the religious scene say between 16 and 17 percent of Mexicans consider themselves evangelical Protestants, perhaps 70 percent of these being charismatic or Pentecostal.[30]

---

[26] "Why Is Latin America Turning Protestant?" *Christianity Today,* April 6, 1992, pp. 28–39.

[27] Tom Houston, *Scenario 2000* (Monrovia, Calif.: MARC, World Vision International, 1992), p. 36.

[28] David Stoll, "A Protestant Reformation in Latin America?" *Christian Century,* January 17, 1990, pp. 44–45.

[29] John A. Coleman, S.J., "Will Latin America Become Protestant?" *Commonweal,* January 25, 1991, p. 59.

[30] "Mexican Churches Growing Rapidly", *Charisma,* October 1993, pp. 68–70.

In El Salvador, where evangelicals have grown from ninety-eight thousand at the start of the 1980s to 1.5 million today, they now comprise between 18 and 25 percent of the population. A notable strengthening of many families has been observed as a result of this evangelical growth: "The evangelical church here teaches that the man who doesn't provide for his family is worse than an animal. . . . Alcohol is strictly shunned, while monogamy, male headship, and paternal responsibility are held up as essential Christian virtues. . . . Many men have turned their lives over to Christ, and they're no longer irresponsible drunkards and adulterers. They've become very hard-working. The change in these men and their families has been so dramatic that even nonevangelicals are beginning to adopt this family structure."[31]

An American priest who recently visited Guatemala described the situation in an interview like this:

> He explored the streets of Guatemala City for five days, walking for hours through areas so stricken with poverty the rubble of a 15-year-old earthquake still blotted the urban landscape. He stepped into unknown cafes; he visited churches; he talked to everyone he met on the street.
>
> The amount of Protestant proselytizing unsettled him. The absence of the Catholic Church's presence stunned him. Here, in the overwhelmingly Catholic country of Guatemala, . . . he witnessed the faltering of the Church in Latin America, and it left him with an empty pit in his stomach.
>
> "Fundamentalism is sweeping the country", the Seton Hall professor . . . says. "Catholics are converting in unprecedented numbers every place you go, while the Church is nowhere to be seen. To a lesser degree, the same phenomenon is occurring across the whole face of Latin America." . . . As much as 45 percent of the country's 8 million Catholics have converted to a Protestant sect in the last several decades.[32]

Upon returning from Guatemala, a scholar friend of mine drafted some personal reflections that he sent me. After commenting

---

[31] "No Longer a Silent Minority", *Christianity Today,* April 5, 1993, p. 72.

[32] Peter Mullen, "In Post-Catholic Guatemala", *National Catholic Register,* May 30, 1993, p. 2.

on the abundance of evangelical and Pentecostal activity, similar
to what we have just heard, he goes on to say:

My hunch—and fear—is that I had a glimpse of a developing
fourth major schism within Christianity.
Major schisms have eerily come at approximate 500 year
intervals. The first—the Nestorian and Monophysite separations in the fifth century—cut off much of the Church in the
lands of its first blossoming, rendering it vulnerable to the
expansion of Islam. It is difficult for anyone visiting Antioch or
Alexandria today to realize that these two cities were once the
major theological centers of the Church.
The second schism, between the eastern Church and the
western Church, became final in 1054. The third major division,
within the western Church, is often dated to Luther's 95 theses
of 1517. These schisms define the major lines of demarcation
among Christians to this day, although the lines have become
more complex with the rise of Pentecostal and independent
Churches in the 20th century.
Even if past schisms do not make a comparable tragedy
around the year 2000 in any way inevitable, they can make us
attentive to the long range implications of current trends.
Pentecostal and evangelical Churches are the most rapidly growing segment of Christianity in many countries today.... If
these trends continue, what will Christianity look like in the
21st century?

In Brazil, barely a tenth of registered Catholics are churchgoers.
This means that, astonishingly, there are more Brazilian Protestants in
church on Sundays than Catholics, since Protestants boast a minimum
of 20 million churchgoers and are expanding twice as fast as the
overall population.[33] Evangelical churches are opening in Rio at
the rate of about one a day.[34] There are 17,000 ordained and
13,000 nonordained full-time ministers in Brazil, while there are
only 13,000 ordained Catholic priests.[35] There are an additional

[33] Ostling, "The Battle for Latin America's Soul", p. 69.
[34] James Brooke, "Pragmatic Protestants Win Catholic Converts in Brazil",
New York Times, July 4, 1993, p. 10. National and International Religion Report,
July 26, 1993, p. 6.
[35] Coleman, "Will Latin America Become Protestant?" p. 60.

6,000 Catholic priests who have married but are not able to function as priests. The situation is so serious that laymen preside at more than 70 percent of Sunday's Catholic services.[36] In addition, of the 110,930,000 professed Catholics in Brazil (the largest Catholic country in the world), 19,843,000 (18 percent) also claim allegiance to spiritist churches. An additional 3,409,000 Catholics profess spiritism alone. (The situation is even worse in Haiti, where 90 percent of the Catholic population also are affiliated with spiritist groups or churches.)[37]

In October 1991 Vatican officials were stunned by low turnouts for Masses led by the Pope. In Brasilia, where the Pope drew 500,000 people for a Mass in 1980, only 100,000 turned out in 1991. On the day of the 1991 Mass one of Brazil's most popular television evangelists drew a total of 400,000 people to outdoor prayer meetings in Rio, Salvado, and Sao Paulo.[38]

Bishop Bonaventura Kloppenburg of Brazil has also noted that Latin America is turning Protestant faster than Central Europe did in the sixteenth century.[39] At a recent major meeting of Latin American bishops, he pointed out that over 300 million of Latin America's Catholics are not practicing their Faith.[40] A Belgian priest who has worked in Latin America for forty years echoes the same observation: "In 20 years Latin America will be Protestant if the Vatican continues its present policies . . . it will be the national church for ceremonial purposes. . . . But the religious life of the poor will be with the sects, as has long been the situation in England."[41]

One bright spot in Brazil, and to some extent in other countries, is the growth of renewal movements such as the charismatic

[36] Michael Kepp, "CELAM Summit Might Be Stormy", *National Catholic Register,* October 11, 1992, p. 10.

[37] David B. Barrett, *World Christian Encyclopedia* (Oxford: Oxford University Press, 1982).

[38] Brooke, "Pragmatic Protestants Win Catholic Converts in Brazil", pp. 1, 10.

[39] Stoll, "A Protestant Reformation in Latin America?" p. 47.

[40] "Falls of the Walls of Old", 30 *Days,* no. 11 (1992): 19.

[41] Gary MacEoin, "In Joust for Latin America, Rome Seeks Option for Rich", *National Catholic Reporter,* November 8, 1991, p. 18.

renewal: "The largest and most quickly growing of these groups is an outgrowth of the 'charismatic renewal'.... There are 5 million Brazilian charismatic Catholics.... The renewal claims that 2,000 of Brazil's 13,800 priests working in 200 of Brazil's 244 dioceses are charismatics, whereas only 150 of them belonged to the movement 10 years ago."[42]

But such growth, as impressive as it is, does not appear to be sufficient yet to turn the tide: "Still, for the moment, the evangelicals seem to be attracting far more adherents than the Catholic renewal. In the 1970s, when evangelicals represented close to 6.3 percent of the Brazilian population, and in the 1980s, 10 percent, today evangelicals represent some 14 percent of the population or close to 21 million people.... The national Conference of Brazilian Bishops estimates that at least 600,000 Brazilians leave the Catholic Church each year to join fundamentalist and evangelical Protestant sects."[43]

Father Eduardo Dougherty, a leader of the Catholic charismatic renewal in Brazil, has some interesting observations on the situation: "Why did the Catholic Church miss the mark? It's a lack of perception of the basic needs of the person—human warmth, healing, a deep spiritual experience.... We have a lot to learn from our Protestant brothers."[44]

But it is not only the Catholic Church that is challenged. The mainline Protestant churches in Brazil (Anglican, Methodist, and Lutheran) have not had much success either.

The historical Protestant churches never went anywhere in Brazil.... Protestantism only exploded because the Pentecostal message touched the most essential part of Brazilian culture, which is both spiritual and pragmatic.... If you talk about spirits to a Catholic priest, he will look condescending and not understand.... The Evangelical will connect. He will look you in the eye and say: "This is the Devil, and he is destroying your life".... Protestant pastors here say that the Catholic church

[42] Michael Kepp, "In Brazil, Renewal Is Thriving", *National Catholic Register*, March 7, 1993, p. 1.
[43] Ibid.
[44] Brooke, "Pragmatic Protestants Win Catholic Converts in Brazil", p. 10.

took a wrong turn in the 1970's when it embraced liberation theology. . . . But two decades later, Rio's religious census has found that the metropolitan region's 3,500 Protestant churches are overwhelmingly concentrated in poor cities. . . . In contrast, Catholicism prevails in Rio's middle- and upper-class beachfront neighborhoods. . . . "The irony . . . is that the Catholics opted for the poor, and the poor opted for the Evangelicals."[45]

It may be, though, that the Holy Spirit is using the reality of the serious decline of the Church in Latin America along with the rise of the "sects" to turn the attention of the Church back toward the basics, to Christ and conversion. At the fourth Conference of the Latin American Episcopate, there was no longer talk of the top priority of the Church being an option for the poor or youth but rather an option for Christ.

The Vatican secretary of state, Cardinal Sodano, who presided over this important meeting in Santo Domingo, underlined the seriousness of the situation and the importance of the shift:

> I would say that in this Conference there was a transition from the dominance of sociological analysis of the reality and its problems to focus on the primacy of Christ's message. . . . Santo Domingo made the option for Christ the only one. . . . Everyone can see how advanced the process of de-Christianization and secularization is in Latin America too and not only in the major cities. Judging by some statistics in circulation during the Conference, religious practice is at a rather low ebb in the great Latin American metropolises. Another issue which is also a source of great concern to the Episcopal Conferences of this continent remains that of sects. And in this case, the statistics speak loud and clear. . . . They have no illusions that they are dealing with a Christian society already constituted. . . . At Santo Domingo, the bishops recognized that evangelization in Latin America must be newly ardent, it must be new as far as its methods and expressions are concerned; and that only by means of a testimony born from the heart of daily life will the message be made effective. Today, as

[45] Ibid.

in the past, we become Christians only if we encounter Christ and live according to Christ.[46]

Asia

The situation in the Philippines, the only predominantly Catholic country in Asia, is very similar to that of Latin America, with great progress being made by Protestant evangelical and Pentecostal mission work. I have been to the Philippines several times, and the presence of the evangelicals and Pentecostals is very noticeable. New, large churches dot metropolitan Manila. The proliferation of these churches is noticeable throughout the country. Frequent crusades, conferences, and rallies, aggressive door-to-door evangelism, and frequent use of the media are characteristic. The opening of seminaries and various leadership-training programs and institutes all attest to the long-range goals and prospects of what is happening. Evangelical churches in this predominantly Catholic country have grown from five thousand in 1975 to 23,200 in 1990. The Evangelical Fellowship of Asia expects the number to double again by the year 2000.[47]

While the Philippines is the only Asian country where Catholics are a majority, there has been remarkable growth among both Catholics and Protestants in South Korea. This has been a significant success story for both Catholic, mainline Protestant, and evangelical and Pentecostal churches. Some of the world's largest congregations and church buildings are to be found among the Pentecostals of South Korea.

Some have noted that the fusion of nationality, culture, and religion that is characteristic of many other Asian countries did not happen in the same way in Korea, thus preparing the way for a greater receptivity to Christianity. At the same time the churches that are growing, across the denominational spectrum, both Catho-

---

[46] Cardinal Angelo Sodano and Stefania Falasca, "Defending the Essential", 30 Days, no. 11 (1992): 24–27.
[47] Charisma, May 1993, p. 87.

lic and Protestant, are generally characterized by a firmness of belief not always characteristic of their sister churches in other countries.

David Yonggi Cho's 650,000 member Yoido Full Gospel Church in Seoul has already committed two million dollars in preparation for reaching North Korea when the doors open. He plans to distribute a Christian newspaper in every major northern city once the peninsula is reunited. Two hundred thousand intercessors recently filled Seoul's Olympic Colosseum to intercede for the reunion of Korea and the opening of the north to the gospel.[48]

Although Catholics are a relatively small minority, the Catholic Church in India has a long and noble tradition and is relatively healthy as regards the commitment of her people. While traveling recently in Europe with a bishop from India, I was encouraged to hear that while in most places in the country the Church was not growing, there were significant conversions among some of the tribes in the north. However, some of the same kind of theological corruption that has so weakened the Catholic Church in other parts of the world is also strongly present in India and other Asian countries, so much so that the same Indian bishop declared, "We are the successors of the apostles, but we don't have the apostles' success. We pray for the Holy Spirit to come, and not much happens."

The theological confusion is such that Rome has begun to speak openly about its concern. Cardinal Josef Tomko, prefect of the Congregation for the Evangelization of Peoples, in a recent address identified India as the "epicenter" of theological tendencies that are radically undermining the basic Christian message and the whole missionary endeavor.[49] Cardinal Tomko sees one reason for the growth of the "sects" in India and throughout Asia as a doctrinal confusion within the Catholic Church that eliminates the explicit proclamation of Jesus Christ: "The spread of sects and the challenge they present to the Church has theological as well as pastoral implications. Doctrinal confusion regarding the

---

[48] *Charisma*, January 1993, p. 40.

[49] Cardinal Tomko, "Proclaiming Christ the World's Only Saviour", *L'Osservatore Romano* (English ed.), April 15, 1991, p. 4.

content of the faith opens the way to the proliferation of sects, to their practical justification, and above all, to a lack of commitment in pastoral care and the explicit proclamation of Jesus Christ, which establishes the Christian community."[50]

Cardinal Tomko sees a misunderstanding about dialogue with the world religions as being a major factor in the doctrinal confusion and practical destruction of the missionary endeavor:

> To make the dialogue equal, either Jesus Christ is downgraded by silence about his divinity, or the founders of other religions are upgraded by making them almost an incarnation of God, or mediators and saviors equal to Jesus Christ. . . . These theologians completely ignore the fact that Jesus not only announced the Kingdom, but *was proclaimed the King in whom the Kingdom of God is made present* . . . without him, "to speak of the kingdom is simply ideology." . . . The abandonment of missionary stations, or preaching the Gospel, and of catechesis by missionaries, the clergy, and women religious, and the flight to social work, as well as the great *reductive* talk about the "values of the Kingdom" (justice, peace) is a widespread phenomenon in Asia and is propagated by some missionary centers on other continents, too. . . . The problem is already so extensive and the theories expounded are spreading so rapidly that the Holy See can no longer remain passive. They are creating a serious danger for faith in Jesus Christ . . . they are weakening the missionary spirit, reducing evangelization to mere dialogue and development, with the abandonment of proclamation, catechesis, and logically, conversions and baptisms.[51]

At the time when the Catholic missionary effort is being undermined from within, the need for a clear Christian witness is needed more than ever. Female infanticide and abortion are but two of the dark shadows plaguing Indian life. One survey of a Bombay clinic showed that of the eight thousand abortions performed in the late 1980s, the great majority were of female babies.[52]

One sign of hope is the rapid growth of Mother Teresa's order,

[50] Ibid.

[51] Ibid.

[52] *National and International Religion Report*, July 12, 1993, p. 5.

the Missionaries of Charity, and their effective communication of the awesome reality of Christian mercy.

Another sign of hope in India is the spread of the Catholic charismatic renewal, which is energizing the faith of large numbers of Indian Catholics. The country now has about ten thousand prayer groups, six thousand of which are in the southern state of Kerala. Healing crusades led by Catholic evangelists draw more than one hundred thousand people. More than a million Indian Catholics are active in this renewal.[53]

The most significant signs of Christian expansion, though, seem to be among the evangelicals and Pentecostals, who hold crusades with literally hundreds of thousands attending and are training pastors and starting new churches at a significant rate. Since 70 percent of India's population is illiterate, "miracle crusades" and a skillful use of audiovisual communication are being utilized with remarkable effectiveness.

One radio ministry receives a half-million letters a year in response to its programs. One film on the life of Christ, produced by an Indian filmmaker, has been dubbed into six Indian languages and is shown almost daily to large audiences across the country. Three million Indians have made decisions for Christ publicly as a result of viewing the movie, and plans are under way to stage screenings in six hundred thousand villages, which, of course, are predominantly Hindu.[54]

Another film produced by evangelicals that has had an amazing impact, not only in Asia but also throughout the world, is a film called simply *Jesus,* produced by Campus Crusade for Christ. It had been dubbed into more than 250 languages and shown in over 195 countries by the spring of 1993, with more being scheduled. More than five hundred million people have seen the film in the past ten years. Wherever an open response to the film is permitted, about 10 percent of the audience indicates a desire to place their trust and faith in Christ. The showing of this film is part of a larger project called "New Life 2000", which is dividing the world

---

[53] "Charismatics in India", *New Covenant,* July 1993, p. 30.
[54] *Charisma,* January 1993, p. 28.

into five thousand areas of one million people each to launch evangelistic film teams and training centers in each area. The U.S. Center for World Mission has stated that "no single evangelistic campaign in human history has touched as many lives as the showing of this film worldwide."[55]

This same organization, with their thirty thousand full-time workers, is also planning to establish in cooperation with existing Protestant denominations more than one million new churches. Through the *Jesus* film alone, just in Thailand, where the Catholic Church carries on a quiet and very unevangelistic existence, Campus Crusade has reported more new churches planted in that country in the 1980s than in the previous 150 years of mission work.[56]

Use of media in the former Soviet republics in Asia has also been effective. The Christian Broadcasting Network's use of television in these Asian republics has generated two hundred thousand written inquiries from the region so far. Ten percent of these respondents from Uzbekistan and 23 percent from Kazakhstan said they made professions of faith in Christ after viewing the CBN programs.[57]

One of the most amazing reports about what is happening in Asia concerns China. While both the Catholic and mainline Protestant churches there have heroically survived vicious persecution and exist today as viable Christian bodies, although under severe restrictions and with great difficulty, the growth of a spontaneous "house church" movement, which is predominantly Pentecostal in character, while obviously not a denomination, has brought tens of millions to Christian faith. I have seen videotapes of meetings of these house churches smuggled out of China and have been awed and humbled at the fervor and love expressed in their worship of God and love of one another.

---

[55] Information on the *Jesus* film was taken from a report issued by Campus Crusade for Christ on this project. This information can be obtained by writing to The JESUS Film Project, 30012 Glenn Dr., Suite 200, Laguna Niguel, CA 92677.

[56] C. Peter Wagner, in *Equipping the Saints,* Spring 1992, p. 11.

[57] *Charisma,* January 1993, p. 33.

Some have suffered greatly for their faith, and their stories read like that of the early Christian martyrs.[58]

A September 1992 bulletin released by the Beijing Statistical Bureau revealed that even the government has been forced to acknowledge the undeniable growth of Christianity under even the most bitter persecution. While previously it was acknowledging only ten to twelve million Christians in China, now it acknowledges approximately seventy-five million Christians there, the vast majority "unregistered" and "unrecognized".[59] Of these, twelve million are Catholics, and sixty-three million are Protestants. Sixty million of all these Christians, or 85 percent, are now Pentecostal or charismatic.[60]

In one area of Henan Province, the number of believers has grown from 260,000 to about six hundred thousand in the last ten years. In Szechwan Province—where one out of every forty people on earth lives—nearly two thousand new churches have been started in just the last two to three years, despite renewed government persecution in the wake of the Tiananmen Square massacre.[61]

Africa

In Africa the situation is more complex, but many of the same factors are at work.

In largely Arabic-speaking Northern Africa, the Africa of Augustine where Christianity was once so strong, the Muslim pressure on the small number of Christians still able to live and work there is very intense. Emigration has continued to decimate their relatively small numbers, and the pressure to convert to

---

[58] Danyun, *Lilies amongst Thorns: Chinese Christians Tell Their Story through Blood and Tears* (Bognor, W. Sussex, Eng.: Sovereign World, 1991), excerpted in *Prophecy Today* (May–June 1993).

[59] Ibid., p. 36.

[60] "Chinese Government Counts 75 Million Christians", *AD 2000*, Spring 1993, p. 3. "World Notes: More Christians in China?" *National Catholic Register*, August 1, 1993, p. 7.

[61] Ibid., p. 38.

Islam is having its effect: "The authorities prefer not to discuss the issue but a vast number of Christians convert to Islam every year. No one, in contrast, takes the opposite step. . . . 15,000 a year of the Orthodox Copts in Egypt become Moslems. It is as if every year, in the homeland of St. Athanasius and St. Anthony Abbot, the father of the monastic life, all the inhabitants of an average-size city were to abjure their faith."[62]

In sub-Sahara Africa the preparation of the African people by their traditional religions and the dedication of the missionaries have resulted in a phenomenal growth of Christianity. A hundred years ago or so, the estimated number of Christians in Africa was half a million. Today, one authoritative estimate is about three hundred million. Of these, about 122 million are Roman Catholic, eighty-seven million are Protestant, and perhaps another sixty-one million belong to rapidly growing independent, largely Pentecostal, church bodies. In addition, there are another twenty-eight million, mainly in Ethiopia and Egypt, who belong to the Oriental churches. Islam is also growing in Africa and counts about 278 million adherents.[63]

During an extended trip to five African countries a number of years ago and in subsequent contact with Africans since, I have discovered many strengths in the Catholic Church in Africa but also some significant and, for me, unexpected weaknesses. Some of these problems are unique to the African situation; many are problems that the entire Church faces.

Although the Catholic population continues to grow, the percentage of Catholics showed a drop from 13.93 percent of the total African population in 1989 to 13.85 percent in 1991, and although

[62] Stefano M. Paci, "News Report", 30 *Days*, no. 9 (1993): 30.
[63] 1993 *Britannica Book of the Year* (Chicago: Encyclopedia Britannica, 1993), p. 270. The statistics given at the 1994 African Synod were somewhat different: 95,613,000 Catholics. It was also reported that the hierarchy is now predominantly African, as is the diocesan clergy, while the religious order clergy is still predominantly non-African. Out of all the religious order women, about 60 percent were African; out of the clergy, 65 percent. (Cardinal Joseph Tomko, "The Situation of the Church in Africa and Madagascar—Some Aspects and Observations", *L'Osservatore Romano* [English ed.], April 27, 1994, p. 18.)

vocations are growing, a majority of apostolic workers in Africa are still foreign missionaries.[64]

The quality of Christian life in African Catholicism has its weak spots. I found the numerical growth of African Catholicism to be deceptive in relation to the number of converts who were actually living a dedicated Christian life. In many ways, African Catholicism has similarities to the cultural Catholicism that is found in many other parts of the world, a Catholicism that observes certain religious practices and ceremonies without adequately understanding them, experiencing their reality, and living them out in daily life.

As Cardinal Thiandoum from Senegal put it at the African Synod of Bishops, "In many areas the Christian faith is shallow and needs to become more rooted."[65]

Many other bishops from all over the continent echoed his concern:

The Archbishop of Dar-es-Salaam, Tanzania:

> The life of many Tanzanian Christians today is characterized by a deep dichotomy regarding the professed Christian faith and the concrete day-to-day living. While theoretically the faith may be expressed in very orthodox terms, concrete life is often so contradictory to the professed faith that one remains stunned by the mere possibility of the two attitudes coexisting in a single individual. . . . The resulting plight is comparable to that of the Gerasene demoniac. . . . That plightful situation in which so many Tanzanian Christians find themselves needs the saving message of Christ. . . . Christ and his Gospel must take precedence; he must be given absolute primacy.[66]

A bishop from Nigeria:

[64] Archbishop Jan Schotte, Address to the African Synod, "African Synod Is Special Moment of Grace", L'Osservatore Romano (English ed.), April 20, 1994, p. 4.

[65] Cardinal Hyacinthe Thiandoum, "The Gospel, Inculturation and Dialogue", L'Osservatore Romano (English ed.) April 20, 1994, p. 9.

[66] Archbishop Polycarp Pengo, "Christian Faith Must Be Deepened in Daily Life", L'Osservatore Romano (English ed.) April 27, 1994, p. 8.

They are usually caught up in the clan and tribal interests. . . . Where the Church is built, where the parish centre is situated, where the Bishop comes from, where he lives, are all more important than what they are and stand for . . . exaggerated ethnicism. . . . This mentality is so pervasive that the saying goes among the Africans that when it comes to the crunch, it is not the Christian concept of the Church as a family which prevails but rather the adage that "blood is thicker than water." And by water here one can presumably include the waters of Baptism.[67]

A bishop from Côte D'Ivoire: "Faith is still fragile here. . . . A syncretism which mixes fetishism and Christianity seems to persist."[68]

Another bishop from Nigeria: "To date, Christian family life leaves much to be desired. Many of the customs and traditions and even philosophy have been carried over to the Christian life by our African converts. They live double standards of lives, one to suit their village standards, and the other to suit Christianity."[69]

The Archbishop of Khartoum, Sudan:

My Diocese baptizes an average of 3,000 to 5,000 adult catechumens every year during the Easter Vigil. We notice however that they soon join the large number of marginal Christians which might include Bishops, priests and religious. . . . We need to revise our sacramental theology and ground it in a sound understanding of the forms and dynamics of conversion. We prepare people to receive the sacraments but seem not well equipped to help people live the sacraments they receive, and understand and accept the demands of each sacrament.[70]

A missionary priest who has worked in Africa for twenty years:

[67] Bishop Albert Kanene Obiefuna, "Present the Church as a Family to Christians in Africa", *L'Osservatore Romano* (English ed.) April 27, 1994, p. 9.

[68] Bishop Auguste Nobou, "The World Expects a Witness of Missionary Co-operation", *L'Osservatore Romano* (English ed.), April 27, 1994, p. 11.

[69] Bishop Joseph Edra Ukpo, "Give Life to an 'African Christian Marriage' ", *L'Osservatore Romano* (English ed.), April 27, 1994, p. 12.

[70] Archbishop Gabriel Zubeir Wako, "Inculturation of Faith and Involvement of Community," *L'Osservatore Romano* (English ed.), May 25, 1994, p. 6.

The African Church is in danger of undergoing a genetic mutation. . . . Why are the sects and Islam spreading? Because they're fascinating. Whereas a great many Church situations no longer are. The genetic change is taking place. Christianity has ceased to be an event, a story, and has turned into a moral and cultural guide. There are too many situations where the Church presence is already in decline, where the initial capacity to stir wonder and encounter Christ has been lost. . . . Catholics are flitting en masse to the sects.[71]

A bishop from Zambia: "Perhaps for too long we Christians have looked upon our mission of evangelizing as a 'spread of religion' rather than a 'call to conversion'."[72]

This qualitative weakness of African Catholicism stems in large part from the way in which both the missionaries and the Africans have approached conversion to Christianity. Often when Christianity arrived, it appeared as the religion of the victorious and powerful colonial powers. People saw it as the religion that went with firearms, material prosperity, technological advance, the amenities of Western civilization, and—very significantly—schools and hospitals. For many years virtually the only schools and hospitals in Africa were those operated by the missions.

Conversion to Christianity was frequently intertwined with a decision to try to get ahead and benefit from the white man's civilization. As one African priest put it, "Baptism was part of the school curriculum." Candidates were accepted for baptism if they could recite several prayers, repeat the Commandments, and enumerate the sacraments. The degree of personal understanding of commitment was frequently not taken into consideration. At a certain age it was expected that those in the mission school would be baptized. Many of the conversions to Catholicism in Africa today still come through the school system.

After baptism follow-up was sparse, especially in the rural areas, where most of the people lived. This was another problem that

[71] Stefano M. Paci, "Father Tiboni: Africa's False Dilemmas", 30 Days, no. 3 (1994): 28.
[72] Bishop Telesphore George Mpundu, "Commitment and Witness for Justice and Peace", L'Osservatore Romano (English ed.), April 27, 1994, p. 5.

contributed to the weakness of Christian life among a large number of African Catholics. In the early days a village might see a priest only once a year. With such a weak follow-up there was a natural tendency for the social ties of the traditional African family life and culture to be stronger than the new, but somewhat superficially prepared for and experienced, Christian life. An individualistic approach to the Christian life provided little social support for a truly new way of life. Today this is still a major problem. It is not uncommon for people in many areas to see a priest only once every several months. Many priests have such a large number of outlying stations that they can visit them only infrequently. Despite the flowering of vocations in some areas, the general situation in terms of the ratio of priests to people is still very poor.[73]

Because of the lack of adequate preparation and of a living Christian community as a support for a deeper Christian life, for many persons baptism, confirmation, and the Eucharist have remained actions that have little connection with real life. Many African Catholics have not experienced much in the way of a personal relationship with Christ, the real power of the Holy Spirit, and deep bonds with brothers and sisters in Christ. As a result many African Catholics are not experiencing the power to live a new life in Christ. This shows up in many areas, particularly in sex, marriage, and family life.

In many parts of Africa only a small percentage of baptized Catholics receive Communion at Mass. One African priest told me that perhaps only 3 percent of the baptized Catholics in the large territory for which he was responsible received Communion. Several factors account for this. Polygamy is still a significant factor in African life, and numbers of Catholics are still involved in this situation, which is too complex to be addressed adequately here. Another reason is that fertility is highly prized in African culture; traditionally marriage is not considered consummated until the first child is born. Today many young African Catholics

---

[73] Cardinal Hyacinthe Thiandoum, "The Gospel, Inculturation and Dialogue", *L'Osservatore Romano* (English ed.), April 20, 1994, p. 9.

are reluctant to enter into Christian marriage, with its ideal of lifelong fidelity, until they assure themselves of their fertility by producing a child. Even then, many are still reluctant because of the cost associated with a church wedding—the white dress, the cost of alcohol, the reception, and so on.

Ironically, the mission schools themselves have contributed to a moral laxity. Almost all these schools have been boarding schools, since the students need to travel large distances that make daily commuting impractical. Young people away from home in the schools or the cities are left without the social network that used to be effective in supporting morality.

Many children are born to Christians outside of marriage. At one predominately Christian college I visited, a staff member told me that many of the female students were pregnant at the time of my visit, most of them unmarried. Fortunately, the extended family systems of the African cultures are able to provide care for these children of unwed mothers.

Problems are not limited to the laity. One African bishop told me that it was not uncommon for an African to become a priest as a way to "wear shoes, eat European food, and rise above his people". Another African bishop confided that he has lost many fine young men who might have served the Church because they have gone to seminaries and been disillusioned by what they found there. He added that those who finish the many years of academic training are often culturally alienated from their people and thus unable to share the people's life and minister to their needs. Frequently, he said, he felt he would rather ordain his lay catechists because of their effectiveness in serving the people.

Like the laity, the African clergy often encounter problems when they are asked to live the Christian morality without experiencing all of the power that should come from real conversion to Christ and the gifts of his Holy Spirit. African priests told me about the great difficulties in living clerical celibacy in a culture that so highly prizes children, and with so little community support, in isolated pastoral outposts. One bishop told me that many of the African priests in his ecclesiastical province were faced with the burden of providing for their unofficial wives and often rather sizable families. In each of the countries I visited I was told by responsible Church leaders that this was a widespread problem to which the bishops as a whole were not facing up. Just recently a priest who has worked in Africa for many years described the heartbreaking situation of the Catholic Archbishop's residence in his city being filled with priests dying from AIDS.

This apparent reluctance of the African bishops to face a widespread and serious problem in the life of their priests stems in part from a tension found throughout the African church between being loyal to the shape, style, and discipline of Roman Catholicism as woven into the fabric of Western culture and finding an authentic African style of Catholicism that could abide more deeply in the daily lives of the African people and build more on their traditional strengths and values—which the early missionaries tended to condemn, often out of ignorance.

Although there are some promising attempts toward Africanization that have resulted in the incorporation of some African dancing, drumming, and music into the liturgy, their impact is limited. Often they do not measure up to the more serious problems of cultural alienation, the failure to bring about basic Christian conversion, and the lack of some measure of community life centered on Jesus. Hopefully the special African Synod, held in the spring of 1994, will be an impetus to the solution of some of these serious problems.

In the meantime, many African Catholics are finding needs and problems in their lives with which they believe the Church cannot help them. For example, problems with evil spirits are quite common in Africa. Witchcraft and sorcery are seriously and effectively practiced arts. One day, while I was visiting a particular country, there was a report on the front page of the capital's daily paper on the trial of two witches, who described how they had followed the commands of evil spirits by killing some children.

Many Africans live in fear that someone who does not like them will enlist the aid of someone who has made a pact with evil spirits to put a curse on them and send evil spirits to torment or harm them or their family members. Many of the leaders of the

Church today generally ignore, make fun of, or discount the reality of these powers. The people do not. Since the Church does not help them, they go to the traditional medicine men and village healers for help and protection.

The same is true of healing. Disease is common in Africa, and Western medicine is not always available or effective. Many of the most educated and faithful African Catholics, when they experience trouble, disease, or feel they are tormented by evil spirits, go to traditional medicine men. Leading African catechists, parish council members, and university professors have all told me this. They have also told me that few Africans will dare tell the missionaries about this part of their life for fear it will not be taken seriously.

Besides going to the traditional tribal practitioners in times of trouble, a growing number of Catholics and mainline Protestants are frequenting the rapidly growing independent African church bodies. These bodies generally adhere to basic Christian doctrine (many are Pentecostal), but some are syncretistic and not truly Christian. Many of them provide strong and effective healing and deliverance ministries, which are seldom found in the Catholic and Protestant churches. Some of the Catholics I met told me that they and their friends still go to Mass on Sunday morning but then go to independent African congregations in the afternoon for prayer for healing and deliverance, for freer worship and warmer fellowship.

This situation was referred to often at the African Synod.

New Churches and religious movements are being born daily in most parts of Africa. They often claim to be non-denominational, but very often they have the Catholic Church as their target. It's sad to acknowledge that most of the adherents are women, Catholic women, for that matter. Investigations have shown that these women feel that their basic African needs are not being catered to in the Catholic Church at the present time. Childlessness and the fear of evil spirits are real concerns, which in Church circles are very often laughed at, dismissed as imaginary and non-existent.

But, to the suffering African woman, these problems are

real. These movements or sects are winning our Catholic women over because they seem to be responding to their real needs.[74]

A bishop from Zaire:

In Zaire, as in many other countries in Africa, sects proliferate in a disconcerting way. To tackle this phenomenon the Catholic Church in Africa must:

—proclaim the Word of God with all her strength to reach Africans in their daily life as a Word which creates, transforms and heals;

—pay attention to the phenomena of witchcraft, magic, the action of spirits and the dead, phenomena which have a real impact on the life of many Africans, even the baptized;

—reassert the value of the Sacrament of the Sick and the ministries such as exorcism, prayer over the sick and deliverance from evil spirits;

—correctly supervise the renewal in the Spirit groups which already serve as schools of prayer, places of conversion and spiritual and physical healing.[75]

While in Nigeria I had the opportunity to visit one of the new independent churches and attend one of their services. This particular church, founded about forty years ago, now has more than five hundred congregations all over Africa and even beyond. Some of these African Pentecostals are now serving as missionaries to the former Soviet Union and other places in Eastern Europe. This church's founder, reputed to have raised more than fifteen people from the dead and to have been instrumental in thousands of healings and deliverances, is still alive. The body of elders of this particular congregation was a solid group of educated men, many of whom had been leaders in more established Christian churches before experiencing personal conversion, healing, power, and joy in worship in this new congregation. They seemed to be a group of balanced men who were leading a sizable congregation in a fervent spiritual life.

[74] Kathryn Houwa Hoomkwap, "Their Voices Are Heard", *National Catholic Register*, May 22, 1994, p. 5.

[75] Bishop Nextor Ngoy Katahwa, "Tackle the Problem of Sects in Africa", *L'Osservatore Romano* (English ed.), May 11, 1994, p. 11.

The Pentecostal growth in other countries is also very striking. Although the Assemblies of God, a Pentecostal denomination based in America, had only 2,065 churches in all of Africa in 1970, by the end of 1991 they had 13,950 churches.

In Burkina Faso, where eighty thousand Assemblies of God women devote one day a week to fasting and prayer, church membership has grown from twenty-five thousand to more than 350,000 in the past two decades. About fifty thousand of these converted from Islam.

In Ghana, the Assemblies of God have added 153 churches and two hundred pastors in the past two years.

According to Loren Cunningham, founder of Youth with a Mission, Mauritius, which was 75 percent Hindu in 1985, is today over 50 percent Christian.[76] Recently the king of Tonga, a Pacific island kingdom, gave Youth with a Mission fifty acres of prime land on which to build a Christian training center for the Pacific region.[77]

One of the most well-known evangelists in Africa at this moment is German Pentecostal Reinhard Bonnke, whose average audience is one hundred thousand. In 1991 half the population of Lomé, Togo, attended his crusade.

In Sierra Leone 90 percent of those who were healed at Bonnke's crusades were Muslims. Often there are national television and radio coverage and invitations to meet the president of the country or to address the parliament.[78]

In Transkei, South Africa, in November 1992, one local Pentecostal church baptized seventy thousand new converts in one day. According to eyewitness reports, "physical healings, deliverance from demons, and other spiritual manifestations took place as the newly baptized came up from the water."[79]

On one occasion I had the opportunity to share with a man who has considerable responsibility for the African Catholic Church, and I made some of the above observations. He replied

[76] "Bright Hope in a Land of Crisis", *Charisma,* January 1993, p. 50.
[77] "God's Love Stirs the South Seas", *Charisma,* January 1993, p. 44.
[78] Ibid., pp. 52–53.
[79] Vinson Synan, *Timelines,* Winter 1993, p. 4.

that yes, there were serious problems but that recent liturgical reforms would solve them and that the African Church needed just a little renewal, but not too much. If he meant that the African Church did not need a lot of the psuedorenewal that has swept through the West, I can certainly agree with him. Unfortunately, I think he was underestimating some of the very great needs facing the Church in Africa. I believe that the Church in Africa, like the Church in most parts of the world, needs a lot of genuine spiritual renewal. The danger there—in a Church pressed by the rising tide of Islam, a growing gap between rich and poor, the devastating spread of AIDS (as many as one of every seven Ugandans may be HIV positive),[80] periodic famine and civil war, continued instability and corruption in many governments, the continued weakness of a confused West—is of too little genuine renewal, too late.

As one Christian psychologist in Kenya, Gladys Mwiti, put it recently: "People may go to church, but their religion is skin deep. They have not been made to realize they own the faith. It has not become part of their lifestyle . . . a value vacuum looms from one end of the continent to the other. . . . Unless the church of Jesus Christ realizes what is happening, then our ministry will not be relevant."[81]

Recently I was a speaker at the National Catholic Charismatic Conference in Italy, and I had a chance to spend time with a Nigerian bishop, Gabriel Ganaka, who was also a speaker. This bishop is well known in Africa and has held many leadership positions both within and without Nigeria. He has since become an archbishop and has been elected president of the Symposium of Episcopal Conferences of Africa and Madagascar. He has spent time with us in Ann Arbor in connection with a conference on John Paul II and the new evangelization which our mission organization, Renewal Ministries,[82] sponsored. He told me that

---

[80] *National and International Religion Report,* February 22, 1993, p. 2.

[81] *National and International Religion Report,* June 28, 1993, p. 7.

[82] Those interested in receiving the monthly newsletter of Renewal Ministries can request this by writing: Renewal Ministries, Box 7712, Ann Arbor, MI 48107.

since my visit to Africa the economic situation had become even worse and that even when Western medicines were available most people could not possibly afford them and were indeed seeking out healing from both traditional native healers and churches which prayed with people for healing. He has taken it upon himself to encourage about fifty African priests in his country to pray for their people for healing of sickness and deliverance from evil spirits and is seeing very worthwhile results. As Archbishop Ganaka strikingly put it: "We need the power of the Holy Spirit and the focus on the person of Jesus that Peter had in the early days of the church, as described in the Acts of the Apostles; on one day Peter preached one sermon and three thousand people converted; we preach three thousand sermons and no one converts."

God is coming to help the Church in Africa face her great challenges. He is raising up the prophets and apostles of the new Pentecost and the new evangelization that John Paul II has called for.

As the closing message of the African Synod put it: "But the culture which gave its identity to our people is in serious crisis. On the eve of the 21st century when our identity is being crushed in the mortar of a merciless chain of events, the fundamental need is for prophets to arise and speak in the name of the God of hope for the creation of a new identity. Africa has need of holy prophets."[83]

He is sending them.

Western Europe

More than a hundred years ago the German philosopher Nietzsche saw that modern European society had cut so many ties with God that for all practical purposes "God was dead", but the full impact of this accumulation of choices would not be felt until the twentieth century.

[83] "Message of the African Synod", *L'Osservatore Romano* (English ed.), May 11, 1994, p. 7.

A number of Catholic writers from Europe in the first half of this century saw the depths of the problem and wrote about it with anguish because so few in the Church were willing to face it. As Charles Péguy wrote: "This is the novelty. This is what has to be recognized. Everything is un-Christian. Perfectly de-Christianized. This, then, is what churchmen will not see; what they will refuse to see; what they will stubbornly deny; and with them this is what many Catholics will refuse to acknowledge, what all Catholics, with them, following them, will deny and refuse to acknowledge, stubbornly, no less stubbornly."[84]

And Emmanuel Mounier wrote: "Modern Christianity continues to make preparations for its own death: this will be so brutal, so total, that one will feel that Christianity has been wiped out of Europe.... In my view, the more I go into the initial reality of Christianity, comparing it with the present situation of modern Christianity, the more I am persuaded that we will all find the true faith again only after a collapse of modern Christianity so complete that many will think that they have come to the end of Christianity. But those who will bear the consequences of this general apostasy will not be the new generations: they will not bear the burden at the Judgment, but all the rest of us will, the false witnesses for more than four centuries."[85]

Today, the evidence for the profound de-Christianization of the Christian "heartland" is painfully clear. Cardinal Ratzinger speaks of the situation in these terms: "Undoubtedly de-Christianization has reached levels that were unimaginable when the Council closed. Suffice to consider that in former Communist Germany today just over ten per cent of the population is baptized: we are witnessing paganism's incredible rate of progress and Christianity, which still seemed present 30 years ago, is disappearing from life and from the public conscience."[86]

[84] Cited in Massimo Borghesi, "A New Beginning", 30 *Days*, no. 12 (1993): 62.

[85] Ibid., p. 64.

[86] Andrea Tornielli, "Interview with Cardinal Ratzinger: Testimonies in the Pagan Age", 30 *Days*, no. 11 (1992): 29–30.

When God judges something, he starts by removing things (cf. Isaiah 3:1–6).

The situation in the various countries of Western Europe is similar in many ways to what we have seen the case to be in North America, but in many countries the decline in faith and morality is even more advanced.

In Great Britain 75 percent of Catholics do not agree with the Church's teaching on contraception, 67 percent do not agree with the teaching on premarital sex, and the same percentage disagree with the teaching on divorce and remarriage.[87] The dominant Anglican Church is in even worse straits, with only 2 percent of its nominal membership attending church regularly.[88]

Among Catholic youth, as is the case in many other countries, the situation is very difficult. Even among those youth attending Catholic schools, half are abandoning the practice of their Faith by the age of fifteen.[89]

Even in Catholic Ireland the same trend was at work and showed up in surveys as early as 1977. At that time almost 10 percent of the general population did not attend church regularly, but already 25 percent of the youth did not attend regularly, and in the intervening years both numbers have increased, and the pressures to legalize abortion and divorce have made significant headway.[90] Of course, church attendance itself is not a reliable indicator for the depth of belief or commitment, as a rhyme recited by Cardinal O'Feigh, the recently deceased Primate of Ireland, at a synod on the laity, indicates: "Paddy Murphy went to Mass and never missed a Sunday, but Paddy Murphy went to hell for what he did on Monday."

The situation in France is even more difficult. Father Yves Congar, one of the greatest French Catholic theologians of this century, describes the situation as "dramatic": "It is dramatic in

[87] Michael P. Hornsby-Smith, "Catholicism in England", *America,* May 22, 1982, pp. 396–99.

[88] Andrea Tornielli, "The Theologian's Reasons", 30 *Days,* no. 12 (1992): 45.

[89] "Young British Catholics Abandoning Ship", *Catholic Weekly* (London), December 19, 1975.

[90] "Will the Irish Remain Christian?" *Faith Today* (Dublin), 1977.

many respects. There is no need to talk about it because the statistics say it all. Fourteen per cent of adults and only seven percent of young people go to church. . . . And then there is a desperate lack of priests. In the parish where I grew up only one Mass every two months is celebrated. I remember that in my town there were fifteen priests in a very small area. Today there are three. Inevitably the young are returning to paganism. There is no more religious practice. Yes, the situation is dramatic."[91]

The results of the most recent study of French Catholicism indicate that a great ecclesiastical "undoing" is under way. Nineteen percent of French people between the ages of fifty and sixty describe themselves as practicing Catholics. Only 10 percent in the forty to fifty age group describe themselves as such, and only 6 percent of those twenty-five to forty years old. For Catholics below the age of twenty-five, only 2.5 percent are practicing.

In 1958 92 percent of French babies were baptized. In 1984 only 60 percent were baptized. In 1948 there were 42,650 French priests, 35,000 in 1975, and 28,700 in 1987. Only 10 percent of the priests are under the age of forty.[92]

The rejection of faith in France seems to have penetrated beyond simply not attending church or disagreeing with certain moral teachings, as important as they are, but touches the very core of the Faith. Among the relatively small number of *practicing* French Catholics, 24 percent do not believe in the Resurrection of Jesus and 48 percent do not believe in the resurrection of the dead as they recite it in the Creed.[93]

A French professor who teaches at the Gregorian University in Rome sums up the situation like this: " 'Entertainment' has killed the metaphysical fiber in man's heart and sealed him off from the supernatural. The recent appeal of the Holy Father to the Church in France resounds for all of the West: 'What have you done with

[91] Yves Congar, O.P., "The Pope Also Obeys", 30 *Days,* no. 3 (1993): 29.

[92] Stefano Paci, "The Church in France: Could Paris Be Our Future, Too?" 30 *Days* (January 1991): 32–38.

[93] Antonio Socci, "The Theologian Who Cannot See or Touch", 30 *Days,* no. 6 (1992): 59.

your Christianity? What have you done with the promises of your baptism?' "[94]

The situation in Germany is also very difficult, with church attendance in the large cities estimated as between 10 and 24 percent of those who call themselves Catholics.[95]

In Spain, one of Europe's traditionally most Catholic countries, there has been a drastic falloff in religious practice in recent years. Eighty percent of Spaniards still describe themselves as Catholics, but only 30 percent attend church: "In a country that was long considered one of Europe's most Catholic nations, the prosperity that has followed the return of democracy here barely a decade ago has fed an extraordinary process of secularization that is rapidly eroding the church's traditional influence over society.

"Having lost its role as moral guardian and political arbiter of the nation's affairs, the Spanish church is experiencing a deep internal crisis as it struggles to find a new place for itself in a contemporary Spain seemingly more interested in mammon than God."[96]

A similar situation obtains in the Pope's own backyard. In 1984 25.6 percent of fifteen- to thirty-year-olds attended church regularly. Five years later the figure had dropped to 15.5 percent. Also, Catholic Italy, in defiance of the Church's teaching, enacted liberal divorce and abortion laws.[97] Just recently Italy achieved the distinction of having the lowest birthrate in the world: 1.3 babies per family.[98] The growth of occult practices in Italy is also reported to be a significant factor in the lives of even many Catholics.

At a special consultation sponsored by the Pontifical Council for the Laity, Father Dino Foglio, a distinguished Italian priest, described the situation in Italy like this:

---

[94] Xavier Tilliette, "I Have Faith, but We Are Beginning Again from Zero", 30 Days (December 1988): 53.

[95] Tommaso Ricci, "The Honeymoon Is Over", 30 Days (March 1990): 32.

[96] Alan Riding, "Church Stifled by Good Life's Roar", New York Times, August 4, 1989.

[97] Jean-Marie Guenois, "The Mass Is Ended", 30 Days (October 1989): 22.

[98] "Empty Cribs", Catholic World Report, March 1993, p. 9.

The majority of our Christian communities seem to be sluggish, lacking in vitality and apostolic fruitfulness. There are many causes of this, but the first and the most radical of all is certainly the fact that very few of our baptized Christians have really experienced God. We therefore have to admit that there has not been any real choice for Christ. This being so, all of our pastoral work remains precarious, because it is like building a house without foundations.

Now if the traditional structures for socializing the faith do not attain the purpose for which they are created, the whole system must be reviewed, and other paths must be sought out in the light of the Holy Spirit.[99]

Perhaps Cardinal Hans Groër, of Vienna, Austria, sums up the situation in Western Europe most succinctly: "The Church has never had so many baptized and yet there have never been so many people who do not believe."[100]

The situation of the Catholic Church in Australia and New Zealand is very similar to that of Western Europe and North America. In a recent meeting with Australian bishops the Pope lamented the continuing decline in Sunday Mass attendance.[101]

Eastern Europe

The situation of the Catholic Church in Eastern Europe and the former Soviet Union is one of both great difficulty and great opportunity. Over the past several years I have had the opportunity to visit several of the Eastern European and former Soviet countries more than once and to visit at length with Church and government leaders in those countries.

On one of these trips, to Poland, I stayed in a hotel in Warsaw

[99] Fr. Dino Foglio, "New Life in Christ", published in *Spectacle of Holiness for the World,* the 1991–1992 Bulletin of the Pontifical Council for the Laity, p. 57.

[100] Cardinal Hans Hermann Groër, "From Values to Reality", 30 *Days,* no. 5 (1993): 60.

[101] Pope John Paul II, "Bring All Catholics Back to the Weekly Eucharistic Celebration", *L'Osservatore Romano* (English ed.), June 2, 1993, p. 4.

for part of the trip and was struck at how it was swarming with businessmen from North America, Europe, and the Orient, all flooding into Poland to establish a commercial foothold. Economic and political freedom can certainly be a blessing, but what a tragedy if the Polish Church, having defeated one kind of oppression and slavery, falls into an even worse slavery, the slavery of the soul that is Western secularism.

People told me that Warsaw had no neon signs a few years ago; now they are common. The city shows the growing influence of Western television, music, and fashions. Pornography is sold openly. In a few years some streets of Warsaw will probably look like Broadway. Western materialism is making strong inroads, particularly among the youth, many of whom are turning away from the Church now that she is no longer the only alternative to communism.

A recent survey shows that although 97 percent of Polish citizens describe themselves as Catholics, between half and two-thirds refuse to accept Church teachings on abortion, contraception, and premarital sex.[102] Church leaders in Poland told me that in 1989, twenty-eight million of Poland's thirty-eight million people attended church regularly. In 1993 only ten million were regularly attending church, and trends for the future do not look bright. Religious education has been restored to Polish schools, and over 90 percent of youth in the schools attend the religious education classes, but only 25 percent go to church.

In recent elections the Catholic Coalition won only 7.1 percent of the vote, shocking the Church. Some are warning that the Church is depending too much on winning for herself a privileged position in the Constitution and not enough on Jesus Christ, and him crucified.[103]

In Hungary, there were many similarities. With a less rigid communism than many other countries, Hungary was among the first to be hospitable to Western business and other influences.

---

[102] "Looking East: Uncertain Church Loyalties in Poland", *National Catholic Register*, January 31, 1993, p. 3.
[103] Luigi Amicone, "The Clinton Effect on Warsaw", 30 *Days*, no. 9 (1993): 21.

While I was there I was able to share with friends a full-page advertisement that appeared in the *New York Times* a few years ago, celebrating the launching of the Hungarian edition of *Playboy* magazine. The ad illustrated well the challenges that Hungarian society will be facing.

The text of the ad reads:

> On November twenty-ninth, Hungarians came one step closer to something they've been fighting for since 1956. Freedom. Not just political freedom, but freedom of the press. And the first American consumer magazine published in Hungarian was *Playboy.* No surprise, since we're the magazine that led a social revolution in America by standing for personal, political, and economic freedom.
>
> That's the power of *Playboy.* A power that reaches 15,000,000 readers worldwide. And it's continuing to grow.
>
> 15,000,000 readers are devoted to us because we're devoted to them. That's why more Americans buy *Playboy* each month than *Esquire, GQ, Rolling Stone,* and *Business Week* combined. Making us the largest selling men's magazine — not just in the country — but in the world.
>
> So here's to freedom. Or, as they say in Hungary, *Eljen a Szabadsag.*

While the Catholic Church in Hungary is slowly adjusting to her new situation, the fastest-growing church in the country is led by Sandor Nemeth, a former Catholic: the five-thousand-member Faith Church in Budapest, which has already started more than eighty satellite churches throughout the country. While aware that he is rocking the boat of the religious establishment in Hungary, this leader finds many Hungarians, particularly the young people, "disillusioned with both communism and the Catholic establishment, and cult groups like the Hare Krishnas, Sun Myung Moon's Unification Church, Scientologists, Mormons and Jehovah's Witnesses are recruiting followers."[104]

In another major Hungarian city two friends from the Franciscan

---

[104] Lee Grady, "Hungarian Officials Target Churches", *Charisma,* April 1993, p. 52.

University of Steubenville are teaching English at a Catholic high school and witnessing to their faith, but they are outnumbered in that same city by ten Pentecostal missionaries from Southern California who are busy starting churches.

Shortly after my return from Hungary a new report hit the American press about the latest "gift" that American business was offering to the former Soviet Union: "Half a million people jammed an airfield Saturday to see AC–DC, the Black Crowes, and Metallica play at the Soviet Union's biggest Western rock concert, touted as a gift to Russian youth. . . .

"The show was 'in celebration of the successful defense of democracy as a gift to the youth of Russia. There is nothing commercial connected to it, no live telecasts, no HBO specials, nothing', said Marilyn Harris, corporate communications director for Time Warner."

The first hit is always free.

On trips to Lithuania, which has the highest percentage of Catholics of any of the countries of the former Soviet Union, significant conversations with Catholic bishops and youth revealed a difficult situation. The long years under communism have demoralized many of the priests, and interest in renewal or new initiatives is not high. Among many priests there is a strong tendency just to keep doing what was done to survive under communism and not make waves. Others are still primarily focused on the political issues and have not yet readjusted to the present needs of the Church for a great work of reevangelization. In the midst of this the strong materialist, secular influences from the West are gaining sway, and many of the youth are losing interest in what is perceived as a paralyzed, traditional, nondynamic Church.

Another factor that was particularly noticeable in Lithuania was the arrival of great numbers of evangelical and Pentecostal missionary groups as well as non-Christian religious groups from the West. In the face of the paralysis and poverty of the Catholic Church, these groups are making great strides, and many are joining them. The largest church building in the country will soon be not the Catholic cathedral but a church being built with help from Swedish Pentecostals for a burgeoning Pentecostal church in Lithuania. If it had not been for the welcoming attitude of one bishop in particular, many of the finest Catholic youth leaders we met would have left the Church for more dynamic Protestant groups. On one trip, Father Michael Scanlan, president of the Franciscan University of Steubenville, and I gave a one-day mini-rally at which hundreds of Catholics responded to opportunities to give their lives to Christ and pray for a fuller release of the Holy Spirit in their lives. Some had never been baptized. We also had the opportunity to offer some young Catholic women who were on their way to live with Mormon families in Utah and attend a predominantly Mormon university the opportunity to attend Franciscan University, where they are presently enrolled.

Throughout the former Soviet Union and the former satellite countries, more than a thousand non-Catholic *organizations* (not including individual congregations and individuals) from all over the world are working vigorously to proclaim the gospel (most often the Christian gospel, but sometimes the gospel of non-Christian sects and cults) with remarkable results. Hundreds of thousands are attending crusades, rallies, training schools, and seminars, and thousands of new churches are being started. Many are being brought to other countries for additional training and studies. American evangelical and Pentecostal evangelists and organizations are prominent in this effort, but so are evangelists and organizations from Africa, Korea, the Philippines, Sweden, and many other countries.

Listen to the eyewitness report of someone involved in such a mission:

> I recently returned to the United States from the city of Moscow where a number of American ministries sponsored a leadership training seminar . . . bringing nearly 1500 pastors and ministers from throughout Russia and the surrounding republics. We held two back-to-back leadership conferences in which a wide variety of training, teaching and equipping was offered. Needless to say, the whole occasion was charged with the presence of the Lord and with the prophetic excitement that characterizes these days of harvest.
>
> Often, as I faced the Russian disciples—most of them very

young both in years and in the Lord—I wondered who is really being trained, them or us! The fire in their eyes, the zeal in their hearts and the excitement and abandonment with which they cast themselves upon the Lord brought us both conviction and great joy.

Expecting to find a persecution-minded and dispirited group of believers (which was true for years), we were met with very lively, excited and prophetic disciples. As they came to the conference, traveling hundreds of miles on trains and buses, they were already positioned toward the Lord and were quick to enter into intense intercession and corporate worship. They were so young in some ways, and yet so mature in others. Indeed, as dark as the Russian landscape may be, the brightness of the emerging church is already drawing the multitudes to God's embrace.

Not only are these disciples and leaders hungry for God's presence and eager to grow, they also possess a very contagious prophetic vision for their land and for the entire earth. I remember a group of these Russian believers describing to us how they fully expect, after building the house of the Lord in their lands, to be sent southward to the Moslem republics. And after evangelizing them, paying the price of suffering and martyrdom, they believe God will open the Moslem world before them—sending them on to India, China and all the way to Jerusalem, where they expect to welcome the Lord's return! Oh, for such vision and fervor for us all![105]

In a recent interview the four Catholic bishops appointed to care for Catholics in various regions of the former Soviet Union gave witness to this situation:

As far as the sects are concerned, they have arrived in the Asian republics too and they are converting so many people. . . . Last summer the sects were also filling the stadiums here [Siberia]. They come from South Korea and America and tens of thousands flocked to listen to what they had to say. They represent a remarkable phenomenon. . . . The Protestant preachers are dominating television air-time, with hours and hours of broadcasts a week never mind the stadiums they rent throughout Russia.

[105] Reuven Doron, "The Lord of the Harvest", *River of Life Ministries,* May 1993, p. 1.

They even hired a boat on the Volga. . . . And in the meantime, the Catholic West sleeps on. It is allowing the sects to carry on with the "new evangelization". We received requests from Omsk for missionaries—either laymen or priests—to teach Catholicism. Down there we have just one priest. . . . Of course there is no comparison between the missionary work of Protestants and that of Catholics. I read about one Baptist project in the paper. In the West they pledged to build a thousand prayer houses for themselves in the former Soviet Union. And we've been trying for the past three years to put up a couple of Catholic churches but we still haven't laid the foundations. . . . I also read that Sweden alone has pledged to finance the building of 500 houses. They certainly get the job done. . . . It's true. They have an endless source of money. But I would like to say this. Our approach is wrong. We think it our duty to stay in the church and wait for the people to come to us and become Christians. But this is an illusion. The Christian proposal will only be convincing if lay witness flourishes, if people in their own environment bear witness. . . . At the time of the Iron Curtain everyone wanted to help us. Now it seems that no one, either religious congregations or Church movements, feel like coming here. And only God knows how much we need them.[106]

Just one Pentecostal church, in Tulsa, Oklahoma, has concentrated on the city of St. Petersburg, for example. In sixteen months it has held monthly crusades that draw twelve to fifteen thousand people each month. So far over four hundred thousand have put their faith in Christ in response to these crusades. The first church they helped start tripled after three months. A Russian Bible school they started has nine hundred students studying five days a week. While people travel monthly from Tulsa to St. Petersburg to help, some taking vacation time to do so and raising their own money, one family has sold their sporting goods store and moved there with their three school-age children to provide regular guidance for the church and Bible school.[107]

---

[106] Lucio Brunelli, "Gorby, Wish You Were Here", 30 *Days,* no. 12 (1992): 17–19.

[107] Natalie Nichols, "Tulsa Church Heads to Russia", *Charisma,* April 1993, p. 50.

Officials in the Russian government are amazingly welcoming of Christian help in restoring morality and character to the Russian people:

> Never mind Big Macs. The former Soviet republics are now opening their public school doors to teaching about Christianity.
>
> Russian officials from the Ministry of Education say they are inviting a consortium of 60 US evangelical groups and Christian colleges, calling itself the CoMission, to train educators in 120,000 public schools how to teach Judeo-Christian principles.
>
> CoMission leaders say they'll recruit 12,000 lay people and college students to spend a year each in the former Soviet Union.... "Seventy years ago, we closed God out of our country, and it has caused so many problems in our society we cannot count them", deputy education minister Evgeniy Kurkin said in a prepared statement recently. "We must put God back into our country, and we must begin with our children."
>
> Deputy minister of education Aleksandr G. Asmolov calls it a miracle that the Christians of the USA would help those in Russia.
>
> "Instead of hostilities, which we saw 10 years ago, we see kindness. That's why I can only say, praise God."[108]

Russian officials have invited Catholic, Orthodox, and traditional Protestant groups, Jews, Muslims, and Buddhists to help also. "So far, however, practically the only groups with the money, materials and will to respond have been evangelical and fundamentalist Protestants from the United States."[109]

Another evangelical organization from the United States, Bill Gothard's Institute in Basic Life Principles, is also doing extensive work in the former Soviet Union and has just announced that the Moscow City Council has asked them to distribute materials on building character to all 2.5 million families in their city. The

---

[108] Dennis Kelly, "New Russia Welcomes Christianity", *USA Today* (International ed.), November 11, 1992, p. 7A.

[109] Kenneth L. Woodward with Clinton O'Brien in Moscow, "Iisus Khristos Loves You", *Newsweek,* January 4, 1993, p. 45.

Russian air force has offered to transport the material free of charge.[110]

Another organization, Missouri-based Revival Fires Ministry, has been asked to provide Bibles to be used as textbooks for all seven thousand public schools in the capital.[111]

Still another organization, Youth with a Mission, has been asked to work alongside education officials in Albania to develop educational materials with Christian principles.[112] This particular evangelical organization has more than seven thousand career missionaries and more than twenty-five thousand short-term missionaries, operating in more than eighty countries.[113] I have encountered members of YWAM on my travels in various countries and find them unusually willing to work with existing churches, including the Catholic Church, and to make their contribution in a way that builds up the local church, when there is an openness to that, rather than start a new church: "Al Akimoff, YWAM's director for Slavic Ministries, says YWAM's missionaries are not aiming to lure Catholics out of their churches. Instead, he says, they are introducing Catholics to the knowledge of Christ and helping to establish Christ-centered, evangelistic Catholic communities."[114]

Also in Albania, the Christian Broadcasting Network has distributed 575,000 gospel booklets to every Albanian schoolchild in grades one through eight and has broadcast its animated children's television series on Albania's only television network.[115]

One bright spot for the Catholic Church in Albania was the appointment of Archbishop Ivan Diaz as papal nuncio. Archbishop Dias is known as a dynamic, Christ-centered bishop.

---

[110] This information is available from the Institute in Basic Life Principles, Box 1, Oak Brook, IL 60522.

[111] Elizabeth Farrell, "Religion Welcome in Slavic Schools", *Charisma*, March 1993, p. 60.

[112] Ibid.

[113] Robert L. Romaker, "One Good Turn Deserves Another", *Ann Arbor News*, January 9, 1993, p. A7.

[114] Julia Duin, "YWAM Builds Bridges to Catholics", *Charisma*, August 1993, p. 78.

[115] Susan Norman, "New Day Dawns in Atheist Albania", *Charisma*, June 1993, p. 76.

All in all, though, the Catholic and Orthodox church authorities of the former Soviet-bloc territories seem to be hampered in their efforts at pastoral and spiritual renewal and evangelization by their preoccupation with reclaiming confiscated church buildings and monasteries, disputing about territorial rights, and placing limits on one another in the name of ecumenism.[116] Meanwhile, the Protestants are coming.

As one Russian Orthodox theologian has put it: "Russian society and the Church are becoming strangers to each other. . . . People expected an answer to their questions. But the Church had been contaminated by the evils of Soviet society, the lack of truth, stereotyped language. . . . In 1989 there was great enthusiasm when priests spoke on television. Today nothing remains of this enthusiasm. Because the Church had nothing to say apart from banal generalities."[117]

Reflections like this are borne out in interviews with some of the Russians who are attending the new charismatic churches in Russia: "I go to the Orthodox church as well, but everything there is so complicated, with the priest and icons. Here everything is from the Bible, everything is understandable, and these pastors are so nice. We feel we're welcome here. . . . It's impossible to understand the priests; you don't feel welcome."[118]

And a prominent Catholic priest in the former Czechoslovakia warns against idealizing the current condition of the Catholic Churches of the East that have survived persecution:

> We should not be sentimental about the Catholic Church in the formerly Communist world. . . . There were, to be sure, martyrs in our church and many honest Christians who even under the hardest conditions have preserved their faith. However, there were also many who wanted to compromise, and there

---

[116] "Rifts in East Are Stubborn", *National Catholic Register,* November 29, 1992, pp. 1, 10. Lucio Brunelli, "The Ukrainian Hitch", 30 *Days,* no. 12 (1992): 25–27.

[117] Viktor Popkov, "At the Turning Point", *Catholic World Report,* December 1992, p. 19.

[118] Serge Schmemann, "Religion Returns to Russia, with a Vengeance", *New York Times,* July 28, 1993, p. A1.

were collaborators and even agents of the State Security. And if we count ourselves lucky because we don't have any problematic theologians with us, we should not fail to add that, unfortunately, we cannot provide a healthy, modern theology which could combine faithfulness to tradition with sensitivity to the needs of our time. For orthodoxy does not in any way mean anxious and uncreative repetition. He who boasts of his lack of tooth decay should ask himself if that is so because he has a set of artificial teeth.

Father Halik then points out that "our proverbial faith in relation to Church authority, too, may have been a little easier during the times when there were almost no bishops, or when our bishops were imprisoned . . . only now do I realize that it is not so simple to respect the authority of superiors whose natural human limits and weaknesses cannot be ignored. Loyalty to the persecuted church, too, was in a way humanly easier than solidarity with the public institution, for at times, some of its external manifestations were enough to make one blush with shame."

And while acknowledging the legitimacy of the Church's claims for the return of her possessions, he warns, "We should not overvalue the economic and institutional problems, but place our main emphasis on spiritual renewal . . . it may be good to remember that the Church does not live from the 'administrative' alone."[119]

The pastor of what may be the fastest-growing church in Czech lands, a Protestant charismatic, Daniel Drapal, who is attempting to build bridges and stand alongside Catholics, echoes this concern. He claims that the incessant demands that Catholic leaders have made for the return of Church property has diminished their respect in the country.

"If the only thing the people really know about the church is that it wants its property back . . . it's very difficult to tell people about Jesus, who said to sell all your property and give it to the poor."[120]

---

[119] Fr. Thomas Halik, "No Model for the West", *Catholic World Report,* June 1993, pp. 22–25.
[120] Randy Tift, "Czech Pastor Seeks Healing of Europe", *Charisma,* April 1994, pp. 60–61.

While speaking with leaders of the Ukrainian Greek Catholic Church in Lviv, in Western Ukraine, on a recent trip the same thought occurred. While these leaders are experiencing a large measure of success in retrieving Church buildings that formerly belonged to the Church and are working on the difficult problems of integrating priests from the underground with Russian Orthodox priests who have come over to the Greek Catholic Church and the Canadian and American Ukrainians in exile who have returned in leadership positions, the pastoral and spiritual problems of the population are daunting and are just beginning to be addressed.

A special report issued by the vicar general of the Archeparchy of Lviv details the "great ruin" of spiritual, moral, and ethical values suffered under the decades of communism. The lack of motivation to work, the widespread corruption and dishonesty as a way of life, the widespread alcoholism and substance abuse, the large numbers of abortions (in 1991 950,000 abortions were officially registered in Ukraine), the frequency of divorce and separations and sex outside of marriage, out-of-control crime, robberies, and now organized crime "families" provide daunting pastoral challenges.[121]

As in other countries, evangelical missionaries from the West are active and have a significant presence on the television channels, while a fledgling Catholic television effort struggles to get off the ground.

As previously noted, a major American Christian magazine ran a cover story titled "Why Is Latin America Turning Protestant?"[122]

---

[121] Msgr. Iwan Dacko, *The New Situation of the Ukrainian Greek-Catholic Church in Ukraine,* published by the Archeparchy of Lviv, September 14, 1992. See also the January–February 1994 issue of *Catholic World,* devoted to an analysis of the situation of the Church in Eastern Europe.

[122] *Christianity Today,* April 6, 1992. Two full-length books have also been published that deal with the phenomenon of evangelical and Pentecostal growth in Latin America; David Stoll, "*Is Latin America Turning Protestant? The Politics of Evangelical Growth* (Berkeley, Calif.: University of California Press, 1990); and David Martin, *Tongues of Fire: The Explosion of Protestantism in Latin America* (Cambridge, Mass.: Basil Blackwell, 1991). An interesting review of these books, by Joseph E. Davis, appeared in the May 1991 edition of *First Things.* Joseph Davis has also written an article for *America,* January 19, 1991,

Unless the Catholic and Orthodox churches turn their energies to the kind of internal spiritual renewal, repentance, and conversion that prepares the way for the preaching of the gospel and the moving of the Holy Spirit, it will not be too many more years before we read another headline: "Why Is the Former Soviet Union Turning Protestant?" But even graver things are at stake.

As Father Werenfried Van Straaten, leader of a major Catholic aid agency, recently said: "If Christ is not preached in these countries, the whole former Soviet block will crumble into ruins. It will become like a decomposing corpse on our doorstep, a corpse 10 times the size of Western Europe. But a corpse whose poisons and stench will weaken the forthcoming millennium right from the start. Without Christ diplomatic efforts to halt the imminent decline will be to no avail."[123]

The results of alcoholism, environmental pollution, multiple abortions, and the breakdown of the health-system infrastructure in Russia, as well as perhaps more accurate statistics, have led to deaths exceeding births by nearly eight hundred thousand last year, making Russia the first industrialized nation to experience such a sharp decrease for reasons other than war, famine, or disease. Life expectancy of adult men has plummeted to sixty years, which means that men in Indonesia, the Philippines, and parts of Africa now live longer than the average man in Russia. If the trend continues, the country's population of 148 million will shrink sharply in the coming years.[124]

But rather than despair, Father Van Straaten is calling for prayer and conversion: "Now we are throwing ourselves heart and soul into a worldwide ecumenical campaign of prayer. Its objective is that the Church in the West and the Church in the East might be converted together and together take the last step along the road to reconciliation. That we might rise again together

---

pp. 37–46, "The Protestant Challenge in Latin America", which deals with these themes.

[123] Gianpaolo Barra, "A Decomposing Corpse", *Catholic World Report,* February 1993, p. 37.

[124] Michael Specter, "Russian Population Shrinks", *Ann Arbor News,* March 6, 1994, p. A6.

from the spiritual ruins of the twentieth century and together proclaim the Gospel credibly to a generation which has lost faith in Marx and is now called to be the herald of the Kingdom of God in the third Christian millennium."[125]

Despite the great challenges the Church is facing and the great weaknesses and failures that we must necessarily consider here, we must not lose sight of the providential hand of God, which is even now using even the most negative of circumstances to prepare his Bride, the Church, for the coming of his Son.

Julian of Norwich, the fourteenth-century English mystic, puts it well:

> Holy Church will be shaken in sorrow and anguish and tribulation in this world as men shake a cloth in the wind; and in this matter our Lord answered, revealing in this way: Ah, I shall turn this into a great thing, of endless honour and everlasting joy, in heaven. Yes, I even saw that our Lord rejoices with pity and compassion over the tribulations of his servants; and he imposes on every person whom he loves, to bring him to his bliss, something that is no defect in his sight, through which souls are humiliated and despised in this world, scorned and mocked and rejected. And he does this to prevent the harm which they might have from the pomps and the pride and the vainglory of this wretched life, and to prepare their way to come to heaven, into endless, everlasting bliss. For he says: I shall completely break down in you your empty affections and your vicious pride, and then I shall gather you and make you meek and mild, pure and holy through union with me.[126]

The pattern of purification and transformation for the Church is the same as for the individual; it is the pattern of the Cross. But we must not forget, even at the darkest moments, the surpassing glory of the subsequent Resurrection, already prefigured in Christ himself.

---

[125] Fr. Werenfried Van Straaten, *Aid to the Church in Need Mirror,* no. 7 (October 1992): 1.
[126] Julian of Norwich, *Showings,* chap. 28.

Chapter Three

The Lifting up of Jesus

While we have surveyed the situation of the Catholic Church in the various continents at least in regard to some of the challenges that she faces, I would like now to gather together some of this information and focus it in a way that prepares us to begin to see the great work the Holy Spirit is doing within the Catholic Church to prepare her for the situation we are in. I realize that, for many reasons, it is hard to take so much "bad news" all at once, but I assure you it is only so we can better understand and appreciate the great good news that is God's gift to the Catholic Church, even in this hour and indeed to all humanity.

At a certain point Jesus said to his disciples, "I, when I am lifted up from the earth, will draw all men to myself" (Jn 12:32). As we look around the world to try to ascertain what the Lord is doing, what the signs of the times are signifying, we are struck by how many are turning to Jesus when he is clearly and confidently proclaimed in the power of the Holy Spirit. For many reasons, it is difficult for Catholics really to see what is happening in this regard.

One of the real surprises of the last part of the twentieth century is the growth rate of those segments of the Christian church that are commonly called evangelical or Pentecostal, in comparison to the mainline Protestant, Catholic, and Orthodox churches. The documentation of such rapidly growing movements is challenging and sometimes unreliable, but church historians and researchers such as Vinson Synan, Peter Wagner, and David Barrett have attempted to chart this growth in a way that is useful to look at for our purposes.

The *Yearbook of American and Canadian Churches* publishes membership figures yearly for the churches in the United States and Canada. Between the years 1965 and 1989, some churches declined in membership while others grew, some significantly.

United Methodists lost 19 percent, the United Church lost 21 percent, the Episcopalians lost 29 percent, the Presbyterians lost 32 percent, and the Disciples of Christ lost 45 percent. Catholics gained 25 percent, Southern Baptists gained 38 percent, Church of the Nazarene gained 63 percent, Seventh Day Adventists gained 92 percent, Assemblies of God gained 121 percent, Mormons gained 133 percent, and the Church of God gained 183 percent.[1]

It is clear that by 1982 some very significant changes had occurred in worldwide Christianity. Nonwhite Christians exceeded white Christians for the first time, and this was in good measure because of the growth of the Pentecostal and charismatic denominations and movements. Over 70 percent of this rapidly growing segment of Christianity is nonwhite. In 1982 the Pentecostal denominations (not including the members of historical churches that are involved with the charismatic renewal) became the largest Protestant family of churches, larger than any of the Baptist, Methodist, Lutheran, Presbyterian, or Anglican groupings. Given that the history of the Pentecostal denominations encompassed only about eighty years, and the churches of the Reformation more than four hundred years, this was an extraordinary development.[2]

By 1990 the Pentecostal denominations had surpassed the Eastern Orthodox churches in numbers and had become the second largest grouping of churches after the Roman Catholic Church. The Eastern Orthodox counted approximately 179 million members in 1990, the Pentecostal denominations counted 193 million, and the Roman Catholics counted 962 million. In addition to the 193 million members of Pentecostal denominations there were,

---

[1] Figures presented in chart form in *Time,* April 5, 1993, pp. 46–47.
[2] Vinson Synan, *The Spirit Said "Grow"* (Monrovia, Calif.: MARC, 1992), p. 5.

according to Synan, an estimated fifty million Chinese Pentecostals unaffiliated with any denomination in underground "house
churches" in China, fifty-five million members of mainline Protestant churches involved in the charismatic renewal, and seventy-
two million Roman Catholics involved in the charismatic renewal.
All together the Pentecostal and charismatic expression of Christianity comprised 21.4 percent of world Christianity in 1990 and
was clearly the fastest-growing segment.

By 1992 the numbers of Pentecostals and charismatics had
grown to over 410 million and now comprised 24.2 percent of
world Christianity.[3] Researchers such as Peter Wagner of Fuller
Theological Seminary claim that a majority of active Christians
throughout the world are now Pentecostal or charismatic: "Any
careful observer visiting churches internationally would know for
certain that the considerable majority of committed Christians
worldwide would be regarded as part of the Pentecostal-charismatic
stream. . . . My research has led me to make this bold statement: *In
all of human history, no other non-political, non-militaristic, voluntary
human movement has grown as rapidly as the Pentecostal-charismatic
movement in the last 25 years.*"[4]

While debate is certainly possible on Wagner's point, and while
the impact of his point depends on his definition of what consti-
tutes an active or committed Christian, it is nevertheless striking
that someone with such solid credentials and such extensive research
travel would make such a bold statement.

It is instructive to look at some of the statistical information in
chart form. While some of the rapidly growing churches are
growing from small bases and relatively small absolute numbers
compared to the larger historical churches and therefore the early
growth in percentage terms is understandably striking, nevertheless the information is important.

As noted in the previous chapter, a significant portion of this
Pentecostal growth is composed of millions of former Catholics

[3] Ibid., pp. 9–11.
[4] Ibid., p. ii.

CHURCHES IN AUSTRALIA
DECADAL GROWTH RATES 1976–1981

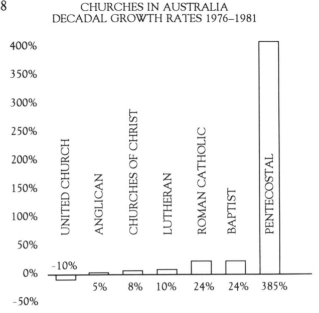

CHURCHES IN GHANA (EAST AKIM)
DECADAL GROWTH RATES 1976–1986

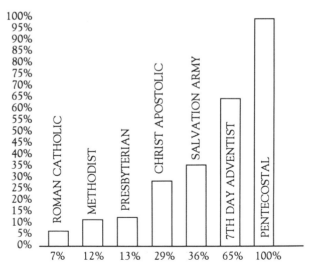

Charts compiled by Peter Wagner and used with his permission

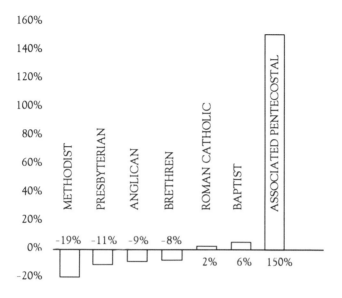

CHURCHES IN NEW ZEALAND
DECADAL GROWTH RATES 1971–1981

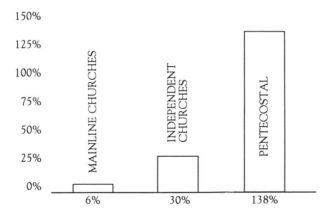

CHURCHES IN SRI LANKA
DECADAL GROWTH RATES 1969–1978

CHURCHES IN THE U.S. AND CANADA
DECADAL GROWTH RATES 1965–1989

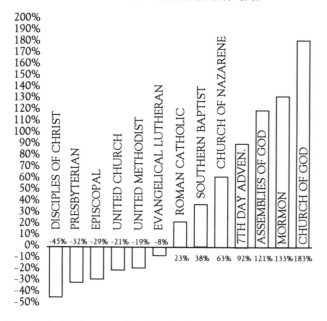

Source: *Yearbook of American and Canadian Churches*, 1965, 1989.

CATHOLIC CHURCH STATISTICS
1991–1992

Country	Total number	Percentage of total population
Australia	4,762,000	27.5%
Canada	11,971,562	45.0%
England	4,179,177	9.0%
Ghana	1,958,000	12.6%
New Zealand	476,000	14.0%
Sri Lanka	1,156,000	6.7%
United States	56,398,696	22.0%

Source: *Yearbook of American and Canadian Churches*, 1965, 1989.

who claim not to have found a living relationship with God that made a difference in their daily lives in their contact with the Catholic Church.

One such former Catholic, who obviously retains a deep love and respect for the Catholic Church, published his reflections on why Catholics such as himself leave the Church:

> Time and time again, however, defectors like myself say that the difficulty we had with Catholicism was that this same powerful force that has done such great things in history also overshadows and obscures Christ. The effect of the obscurity for me was that, while I certainly grew up knowing about Jesus, I never realized who He is or why He came to earth in the first place. I knew Catholicism ... I have been shaped by Catholicism as religious system and culture—but, I never heard the Gospel.
>
> I can just see Catholic religious leaders pulling their hair out at that statement: "What do you mean you never heard the Gospel! What do you think we've been proclaiming the last 2,000 years in the Eucharist?" Yes, I realize the preeminent place Christ holds in the Mass. I know Scriptures are read every Sunday. I know the magnificence and purity of the Nicene Creed and its unchanging call to recommitment. I've no interest in slandering an institution for which I hold tremendous respect. I have to report, though, what I hear coming from the mouths of ex-Catholics as they describe their number-one reason for leaving Catholicism: "How could it be that I spent 22 years in the Catholic Church", one friend spoke angrily, "and never heard the Gospel?" ... We left because we met Jesus Christ, and He changed our lives in a way that we never knew in the Catholic Church. I left because someone shared with me the same Gospel that gripped St. Peter and the apostles and martyrs and thousands of Catholic and Protestant saints since. I came to understand who Jesus is and why He came to earth ... to free us from the encumbrance of sin, providing us with what we could not do for ourselves: restore us to God for eternity.... For reasons I don't nearly understand, millions of other former Catholics beside myself couldn't hear this Gospel within the Catholic Church. I urge Catholic leaders in this country to ask themselves why

their most potentially ardent members must go elsewhere to find their spiritual food.[5]

These reflections match what hundreds of Catholics and former Catholics have told me over the years and in the mail I receive in response to our weekly television and radio programs.[6] Just as I was thinking about this issue in preparation for writing this chapter, I received two letters, which I will excerpt here, that are typical of many that I receive:

> I realize you must receive a multitude of mail, but I do hope and pray that this note reaches your hand personally. . . . My husband and I are Catholics. . . . Our church is the only Catholic church here in. . . . We have always been Catholic, and we realize the importance of the Eucharist, which we love. We believe that the Catholic Church is the one true Church; however, we believe you don't have to be Catholic to get to heaven. We are not learning or growing here in our parish. In fact, we are dying—slowly drowning and knowing it. We are most concerned for our children. The CCD program is lacking in many areas. When I was growing up we heard God loves us, but we were also taught very definite rights and wrongs. Today everything is watered down. We want our children to grow up secure in the Lord and their relationship with him. We want them to have a Church that encourages and supports them when they stand up for what is right and that is there for them when they fall. We have been very frustrated for a long time. Our son will be entering kindergarten, and maybe that's why we are thinking about it so much. . . . The Knights of Columbus are an active group in our parish, but many of their meetings are beer-drinking ones. They were also responsible for starting

[5] Mark Christensen, "Coming to Grips with Losses: The Migration of Catholics into Conservative Protestantism", *America,* January 26, 1991.

[6] For more than ten years I've hosted a weekly Catholic television and radio program called "The Choices We Face". Besides airing on the EWTN network in the United States and the VISION network in Canada, it is transmitted over regular broadcast stations in many other cities as well. Those wishing a listing of times and stations where the program is available can obtain this information by writing to The Choices We Face, Box 7712, Ann Arbor, MI 48107.

bingo in our parish hall open to the public with large cash winnings. We are ashamed of this because we feel this is gambling and a bad influence on our young. . . . We have considered leaving the Church here and joining the Assemblies of God. There is little to no Christian friendship here . . . we've tried prayer meetings, yet nobody comes. Our pastor is burned out and frustrated with the lack of participation . . . yet so many people from the Assemblies have been there for my husband and me in prayer and support many times when we needed it. We visit their church occasionally. My husband and I feel very pulled apart by all of this. . . . We feel the need to seek the Lord where he may be found, for our own sakes as well as our children's.

Another person writes:

I work at a Catholic hospital as a counselor and love being near the Blessed Sacrament all day, though my unit is very anti-Catholic in subtle ways. But I can't meet Catholics who are excited and committed to Jesus either here or at my parish. I've tried for ten years. I've taught CCD, worked in the St. Vincent de Paul Society, but our parish is so cold and hardly anyone knows my name even though I've taught there for eight years. . . . I started going to Protestant churches because they met me in my need when I was pregnant and needed help right after having the baby; they helped me move, invited me to a Bible study, and prayed with me. . . . I have tried to hang in there as a Catholic and light a candle rather than curse the darkness, but I no longer feel any strength to continue to try. . . . I've never written a letter to anyone I didn't know before, but my heart aches about this.

Or as a recent news article put it:

One of the fastest-growing churches in the . . . Archdiocese is Southeast Christian Church, a Protestant church whose congregation is 60%–65% former Catholics, which takes in an estimated $126,000 a week in its Sunday collection, and which is building a new $4–$5 million place of worship for its expanding community.

Faithful Catholics in the archdiocese . . . say they are now growing despondent. . . . Reluctantly, they now say, the archbishop cannot grasp the serious crisis afflicting the local Church, or he is ignoring it, since many Catholics have tried to alert him to the problems of diminishing numbers, the lack of zeal and low Mass attendance, the widespread liturgical aberrations, the falling away by many Catholics from a sacramental life, and the high rate of divorce among Catholics . . . a majority of archdiocesan . . . priests have called for the ordination of women and relaxation of the Church's rule of clerical celibacy as a way to solve the Church's problems.[7]

In recent years this has not escaped the notice of significant leadership in the Catholic Church. Initially prevalent attitudes of blaming Protestants for "proselytizing" Catholics or, in Latin America, conspiracy theories involving the CIA[8] have given way to serious reflection that is identifying significant weaknesses in the pastoral situation of the Catholic Church today.

That is precisely the approach that Cardinal Vidal, Archbishop of Cebu, Philippines, has taken in his region: "The presence and activity of fundamentalists in our midst, far from discouraging our own efforts, stimulated us to work on five fronts: (1) reading, study and prayer with the Bible in hand; (2) catechesis leading to mature personal commitment; (3) a pastoral approach that reaches out to all, especially the marginalized, and makes them feel they really belong to the church, either through parishes or small communities; (4) the liturgy must become warm, fraternal, with biblically based homilies; (5) recruit and form lay pastoral agents to confirm their brothers and sisters in the faith."[9]

Cardinal Thiandoum of Senegal, in a speech at the African Synod of Bishops in 1994, expressed a need to learn from the "sects" and even reach out a hand of friendship:

---

[7] Paul Likoudis, "Louisville Priests Tell Archbishop It's Time to Ordain Women Priests", *Wanderer,* November 19, 1992, p. 1.

[8] Joseph E. Davis, "The Protestant Challenge in Latin America", *America,* January 19, 1991, pp. 38–39. Peter Steinfels, "Shepherds, or Wolves? Whatever, Flocks Grow", *New York Times,* October 27, 1992, p. A4.

[9] Peter Hebblethwaite, "Cardinals Study Sects, Digressing to Aim at Other Targets", *National Catholic Reporter,* April 19, 1991, p. 6.

The *Sects* feature in many of the responses to the *Lineamenta*, often as a cause of concern for the Church. This word however covers a diversity of phenomena, even in the same area. Their activities and apparent success often challenge us to look more closely into our methods of evangelization and pastoral care. Should we not acknowledge some of their strong points: zeal for the Gospel, deep conviction, attention to individual needs of body and soul, effective organization in small groups, lively, warm and enjoyable worship? Even in cases of fanatical opposition to the Catholic faith, a positive response on our part in the spirit of dialogue is always possible. The Church, as a patient and indulgent mother, must have an open heart which invites and welcomes everyone.[10]

In an interview in connection with the African Synod of Bishops, Cardinal Arinze, one of the Synod's presidents, made similar points: "We have to accept that the sects are really saying to the Church 'Please, do your homework; please look into your house, ask yourselves why do we attract quite a number of your members? What is it that we have that attracts them that you don't have?'... Why is it that these Independent Churches succeed? What is it that they have which attracts, which perhaps the Catholic Church needs to reflect more about? What is it that we can do to work with them and to convince them that we are members of a Church that is universal?"[11]

In 1986 four departments of the Vatican issued a report, "Sects or New Religious Movements: Pastoral Challenge", that attempted to analyze a broad group of religious movements, including non-Christian movements. While pointing out some of the problems characteristic of these groupings, the report also spoke directly of the need for the Catholic Church to examine herself and make some changes. The report summarized some of its conclusions in a particularly striking way: "The Church is often seen simply as an

[10] Cardinal Hyacinthe Thiandoum, "The Gospel, Inculturation and Dialogue", *L'Osservatore Romano* (English ed.), April 20, 1994, p. 11.
[11] Gerard O'Connell, "Arinze on the African Synod", *Inside the Vatican*, April 1994, pp. 41–43.

institution, perhaps because it gives too much importance to structures and not enough to drawing people to God in Christ."[12]

Bishop Paul Cordes, vice-president of the Pontifical Council for the Laity, when asked why he was working to build unity among the various lay movements in the Church, responded: "The movements are important for the Church today because they have a very Christ-centered vision of faith. They all speak of Christ as the main point in the life of a Christian. Sometimes when I look at the general pastoral goals of the Church I find this lacking. I don't find the emphasis on veneration of God. The mission of the movements is to keep alive the idea that salvation comes from God, and this they can do together."[13]

This echoed a similar direct statement made by the 1985 World Synod of Bishops: "Because of a partial reading of the council, a unilateral presentation of the church as a purely institutional structure devoid of her mystery has been made. We are probably not immune from all responsibility for the fact that especially the young critically consider the church a pure institution. Have we not perhaps favored this opinion in them by speaking too much of the renewal of the church's external structures and too little of God and of Christ?"[14]

The Pope himself has gradually come to recognize that blaming the sects is not an adequate explanation for what is happening: "However, we cannot forget that their success is owed to the tepidity and indifference of the Church's children, who are not up to the level of their evangelizing mission because of their weak testimony of a coherent Christian life, their neglect of the liturgy and the expressions of popular piety, and also because of the scarcity of priests and pastoral ministers, among other causes. The effects of an insufficient catechesis and formation leave many

---

[12] "Sects or New Religious Movements: Pastoral Challenge", *L'Osservatore Romano* (English ed.), May 19, 1986, p. 5, sec. 5, par. 2.

[13] Bishop Paul Cordes, "Voices: Bishop Paul Cordes on the Role of Lay Movements", *National Catholic Register,* June 24, 1990, p. 6.

[14] Synod of Bishops, "The Final Report", *Origins* 15, no. 27 (December 19, 1985): I, 4, p. 445.

faithful in lamentable helplessness before the recruitment work by non-Catholic agents."[15]

In 1991 Pope John Paul II called together a special meeting of the world's cardinals to discuss two topics he considered particularly urgent at the time: one was abortion and other life issues; the other was the growth of the "new religious movements". Cardinal Arinze, head of the Pontifical Council for Interreligious Dialogue, and an African, presented a comprehensive analysis of the "new religious movements" and of the searching questions the Catholic Church needs to ask herself, faced with their success.

Cardinal Arinze pointed out that many of these new religious movements are exposing the pastoral weak points of the Catholic Church. They supply many forceful leaders and evangelists who are trained in a relatively short time, whereas priests are few and scarce. They bring infectious dynamism and remarkable commitment, whereas the Catholic people are lukewarm and indifferent. They focus on salvation only through Christ and take advantage of widespread Catholic confusion regarding the basis of salvation. They develop small communities so that individuals feel loved, appreciated, and given a meaningful role, whereas parishes are too large and impersonal. They assign leadership roles, whereas lay people feel marginalized. They celebrate fervent religious services, whereas the sacred liturgy is celebrated in a cold and routine manner. They urge personal commitment to Jesus Christ and strict adherence to the Bible, whereas homilies are intellectually above the heads of the people. They stress personal relationship with God, whereas the Church seems presented too much as an institution marked by structures and hierarchy.

The Cardinal calls for self-examination: "What makes people join the new religious movements? What are the legitimate needs of people that these movements promise to answer and that the Church should be meeting? Are there other causes of the rise and spread of these movements? What does God want of the Church in this situation? . . .

---

[15] Pope John Paul II, cited in Davis, "The Protestant Challenge in Latin America", p. 44.

"The dimension of religious experience should not be forgotten in our presentation of Christianity. It is not enough to supply people with intellectual information. Christianity is neither a set of doctrines nor an ethical system. It is life in Christ which can be lived at ever deeper levels."

In conclusion, Cardinal Arinze noted, "In front of the dynamic activity of the new religious movements, the pastors of the Church cannot just go on with 'business as usual'. The phenomenon of the new religious movements is a challenge and an opportunity." The Cardinal concludes his presentation by repeating Pope John Paul II's call for a "new evangelization".[16]

It is not just Cardinal Arinze who is pleading with us that we not go on with "business as usual". Listen to the voice of a former evangelical Protestant who is now a Catholic:

> During the past few years, I have come across a number of articles in Catholic periodicals bemoaning the huge numbers of Catholics, especially in Latin America, who are flooding into evangelical Protestant churches. The reasons given always seem to be variations on a theme . . . the overall impression is that the Church is being besieged by an inexplicable, emotionally primitive form of cross-cultural handling.
>
> As a born and bred evangelical who has done graduate work with some of the foremost evangelical mission strategists, has been familiar with missionary circles for years, and who has since converted to Catholicism, I am acutely aware that the evangelical tide sweeping across Latin America and other traditional Catholic communities may not be accurately evaluated in so superficial a fashion. . . . In my experience, evangelical missionaries and mission leaders, teachers and strategists are usually an intellectually and culturally sophisticated crowd, heavily endowed with MA's and PhD's. . . . Evangelicals are convinced that it is of the supreme importance that each human being have the opportunity to know Jesus Christ as Lord and God. This is both disconcerting and puzzling to many Catholics, who tend to think of evangelism as a breach of good taste, if

[16] Cardinal Francis Arinze, "A Pastoral Approach to the Challenge Posed by the New Religious Movements", *L'Osservatore Romano* (English ed.), April 15, 1991, pp. 5ff.

not out-and-out spiritual fascism. We have wandered far from the spirit of Francis Xavier and Teresa of Lisieux. I know many lay evangelicals who have spent years in advanced education in order to be able to enter, in a secular capacity, countries officially closed to mission work so that some living witness to the Lordship of Jesus Christ might be found there. The evangelicals have read our history. It was in just such a spirit that the missionary monks confronted the pagan cultures of their day. Do we really think that business-as-usual cultural Catholicism is going to be able to stand up to that sort of purposeful, self-sacrificial passion? Instead of wringing our hands helplessly, we should be learning from our separated brethren and pray that God will rekindle in us the fire of the Gospel.[17]

And is not the voice of Francis Xavier himself, coming to us from the sixteenth century, still relevant here?

There is now in these parts a very large number of persons who have only one reason for not becoming Christian, and that is that there is no one to make them Christians. It often comes into my mind to go round all the Universities of Europe, and especially that of Paris, crying out every where like a madman, and saying to all the learned men there whose learning is so much greater than their charity, *"Ah! what a multitude of souls is through your fault shut out of heaven and falling into hell!"* Would to God that these men who labour so much in gaining knowledge would give as much thought to the account they must one day give to God of the use they have made of their learning and of the talents entrusted to them! I am sure that many of them would be moved by such considerations, would exercise themselves in fitting meditations on Divine truths, so as to hear what God might say to them, and then, renouncing their ambitions and desires, and all the things of the world, they would form themselves wholly according to God's desire and choice for them. They would exclaim from the bottom of their hearts: *"Lord, here am I; send me whithersoever it shall please Thee, even to India!"* Good God! how much happier and how much safer they would be! With what far greater confidence in God's

[17] Sherry Weddell, "Evangelicals in Brazil", *Catholic World Report,* March 1992, pp. 6–7.

mercy would they meet their last hour, the supreme trial of that terrible judgment which no man can escape! They would then be able joyfully to use the words of the faithful servant in the Gospel: *"Lord, Thou gavest me five talents; behold, I have gained beside them other five!"* They labour night and day in acquiring knowledge, and they are very diligent indeed in understanding the subjects which they study; but if they would spend as much time in that which is the fruit of all solid learning, and be as diligent in teaching to the ignorant the things necessary to salvation, they would be far better prepared to give an account of themselves to our Lord when He shall say to them: *"Give an account of thy stewardship."* I fear much that these men, who spend so many years in the Universities in studying the liberal arts, look more to the empty honours and dignities of the prelature than to the holy functions and obligations of which those honours are the trappings. [18]

In the face of all these difficulties, John Paul II has begun insistently to call the Church to a "new evangelization". It has almost become the major focus of his pontificate. What is this "new evangelization" to which the Pope is calling the Catholic Church as we approach the end of the century? What is its significance in relationship to some of the "signs of the times" that we have been attempting to discern and interpret?

The New Evangelization

Pope John Paul II first called for a "new evangelization" in 1983 in Haiti, a new evangelization that would be "new in ardor, methods, and expression". In 1992 he addressed all the bishops of Latin America on the occasion of the five-hundredth centenary of Columbus' discovery of the New World and its subsequent evangelization and again called for a new evangelization: "The new evangelization does not consist of a 'new gospel'. . . . Neither

---

[18] Letter of Francis Xavier from Cochin, December 31, 1543. Henry James Coleridge, *The Life and Letters of St. Francis Xavier,* 3d ed., vol. 1 (London: Burns and Oates, 1902), pp. 155–56.

does it involve removing from the Gospel whatever seems difficult for the modern mentality to accept. Culture is not the measure of the Gospel, but it is Jesus Christ who is the measure of
every culture and every human action. . . . The new evangelization
has as its point of departure the certitude that in Christ there are
'inscrutable riches' (Eph 3:8) which no culture nor era can exhaust,
and which we must always bring to people in order to enrich
them. . . . These riches are, first of all, Christ himself, his person,
because he himself is our salvation."[19]

In addressing the phenomenon of so many Catholics leaving
the Church as a result of the efforts of what are often called in
Latin America the "sects", the Pope calls the Church to focus on
helping people come into personal relationship with God in her
evangelizing efforts and sees a good part of the new evangelization
as being a reevangelization of those who are perhaps only nomi-
nally Catholic: "The alarming phenomenon of the sects must be
met with a pastoral action that places at its center the whole
person, his community dimension and his longing for a personal
relationship with God."[20]

When speaking of the danger of political and social ideologies
that point to a false salvation in purely temporal terms, the Pope
again points to the person of Christ: "What will free us from these
signs of death? Experience in the world today increasingly shows
that ideologies are unable to defeat that evil which keeps people
enslaved. Christ is the only one who can free us from this evil. . . . It
makes the task that the Church is facing more urgent: to rekindle
in the heart of all the baptized the grace they received. 'I remind
you', St. Paul wrote to Timothy, 'to stir into flame the gift of God
that you have' (2 Tim 1:6).

"Just as the people of the new covenant received life through
the Holy Spirit at Pentecost, only this acceptance will raise up a

[19] Pope John Paul II, "Address to Bishops of Latin America", *L'Osservatore
Romano* (English ed.), October 21, 1992, p. 7, sec. 6.

[20] Ibid., p. 7, sec. 12. The American bishops have also recently issued an
important pastoral letter on evangelization, "Go and Make Disciples", which
advances even further the excellent work being done on this topic. It is
theologically clear, inspiring, and practical as well.

people capable of giving birth to men and women who are renewed and free, and conscious of their dignity."[21]

In his closing words the Pope speaks in a particularly inspiring and prophetic manner:

> Jesus Christ, the faithful Witness, the Pastor of pastors, is in our midst, because we are gathered in his name (cf. Mt 18:20). With us is the Spirit of the Lord which guides the Church to the fullness of truth and renews her with the revealed word in a new Pentecost. . . .
>
> Be faithful to your baptism, in this centenary give new life to the great gift you have received, turn your hearts and gaze to the centre and origin, to him who is the basis of all happiness, the fullness of everything! Be open to Christ, welcome the Spirit, so that a new Pentecost may take place in every community! A new humanity, a joyful one, will arise from your midst; you will experience again the saving power of the Lord and "what was spoken to you by the Lord" will be fulfilled. What "was spoken to you", America, is his love for you, his love for each one, for all your families and peoples. . . .
>
> Church of America, today the Lord is passing by. He is calling you. In this moment of grace, he is once again calling you by name and renewing his covenant with you. May you listen to his voice so that you may know true, total joy and enter into his peace (cf. Ps 94:7, 11)![22]

In 1994 John Paul II identified the "typical style of the new evangelization: a style marked by what is essential and radical, immersed in the mystery of the dead and risen Christ and courageously open to the needs of modern man".[23]

The Theological and Historical Significance of the "New Evangelization"

As I was reflecting on this call to evangelism that Pope John Paul II is making, in continuity with Pope Paul VI, and the upsurge of

---

[21] Ibid., p. 8, sec. 19.

[22] Ibid., p. 10, sec. 30.

[23] John Paul II, "Your 'Way' Builds up Parishes", *L'Osservatore Romano* (English ed.), February 9, 1994, p. 7.

such evangelism in the charismatic renewal as well as in other movements and initiatives, I came across the text of a talk that noted American theologian Father Avery Dulles, S.J., gave that was published in the February 1, 1992, issue of *America* magazine and later printed in pamphlet form by Fordham University.

In this talk Father Dulles points out how significant this call to evangelization is in light of the actual focus of the Catholic Church in recent centuries: "The majority of Catholics are not strongly inclined toward evangelization. The very term has for them a Protestant ring. The Catholic Church is highly institutional, sacramental, and hierarchical in its structures. Its activities are primarily directed toward the instruction and pastoral care of its own members, whose needs and demands tax the institution to its limits. Absorbed in the inner problems of the Church, and occasionally in issues of peace and justice, contemporary Catholics feel relatively little responsibility for spreading the faith."[24]

Father Dulles points out that missionary activity in predominantly non-Christian lands was seen as the job of a specialized few and that in predominantly Christian lands "mission" for Catholics was in bringing Protestants to see the truth of the claims of the Catholic Church: "In predominantly Christian territories Catholics showed no lack of interest in convert-making, but again the thrust was not evangelical; the gospel was hardly at the center. This apostolate was mainly directed to showing, against Protestants, that Christ had founded a hierarchical Church, which was to be accepted as the organ of divine revelation. The focus was more on authority than on content. Catholics were instructed to believe whatever the Church taught precisely because it was Church teaching."[25]

Father Dulles cites the significance of Vatican II in refocusing the Catholic Church on the gospel and on evangelization: "Vatican I used the term 'gospel' only once, and never used the terms 'evangelize' or 'evangelization'. Vatican II, by contrast, mentioned the 'gospel' 157 times, 'evangelize' 18 times, and 'evangelization' 31

[24] Avery Dulles, S.J., *John Paul II and the New Evangelization* (New York: Fordham University, 1992), p. 3.

[25] Ibid., pp. 3–4.

times. When it spoke of evangelizing, Vatican II seems generally to have meant what the kerygmatic theologians meant by the term: the proclamation of the basic Christian message to those who did not yet believe in Christ."[26]

Father Dulles then traces the development of this more evangelical focus in the postconciliar writings of the Popes and concludes with this remarkable summation:

> In my judgement the evangelical turn in the ecclesial vision of Popes Paul VI and John Paul II is one of the most surprising and important developments in the Catholic Church since Vatican II. . . . While both popes have notably broadened the concept of evangelization, they have retained the main emphasis of the earlier kerygmatic concept. For them, as for the kerygmatic theologians, the heart and center of evangelization is the proclamation of God's saving love as shown forth in Jesus Christ. Where the name of Jesus is not spoken, there can be no evangelization in the true sense. . . . All of this constitutes a remarkable shift in the Catholic tradition. For centuries evangelization had been a poor stepchild. Even when the term was used, evangelization was treated as a secondary matter, the special vocation of a few priests and religious. And even these specialists were more concerned with gaining new adherents for the Church than with proclaiming the good news of Jesus Christ. Today we seem to be witnessing the birth of a new Catholicism that, without loss of its institutional, sacramental, and social dimensions, is authentically evangelical. . . . Catholic spirituality at its best has always promoted a deep personal relationship with Christ. In evangelizing we are required to raise our eyes to him and to transcend all ecclesiocentrism. The Church is of crucial importance but is not self-enclosed. It is a means of drawing the whole world into union with God through Jesus Christ. . . . Too many Catholics of our day seem never to have encountered Christ. They know a certain amount about him from the teaching of the Church, but they lack direct personal familiarity. . . . The first and highest priority is for the Church to proclaim the good news concerning Jesus Christ as a joyful message to all the world. Only if the Church

[26] Ibid., p. 4.

is faithful to its evangelical mission can it hope to make its distinctive contribution in the social, political, and cultural spheres."[27]

What Avery Dulles calls "ecclesiocentrism", Father James Doyle, a priest of the Orthodox Church in America, calls "the historic orthodox disease": "Orthodox speakers agree, however, that in practice, Orthodox churches often blur the fundamentals of the gospel message with their emphasis on traditional forms."

"The Church for us is everything", he said. "That's been the historic Orthodox disease."[28]

The Pope links the call for a "new evangelization" with the necessity of a "new Pentecost".[29] Let us briefly consider now some aspects of this "new Pentecost".

A "New Pentecost"

Theologically it is clear why the Pope is linking his call for a new evangelization with the necessity of a new Pentecost. Jesus himself told his disciples, "It is not for you to know times or seasons which the Father has fixed by his own authority. But you shall receive power when the Holy Spirit has come upon you; and you shall be my witnesses in Jerusalem, and in all Judea and Samaria and to the end of the earth" (Acts 1:7–8).

It is difficult if not impossible to be witnesses to the risen Lord except through the encounter with him made possible only by the Holy Spirit. The living, personal relationship with Jesus that makes being his witnesses possible is contingent upon the action of the Holy Spirit.

Recently I have been taking some graduate theology courses at a

[27] Ibid., pp. 13, 16–17.

[28] Joe Loconte, "Peering over the Orthodox-Evangelical Crevasse", *Christianity Today,* November 9, 1992, p. 63.

[29] Pope John Paul II, "May Mary's Prayers Guide Latin Americans to a New Pentecost", *L'Osservatore Romano* (English ed.), Angelus reflection for Sunday, September 23, 1992, p. 8.

nearby major seminary in Detroit. In the course of an ecclesiology course I had the occasion to reread a number of the documents of Vatican II. I had read them all, more than once, years ago, but had not reread them recently. As I did, I was deeply impressed by the strong biblical foundation, Christ-centeredness, and sensitivity to the Holy Spirit that the documents manifested. They are truly documents written with great scriptural, theological, and spiritual depth. One of their remarkable features is the great prominence given to the role of the Holy Spirit in the plan of salvation and the life and mission of the Church. If before the Second Vatican Council it could be said, and it was, by noted Catholic spiritual writers that the Holy Spirit was the forgotten Person of the Trinity, that is clearly no longer the case.

Another factor that has greatly increased the sensitivity of the contemporary Catholic Church to the role of the Holy Spirit has been the unexpected outbreak of a significant charismatic renewal movement within the Church. Cardinal Suenens, one of the four moderators of Vatican II and one of its most eloquent spokesmen for the need to give the Holy Spirit a prominent place in the Council documents, saw in the subsequent outbreak of the charismatic renewal one of the fulfillments of the promise of the Council.

The charismatic renewal in the Catholic Church is present in virtually every country, and some estimates indicate that over seventy-two million Catholics have been significantly touched by this renewal. But it has been able to make a contribution far beyond the actual boundaries of the movement in its influence on music, styles of worship, and focus on "testimony" and "witness" and evangelization. In many parishes in developed countries a substantial portion of those actively involved in service in the parish, in CCD programs, RCIA, marriage preparation programs, and so on, have become active Christians through their contact with the charismatic renewal.

Obviously the charismatic renewal doesn't have a "corner" on the Holy Spirit, and the Spirit is obviously working in a great variety of different ways in many different movements, but it has had a notable impact in the very areas the Pope is focusing on, the new evangelization and the new Pentecost. And while the charismatic renewal, as a movement with its own forms, styles, and structures, is understandably not for everyone, in its essence it is hitting on something very fundamental and very needed in the contemporary Church, an understanding and experience of the possibility of truly encountering the risen Lord in the power of the Holy Spirit, an understanding and experience that are obviously not the property of any movement but of the very essence of the Christian life.

Recently a leading Catholic Scripture scholar, Father George Montague, S.M., former head of the Catholic Biblical Association, and a leading Catholic ecumenical theologian, Father Kilian McDonnell, O.S.B., published a major study analyzing the theological and scriptural aspects of the "charismatic experience". Their findings are quite significant.

In brief, they conclude that the charismatic experience of "baptism in the Holy Spirit" is in essence what Scripture and the Fathers of the Church for the first eight centuries of the Church's life describe as being integral to the experience of the sacraments of Christian initiation.

In describing the preponderance of patristic evidence, they conclude, "Thus, from Carthage in North Africa, Poitiers in Gaul, Jerusalem in Palestine, from Caesarea in Cappadocia, from Constantinople, and from Antioch, Apamea, Mabbug, and Cyrrhus in Syria, we have witnesses to the reception of the charisms within the rite of initiation. . . . *Once again, accepting the baptism in the spirit is not joining a movement, any movement. Rather it is embracing the fullness of Christian initiation, which belongs to the church.*"[30]

What we are talking about here is something as fundamental as conversion, as what the New Testament describes as normal Christian life, as starting out with a "full deck".

---

[30] Kilian McDonnell and George T. Montague, *Fanning the Flame: What Does Baptism in the Holy Spirit Have to Do with Christian Initiation?* (Collegeville, Minn.: Liturgical Press, 1991), pp. 20–21. The longer work on which *Fanning the Flame* is based, by the same authors, is *Christian Initiation and Baptism in the Holy Spirit* (Collegeville, Minn.: Liturgical Press, 1991).

In conclusion, all are called to fan into flame the gift of the Holy Spirit received in the sacraments of initiation. God freely gives this grace, but it requires a personal response of ongoing conversion to the Lordship of Jesus Christ and openness to the transforming presence and power of the Holy Spirit. Only in the Holy Spirit will the church be able to respond to its pastoral needs and those of the world. The challenge is before us and the consequences are clear:

> Without the Holy Spirit, God is far away
> Christ stays in the past,
> the Gospel is a dead letter,
> the church is simply an organization,
> authority a matter of domination,
> mission a matter of propaganda,
> the liturgy no more than an evocation,
> Christian living a slave morality.

But in the Holy Spirit:

> the cosmos is resurrected and groans with
> the birth-pangs of the kingdom,
> the risen Christ is there,
> the Gospel is the power of life,
> the church shows forth life of the Trinity,
> authority is a liberating service,
> mission is a Pentecost,
> the liturgy is both memorial and anticipation,
> human action is deified.

The Spirit calls each of us and the church as a whole, after the pattern of Mary and the Apostles in the Upper Room, to accept and embrace the baptism in the Holy Spirit as the power of personal and communal transformation with all the graces and charisms needed for the upbuilding of the church and for our mission in the world. This mission has its origin in the Father reaching through the Son in the Spirit to touch and transform the church and world to lead them in the Spirit through Christ back to the Father.[31]

---

[31] Ibid., pp. 26–27. The poetic paean to the Holy Spirit is attributed to Metropolitan Ignatios of Latakia, "Main Theme Address", *The Uppsala Report* 1968 (Geneva: WCC, 1969), p. 298.

While the more unusual, to our time at least, features of the charismatic renewal, such as speaking in tongues, prophecy, and healing, tend to draw the most attention, the most important feature is what is spoken about as baptism in the Holy Spirit, or the fundamental encounter with Christ and filling with the Holy Spirit that the New Testament presents as normative for Christian initiation. Terminology can be debated, external expressions can vary, but the underlying reality and experience seem to be something for the whole Church. And indeed, many movements in the Church are witnesses to varied aspects of this same reality. This is the thesis that Cardinal Suenens has held from the beginning: namely, that what is happening in the charismatic renewal is intended as a grace for the whole Church, or the recovery of a grace for the whole Church, and the job of the movement is to lose itself in the wider Church. The beginnings of this can already be seen.

As Bishop Paul Cordes, vice president of the Pontifical Council for the Laity, speaking on behalf of Pope John Paul II, said on the occasion of the twenty-fifth anniversary celebration in Pittsburgh of the charismatic renewal in the Catholic Church: "The charismatic renewal has a great contribution to make in the years ahead to the proper understanding and renewal of the sacraments of Christian initiation so that all God's people may one day experience a greater fulness of life in Christ by being—as you call it—'Baptized in the Spirit'."[32]

Or as a leading Orthodox theologian has put it: "The Apostles and fathers of our faith had the advantage of being instructed in every doctrine and furthermore they were instructed by the Saviour himself; they were spectators of all the graces he poured into human nature and of all he suffered for mankind. They witnessed his death, resurrection and ascension into heaven; yet, having seen all this, they showed nothing new or noble or spiritual that was better than the old state until they were baptized with the Spirit at Pentecost."[33]

[32] Bishop Paul Cordes, "The Call to the Catholic Charismatic Renewal of the Church Universal", given in Pittsburgh, Pennsylvania, June 1992. Text available from Franciscan University of Steubenville press office, Steubenville, Ohio.

[33] N. Cabasilas, cited in Fr. Raniero Cantalamessa, *Life in the Lordship of Christ* (Kansas City, Mo.: Sheed and Ward, 1990), p. 143.

As Father Cantalamessa has put it: "The Spirit of Christ which characterizes the new covenant is not primarily an exterior manifestation of thaumaturgical and charismatic power but it is the principle of a new life. To be really so, a new Pentecost must take place at this depth; it must renew the heart of the Spouse and not only her garments. . . . For each one of us, the entrance to this new Pentecost taking place in the Church is a renewal of our Baptism. The fire of the Spirit was given to us at Baptism. We must remove the ashes suffocating it so that it can flame again and make us capable of loving."[34]

And yet, while "charismatic power" and "charismatic gifts" are not the most important aspects of the first Pentecost or the renewal of Pentecost in our time, they are given by God for an important purpose and, as the Council admonishes us, should be "received with thanksgiving and consolation since they are fitting and useful for the needs of the Church".[35]

In his major encyclical *The Splendor of Truth,* John Paul II again reaffirms the necessity of a free working of the Holy Spirit for the success of the new evangelization:

At the heart of the new evangelization and of the new moral life which it proposes and awakens by its fruits of holiness and missionary zeal, there is *the Spirit of Christ,* the principle and strength of Holy Mother Church. As Pope Paul VI reminded us: "Evangelization will never be possible without the action of the Holy Spirit." . . . As Novatian once pointed out—here expressing the authentic faith of the Church—it is the Holy Spirit "who confirmed the hearts and minds of the disciples, who revealed the mysteries of the Gospel, who shed upon them the light of things divine. Strengthened by his gift, they did not fear either prisons or chains for the name of the Lord; indeed they even trampled upon the powers and torments of the world, armed and strengthened by him, having in themselves the gifts which this same Spirit bestows and directs like jewels to the Church, the Bride of Christ. It is in fact he who raises up prophets in the Church, instructs teachers, guides

---

[34] Ibid., p. 154.
[35] Constitution on the Church *Lumen Gentium,* 12.

tongues, works wonders and healings, accomplishes miracles, grants the discernment of spirits, assigns governance, inspires counsels, distributes and harmonizes every other charismatic gift. In this way he completes and perfects the Lord's Church everywhere and in all things.[36]

I remember when the contemporary manifestations of the charismatic renewal first broke out in the Catholic Church in 1967 some theologians opined that the charismatic gifts of the Spirit were really not necessary in the twentieth century since they were given to the early Church because she lived in the hostile environment of a pagan society and needed such manifestations of the Holy Spirit to confirm the preaching of the gospel.

I hope it is clear from the previous chapters and the witness of our own experience that we are no longer living in a Christian society and that we need all the "power from on high" that we can get. How rapidly Christendom is dissolving before our eyes! How rapidly one age of Church history is ending and another is beginning! How much has changed in the last twenty-five to thirty years! How quickly we are again coming to the situation the early Church was in as she lived her life and preached the gospel in the midst of a pagan society. How desperately we need a new Pentecost!

The noted French Marian scholar Father René Laurentin, in commenting on the significance of the charismatic renewal for the Church, had this to say:

Fervent groups (charismatic or others) play a very important role in the Church of today. Because the Church, and even the Churches (Protestant) are today in the grips of propaganda from the sects which devour them or, more precisely, the churches are on a pathway of decadence. Thus the Catholic continent, Latin America, has been devoured by the sects these past years. They have won over 20% of Catholics, more in certain countries. The most effective antidote today is the charismatic renewal; and one must also add other fine groups such as Focolari, Neo-Catechumenate, Cursillos, as well as the

[36] John Paul II, Encyclical *Veritatis Splendor* (*The Splendor of Truth*), sec. 108.

prophetic messages coming from apparitions of Mary across the
world. They are giving to people today the call and the Presence which they need. . . . One is able to give thanks because
the Renewal has been a specific remedy for the formalism of the
pre-Conciliar American Church and the pastoral ideologies of
the European Church. . . . One is able to give thanks because
the Renewal has bypassed the rationalist and sterile environment,
in recreating a contact, not irrational, but supra-rational, with
God, who is the source of life: "so that they may have life and
have it more abundantly" (Jn 10:10).[37]

Remember, perhaps 75 percent of the Protestant "sects" are
Pentecostal. This is an indication of the importance of the "new
Pentecost" as an accompaniment to the "new evangelization".

Just as I was writing this, across my desk came the story of a
Catholic missionary priest serving in Papua, New Guinea, that
illustrates what we are discussing. The priest shares how there was
a lack of adult attendance and spiritual vitality at Mass in the area
in which he was working. Struck by the vitality of a nearby
Assembly of God (Pentecostal) church, he wondered how the
Spirit could be "so active in that church and not in the Catholic
Church? That's when I became aware of the Catholic charismatic
renewal; and of my own need to pray for the Holy Spirit in my
life."

On a retreat given by two Australian priests, "The Lord really
touched me with the Spirit. I began to understand what baptism
in the Spirit meant and how the Holy Spirit really changes one's
life and revitalizes the church. . . . After the retreats, many prayer
groups formed in the towns and the movement spread out to bush
parishes as well. I often felt that the Holy Spirit wasn't waiting for
priests, brothers or sisters to act but was going right ahead firing
the hearts of the people who demand attention."

Why has this been so effective in bringing life to sluggish
Catholic parishes in New Guinea? "They have a deep hunger for
Jesus and for the Bible. They don't want us priests to come and

---

[37] René Laurentin, "25 ans déjà . . . ", *Il est vivant!* January–February 1992,
pp. 8–9. Translation by Ralph Martin.

preach about just any old thing. They want to really hear the story of Jesus. For example, I can remember going way out into one of the smaller river villages and having a little old lady grab my hand and thank me for coming. 'We are so hungry for Jesus. You must come back and give us more.' Now that was thrilling because women in that country don't usually even speak out.... When I heard of Catholics going off to other sects to find Jesus, I used to resent it but now I understand their needs better. I think we have to acknowledge that renewal begins here in the heart of each of us and until we know Jesus intimately we cannot go out and give him to others."[38]

Of course there are many powerful workings of the Holy Spirit without "unsettling" external manifestations, yet sometimes when there is a strong moving of the Holy Spirit it is not unusual for things to be a little "messy". It was thus in the early Church, in subsequent times of spiritual renewal, and is such today. It is sometimes the price that has to be paid for letting the Spirit blow where he will.

Even the acts of the process of canonization of Ignatius of Loyola, founder of the Jesuits, recount unsettling phenomena similar to those sometimes found today when the "new Pentecost" is being experienced with fervor: "Very strange phenomena were produced in ten or so of his female disciples, during the exercises (but also during the devotional meetings). They were covered by a perspiration of fear and lost consciousness or, losing control over their limbs, they fell to the ground, and, either wholly or partly unconscious, rolled about in spasms on the floor for an hour or so."[39] Were the original "holy rollers" Jesuit retreatants?

Of course, such external manifestations or even interior experiences of the Spirit are in no way to be equated with holiness. Teresa of Avila, in her detailed analysis of such manifestations,

---

[38] "A Testimony: Fr. Edward Bauer, S.V.D., in Papua, New Guinea", *ICCRO Newsletter,* September–October 1993, p. 3.

[39] Cited in Bishop Paul Joseph Cordes, *Charisms and the New Evangelization* (Middlegreen, Slough, U.K.: St. Paul Publications, 1992), pp. 32–33. This book is available in North America from Franciscan University Press, Steubenville, Ohio.

makes the interesting point that such manifestations may be given because of our weakness: "And let none of you imagine that, because a sister has had such experiences, she is any better than the rest; the Lord leads each of us as He sees we have need. Such experiences, if we use them aright, prepare us to be better servants of God but sometimes it is the weakest whom God leads by this road; and so there is no ground here either for approval or for condemnation. We must base our judgments on the virtues. The saintliest will be she who serves Our Lord with the greatest mortification and humility and purity of conscience."[40]

It is interesting to note that Pope Leo XIII opened the twentieth century by issuing an appeal to the entire Church to pray for the Holy Spirit, that Pope John XXIII asked all the Catholics of the world to pray a prayer asking for a "new Pentecost" in preparation for the opening of Vatican II, and as sound a theologian and well-placed observer of the worldwide Church as Cardinal Ratzinger has called the time we are living in "a Pentecostal hour":

> What sounds full of hope throughout the universal Church— and this even in the midst of the crisis that the Church is going through in the Western world—is the upsurge of new movements that no one has planned and no one called into being, but that simply emerge of their own accord from the inner vitality of the faith. What is becoming apparent in them—albeit very faintly—is something very similar to a pentecostal hour in the Church. I am thinking for instance of the Charismatic Renewal movement, the Neocatechumenals, the Cursillo movement, the Focolarini, Communion and Liberation, and so on. All these movements undoubtedly raise many problems, but this is invariably the case in everything that is truly alive.... What is emerging here is a new generation of the Church which I am watching with a great hope. I find it marvelous that the Spirit is once more stronger than our programs and brings himself into play in an altogether different way than we had imagined.... It grows in silence. Our task—the task of the office-holders in the

---

[40] Teresa of Avila, *Interior Castle* (New York: Doubleday, Image Books, 1989), p. 184, 6th mansion, chap. 8.

Church and of theologians—is to keep the door open to them, to prepare room for them. . . .

The period following the Council scarcely seemed to live up to the hopes of John XXIII, who looked for a "new Pentecost". But his prayer did not go unheard. In the heart of a world dessicated by rationalistic scepticism a new experience of the Holy Spirit has come about, amounting to a worldwide renewal movement. What the New Testament describes, with reference to the charisms, as visible signs of the coming of the Spirit is no longer merely ancient, past history: this history is becoming a burning reality today.[41]

It is clear that we are in the midst of a significant act of God in bringing renewal to the Catholic Church, perhaps even a "new Catholicism", as Avery Dulles describes it. It may seem slow sometimes and suffer setbacks, but the Spirit of the Lord is at work in a powerful way. In the words of the Popes, in the grassroots moving of the Spirit among millions of ordinary people, a clear cry is coming forth: *"This is my beloved Son; listen to him!"* Let's do that!

[41] Cardinal Joseph Ratzinger with Vittorio Messori, *The Ratzinger Report* (San Francisco: Ignatius Press, 1985), pp. 43–44, 151.

Chapter Four

What Is the Spirit Saying?

As the life of the early Church developed, the Spirit that Jesus promised to send functioned in all the ways that Jesus promised, including drawing the early Christian communities' attention to things that they were missing or overlooking that should not be missed or overlooked. I believe the Spirit has continued to fulfill that function throughout the history of the Church and is doing so today. Sometimes the Spirit is listened to, and blessing comes to the Church; sometimes he is not, and greater difficulties unfold. It is necessary, as the Second Vatican Council urged, that we "discern the signs of the times"[1] and listen attentively for what the Spirit might be saying to the Church today.

One of the ways we can "discern the signs of the times" is by looking closely at what is happening as it pertains to the Church, and that is what we have tried to do in the first three chapters. In this chapter I would like to share some reflections about the significance of what we have just surveyed for us as a Church and as individuals.

Some of the facts we have looked at can be challenging to accept. While we can justifiably argue with this method of measurement or that, this survey or that, when all the measurements and all the surveys point in the same direction, there is a message to which we need to pay attention. And while we can quite correctly say that the statistics do not tell the whole story and that a lot of positive things are happening, yet there is a message to

[1] Decree on Ecumenism *Unitatis Redintegratio,* 4.

which we need to pay attention. That message, in its simplest form, perhaps could be stated like this: *When Jesus is proclaimed clearly and confidently, in the power of the Holy Spirit, many more people come to faith and there is much more growth to the Church than when he is not.* This is a simple message but with profound implications, and it is a message that is not easy, even for many within the Church, to accept. And why not?

It is difficult for many of us to accept that our beloved Catholic Church could be in such difficult straits as all the available information clearly indicates she is. The very size, geographical spread, and ancient Tradition of the Church, the glory of so many saints and martyrs over the centuries, the faithfulness of her doctrine and moral teaching, the security of her historical continuity, the excellence of her sacraments, can sometimes be so attractive and comforting that anything that would indicate there are serious problems may not be warmly welcomed. None of us likes our security or comfort disturbed, but sometimes they must be if God's purposes are to be accomplished.

In a rare interview, given at the end of 1993, John Paul II called for just such an examination of conscience: "Certainly at the end of this second millennium we should make an examination of conscience: where we are, where Christ has brought us, where we have strayed from the Gospel. It is a subject that would undoubtedly require a deeper analysis."[2]

There is also a tendency to blame factors external to the Church for her difficulties and to suppose that if different political parties were in power or certain laws changed or certain politicians more favorable that the decline the Church is experiencing would be reversed, that secularization and de-Christianization are simply things that happen "out there" for which the Church bears no responsibility and in the face of which she is helpless. Cardinal Angel Suquia, of Spain, in an important address given to the Spanish Episcopal Conference in 1992, addresses this temptation:

> Without doubt there is in modern societies, as something almost inherent in them, a certain component of intolerance that tends

[2] John Paul II, "The Gospel Never Ceases to Be Sign of Contradiction", *L'Osservatore Romano* (English ed.), November 17, 1993, p. 7.

to limit the freedom of public expression of the faith, and that at times even suppresses it violently. But when Christians infer that we attribute primarily to this intolerance the difficulties of the faith in opening new horizons to men, we manifest a notable lack of historical consciousness and a true ignorance of our situation in the world. Above all, we show such a distrust of the redemptive power of Christ that perhaps we ourselves are, and precisely for this reason, the major obstacle of the new evangelization. With this way of thinking, besides, we hide from ourselves our true evils. These evils do not come from outside the Church, but from ourselves. What is surprising is not that the world is the world—what else could it be, if it has not known Christ?—nor that the world . . . opposes the gospel. What is surprising is that, if Christ is who the Church thinks he is, we Christians give such a shameful testimony to him and to the Redemption. It is here that we must first seek the origin of our evils: in the religious weakness of our faith, and in its lack of conviction and of ardor; in its dependence with respect to ideological positions and systems, and in its estrangement from the real life of man; or in the frailty of our ecclesial communion. The worst consequence of this way of thinking that attributes the dechristianization principally to "political" causes, external to the life of the Church, is that in it we shun the supplication, the conversion, and the clarity of the testimony of Christ, which are the indispensable ways of evangelization. . . . To seek the surety of the faith or the possibility of an authentic missionary proposal whose supports do not proceed from the faith itself, but rather from a favorable cultural or social atmosphere, or from the sustenance of the Church by political powers is, at least, a confession of the weakness of our faith, and an unequivocal sign that the new evangelization must begin with ourselves. The dechristianization of Europe has many causes, but certainly it would not have occurred without a certain cultural weakness of Christians, who have yielded to the false alternative that modern life presents to Christianity.[3]

It is easy as a Catholic to develop a form of pride that can become a serious obstacle in our relationship with God and with

---

[3] Cardinal Angel Suquia, "The New Evangelization: Some Tasks and Risks of the Present", *Communio*, Winter 1992, pp. 515–40.

others and a serious impediment to God accomplishing his purposes through the Church. St. Bernard of Clairvaux and many others who have contributed to the theological and spiritual tradition of the Church identify pride as the most serious of sins.[4] As Scripture makes explicitly clear, the proud must be humbled for God's purposes to be accomplished,[5] and I think this is one of the things God is attempting to accomplish in what we see unfolding.

It is embarrassing and humbling when Catholic Italy votes overwhelmingly (68 percent to 32 percent)[6] in favor of legalizing divorce and abortion. It is embarrassing and humbling when 64 percent of American Catholics vote for proabortion candidates.[7] It is embarrassing and humbling when the Church's "dirty linen" is hung out by the media for all to see.

The cases of priests who use their relationships with young boys to have sex with them is sending shock waves through the Church and through society. Over four hundred cases have been publicly acknowledged by the American bishops, and hundreds of millions of dollars have already been paid out in settlements, but the problem is certainly wider than what has currently come to light.[8] By 1995 it is expected that the price of the scandal in judgments from lawsuits will have reached a billion dollars.[9] One American archdiocese has warned it is in danger of having to declare bankruptcy because of the number of sexual abuse cases:

> Faced with dozens of sexual molestation claims against priests in New Mexico, the Catholic Archdiocese of Santa Fe has told

[4] Bernard of Clairvaux, *On Loving God* (London: Hodder and Stoughton, 1985), chap. 2, p. 87.

[5] James 4:6–10.

[6] Gianni Valente, "An Intolerable Realism", 30 *Days,* no. 5 (1993): 43.

[7] Ralph Martin, "The Election: Hard Years Ahead", *New Covenant,* January 1993, pp. 26–31.

[8] "Stresses Pope's Concern for Victims of Pedophile Priests", *Wanderer,* July 1, 1992, p. 1.

[9] Gianni Cardinale, "The Price of Scandal", 30 *Days,* nos. 7/8 (1993): 26.

parishioners that it might have to file for bankruptcy. It has also asked parishioners to help defray millions of dollars in settlement costs and legal expenses to spare it from becoming the first American archdiocese ever to file for Chapter 11 bankruptcy protection.

In a letter read from pulpits or posted on bulletin boards in 91 parishes and missions throughout New Mexico on Sunday, Archbishop Michael J. Sheehan noted that with victims of sexual misconduct demanding up to $50 million in damages and the church's insurers balking, bankruptcy loomed. Acknowledging that he was taking a "drastic" step, he asked each parish to contribute whatever cash and property it could rather than have them seized by the courts. . . .

Church officials here estimate that over a 30-year period as many as 200 people were abused by 45 to 50 priests. The Archdiocese is currently defending itself in 41 separate lawsuits. Another 20 people have said they had claims but have not yet retained lawyers. Nineteen cases have already been settled for $10,000 to $600,000. The payouts have varied with the duration and severity of the abuse, which runs from single unwanted kisses to eight years of oral sex and sodomy.[10]

In the United States, 48 percent of Catholics polled believe that sexual abuse by priests is common, 53 percent believe the Church is handling the abuse issue badly, and 64 percent think the Church is more concerned with her image than with solving the sexual abuse problem.[11] Thirty-seven percent of the Catholics in Canada have indicated their faith has been shaken by the exposure of such sexual corruption among clergy in Canada.[12]

I am afraid this is only the tip of the iceberg. For years ordinary Catholics have written to me telling me of their personal experience with situations such as the ones that are now being exposed and others as well. Priests frequenting homosexual bars, priests

[10] David Margolick, "Facing Costly Sex Abuse Cases, Archdiocese Turns to Parishioners", *New York Times,* December 22, 1993, pp. A1, A11.

[11] "How U.S. Catholics View Their Church", *USA Today,* August 10, 1993, p. 6A.

[12] "A Church at Odds with Its Adherents", *Maclean's,* April 12, 1993, p. 49.

having affairs with married women in their parishes, priests who serve as judges on marriage tribunals granting annulments without hearing the testimony of the other spouse, and sometimes a priest even leaving the priesthood and marrying the woman whose marriage has just been declared annulled.

The issue of annulments is also profoundly troubling to many ordinary Catholics who have been faithful to their marriages despite great difficulties. Almost everybody knows somebody now who has been married many years with four or five or more children, who twenty-five years into the marriage gets a divorce and then an annulment and marries again in the Church. While annulments are a legitimate juridical exercise of the Church's authority, by which she declares that there was such a serious defect in the intentions or capacities of one or both parties at the time of the marriage that they were incapable or unwilling to enter into lifelong Christian marriage, the Pope and high Vatican officials have expressed grave concern about the frequency with which annulments are being granted in the United States:

> Are U.S. Church tribunals becoming the Reno or Las Vegas of the universal Church?
>
> American Church tribunals are offering too many annulments and are guilty of eroding respect for marriage, according to a Vatican official. . . .
>
> It is a view that has been frequently heard before. But Archbishop Vincenzo Fagiolo, president of the Pontificial Council for the Interpretation of Legislative Texts, recently made that argument in a particularly stark and provocative manner at a Vatican sponsored meeting on the rights of families.
>
> He said the number of annulments in the United States is cause for "grave scandal", and that American Church tribunals are too lax in allowing for psychological grounds in granting marriage dissolutions.
>
> Fagiolo noted that 70 percent of all the Church's pending annulment cases come from the United States and that 98 percent of U.S. cases heard end in annulments.
>
> It was a damning indictment of a tribunal system which yearly grants about 43,000 annulments and costs American

Catholics, through subsidies from dioceses and fees paid by petitioners, $22.5 million.[13]

American officials respond that these statistics, while accurate, reflect the greater efficiency of American tribunals. Some canonists claim that such a high percentage of annulments are granted because the weaker cases are screened out from the beginning. It is not a response that is fully convincing to either ordinary Catholics or Rome. It would be far better to admit there have been abuses and efforts are being made to correct them than to pretend that everything has always been fine.

When ordinary Catholics have written to me troubled by matters like this, I have generally counseled them to bring their concerns to their bishop, who often has refused to see them or to respond to letters or, most commonly, who simply transfers the priest in question to another parish, where the problem often recurs.

It was not until hundreds of lawsuits, massive publicity, and hundreds of millions of dollars of damage judgments against the Church were rendered that serious efforts were undertaken that might actually be effective in dealing with the grave problem of priest pedophilia. It remains to be seen whether the even more widespread problems that are no less serious will also be effectively addressed. When an individual or the Church as a whole has no self-discipline, God will often allow the world to do the job that needs to be done.

Cardinal O'Connor, Archbishop of New York, has expressed his spiritual sense of what is happening in the exposure of this moral corruption in the Church: "The church is going through a period of trial by fire, and when fire doesn't destroy, it purifies."[14]

It is important that this trial by fire doesn't destroy our own faith or our faith in Christ's presence in the Church and in his many godly priests.

St. Augustine in one of his letters had some good advice that is

---

[13] Peter Feuerherd, "Take a Closer Look", *National Catholic Register,* June 27, 1993, p. 1.

[14] Peter Steinfels, "Pope Vows to Help Bishops Remove Priests Who Molest", *New York Times,* June 22, 1993, pp. 1, A6.

very applicable to the situation in which we find ourselves today. He was writing in regards to a possible homosexual scandal between a priest and an aspirant to the priesthood.

> Of those who take pleasure from these griefs of ours . . . we have learned to pray for them, and to wish them well. For what other purpose do they sit there, and what else do they aim at, than to assert and contend without any proof, when some bishop or cleric or monk or nun has fallen, that all are like that!
>
> Yet, when some married woman has been shown an adulteress, they do not cast off their wives or accuse their mothers. But when it comes to those who have professed a sacred calling, if some false charge has been rumored, or some true one published, they pick it up, embellish it, spread it about, to make it believed everywhere. . . .
>
> We should not be discouraged, we should not be frightened when we see charity growing cold in the face of increasing immorality, nor depressed at sudden and unexpected events. Remembering those things that were predicted before the end, should we not faithfully persevere to the end, because after the end of time we will be raised to that life without anxiety which will have no end?[15]

This trial by fire is going on in many places, in many ways.

It is humbling to see that the evangelization and catechesis of so many Catholics and Orthodox has been so shallow that vicious fratricidal warfare is once again erupting, and some of the same "Christian" atrocities against the Moslems of Crusade days are being repeated. It is embarrassing to see "Christians" and their leaders silent once again before atrocities carried out by their people. The Catholic Archbishop of Belgrade, Yugoslavia, has spoken of the tragedy of all this: "The hate, crime, and all the kinds of atrocities, as a result of the war in what used to be Yugoslavia, reveal how shallowly the people were evangelized. The communist-atheist indoctrination has ruined the very core of the moral code. So it was that such a hellish atmosphere came into

---

[15] St. Augustine, Letter 78.

being, in which all kinds of serious crimes are being committed. This apocalyptic situation is a great challenge for the Church."[16]

It is humbling and deeply troubling to see millions of our youth in the West carried off into spiritual and moral captivity by a contemporary pagan culture operating through the media, while the Church has remained largely silent. Some courageous bishops are beginning to acknowledge the truth:

> If we had to put our finger on a single force that has caused so much change, resulting in today's lack of morals and values, it is indeed television and the silence of the Church to oppose the media . . . they enter every home of America and stay for hours— often opposing family values—unopposed by parents, church, or government. . . . Unfortunately, the silence of the Catholic Church has been deafening . . . in reflecting on the impact of the Church on television versus the impact of television on the Church and the Church's congregations, we cannot help but note that over the years . . . television has been very willing to take on a silent 2,000 year old Church and bring it to the point of crisis. We have become too complacent, too silent, relying on a 20 minute Sunday homily and an occasional letter from the local bishop to address this situation, as indeed it "grew and grew to be gruesome". Some look on the Church as a business; if so, we are doing a bad job. We are losing our customers![17]

Of course, none of us is without sin, and "we all make many mistakes" (James 3:2a), but sooner or later, if we do not voluntarily deal with our sin and bring it into the light for God's forgiveness and for grace to change, God will bring it out into the light for us or we will find ourselves gradually cut off and isolated from the initiatives that God himself is undertaking, utilizing volunteers. (Here I am, send me!)

I know this has been true in my life, and in ways that are quite parallel to what seems to be happening in a wider way in the Church.

---

[16] Archbishop Franc Perko, "The Edge of Hell", *Catholic World Report,* December 1992, p. 25.

[17] Bishop Robert J. Carlson, Auxiliary Bishop, St. Paul–Minneapolis, and Robert K. Heldman, "A Crossroad in Time", *Wanderer,* April 8, 1993, p. 2.

I have been involved in working for and with the Church in a full-time manner since I left graduate school at Princeton twenty-eight years ago. I have been involved in a leadership capacity with renewal movements that have made a significant impact on the wider Church. First with the Cursillo Movement and then with the charismatic renewal movement, I have seen God touch literally millions of my fellow Catholics and bring them to a deeper relationship with him and involvement in his mission. I have also been active in a particular facet of the charismatic renewal that involves the formation of renewal communities, in our case, covenant communities.

Imperceptibly to me, over the years attitudes of pride, arrogance, and elitism crept into our hearts and into our work. We thought we had solved certain problems that the wider Church had not and had some answers that the Church needed today. While there was definitely a good measure of truth in what we saw and some wider usefulness to what we had experienced, we gradually overrated our own work, tended to underrate the work of others, and built walls between us and others when what God wanted were doors and bridges.

It was not that others had not seen some of these attitudes develop and tried to draw them to our attention. We just were not very well disposed to listen or to understand. We were too concerned with guarding and building the work really to listen to the "little ones" who tried to say that something had gotten out of kilter and was hurting them. We had become owners or proprietors of our work rather than stewards of God's work and servants of his will.

Father Marie-Dominique Philippe, O.P., speaks well of how this attitude of ownership can become a serious obstacle to doing God's will:

> Saint Francis de Sales says that there is always a moment in our lives when God asks whether we prefer His Will to the blessings that we've received from Him. . . . Are we poor with respect to God's blessings? If we are, then we are capable of giving them back to God and accepting His Will over and above His blessings.

If, on the other hand, we grab God's blessings, they can then become an obstacle and can render us incapable of accepting God's Will. And it's terrible to see how quickly we become proprietary! Then you'll see how difficult it is to be poor because our proprietary rights are constantly "growing" . . . then we have to prune during spring, summer, fall, and winter . . . and during each period of our life . . . because they "grow" very quickly . . . ! As soon as God grants us a blessing, we grab it immediately with the best of intentions, "for the greater glory of God". Yes, yes . . . for *our* greater glory . . . and not God's glory. . . . It's striking to see how poverty gives a penetrating gaze. Most of the time our faith isn't contemplative and our hope doesn't go beyond appearances because we are too proprietary. Really, proprietors always have a short term outlook because they consider primarily their possessions instead of the Will of God. Those who love always go beyond their possessions. They are bound to a Person—they are bound to God and neighbor.[18]

Eventually we did listen, but it was late, and there was a lot more pain, confusion, disillusionment, and airing of "dirty linen" than there would have been if we had been able to hear what the Spirit was trying to tell us earlier rather than later.[19]

It is also embarrassing and humiliating to hear millions of former Catholics say they never heard the gospel preached in the Catholic Church! Or to see churches and movements with, to Catholic eyes, inadequate theology, training, and church structures growing rapidly all over the world.

As John Paul II has recently pointed out, recognizing the growth of the "sects" as one of the significant "signs of the times" is a necessary part of the reflection the Church must do today if her mission is to be effective. He goes on to say that "we must humbly acknowledge" that baptized Catholics sometimes do not satisfy their spiritual hunger, "for whatever reason", in the Catholic

[18] Fr. Marie-Dominique Philippe, O.P., *Follow the Lamb* . . . (Laredo, Tex.: Congregation of St. John, 1991), pp. 196, 197, 200.

[19] Ralph Martin, "Community: A Work in Progress", *Faith and Renewal*, January–February 1993, pp. 3–8.

Church.[20] There is a temptation simply to dismiss such testimony and ignore the "upstart" churches of which they are a part. But with the Holy Spirit helping, it seems that slowly the Church is resisting this temptation and starting to look at the facts that need to be looked at.

There is a temptation to point out all the weaknesses and deficiencies of such churches and movements, of which there indeed are many. There is much weakness and imbalance in a lot of this phenomenal growth, and not all of it will bear lasting fruit. Inadequate leadership training, the "revolving door" syndrome, imbalance in theology, faulty Scripture interpretation, moral relativism, sectarian pride, schismatic problem solving, lacks of safeguards and checks and balances in church government and in the prophetic and charismatic dimension, overemphasis on subjective experience, and indeed, arrogance, pride, and elitism are not absent here either. Happily, some of these weaknesses are beginning to be addressed by evangelical and Pentecostal leaders themselves.[21]

But despite the problems and weaknesses, there is a message here, from the Holy Spirit, I believe, that we need to hear. It could be put like this: *The Father is so delighted when his Son is honored and proclaimed, so delighted when people put their faith and trust in him, that he is willing to pour out the Holy Spirit in abundance, even if the theology and Church structures of these situations are not all he would desire. The Father is putting first things first, and perhaps what the Spirit is saying in all of this is that so should we.*

In so many different ways, through so many different voices it seems clearer and clearer that this is indeed one of the important things that the Spirit is saying to the Catholic Church today. The

---

[20] Pope John Paul II, "Church Confidently Awaits the Dawn of a New Missionary Era", *L'Osservatore Romano* (English ed.), March 3, 1993, p. 3.

[21] John Maust, "Evangelical Gathering Stresses Reconciliation", *Christianity Today*, October 26, 1992, p. 72. Samuel Escobar, "Protestantism Explodes", *Christian History*, issue 35, p. 45. "When Latin Americans Evangelize . . . ", *Christianity Today*, April 5, 1993, p. 73. David M. Howard, "Great Things to Come", *Christianity Today*, April 6, 1992, p. 39. *National and International Religion Report*, July 12, 1993, p. 4.

substantial problems of the Church in many parts of the world, contrasted with the rapid growth of the evangelical and Pentecostal churches, are means the Holy Spirit is using to get our attention, so we can again hear the Father speaking: *This is my Beloved Son, listen to him! and turn to him anew, in repentence and faith.*

One of the major ways the Holy Spirit is at work to renew the Church is through the work of the Second Vatican Council, and one of the major ways the Spirit is speaking to the Church is through this Council. It was a Council of reform, a Council of return. Returning to the sources, to the Scripture, to the authentic Tradition, to the proper priorities, to real spiritual life—most of all, turning to the Person of Christ. A few months after he was elected Pope, Pope Paul VI opened the second session of the Council with these important words:

> What, dear brothers, are we going to make our starting-point? What path must we tread if we are going to be guided by God's law rather than by any reasons so far expounded? What goal are we to set ourselves? . . . These three questions . . . have one and the same answer—Christ. We who are gathered here together on this solemn occasion have to remind ourselves of this, and proclaim it to the whole world. Christ is our starting-point, Christ our leader and our way, Christ our hope and our goal.
>
> May this Ecumenical Council have a clear realization of that bond which binds us to Jesus Christ. . . . It binds us, the living, holy Church, to Christ from whom we come, through whom we live, toward whom we tend. May this our present assembly shine with no other light than Christ, the light of the world. May our minds seek no other truth than that proclaimed by the words of the Lord, our only teacher. May our sole ambition be to give whole-hearted, loyal obedience to His commands. May no other confidence sustain us than that which strengthens our own poor frailty—relying on His words: "And behold I am with you all through the days that are coming, until the consummation of the world." . . . Our Lord Jesus Christ . . . the Word incarnate, Son of God and Son of Man, the world's redeemer. He indeed is the hope of the human race, its one supreme teacher and shepherd, our bread of life, our High Priest and our victim, the one mediator between God and men,

the savior of this world and king of the eternal world to come.... Christ is invisibly yet really our founder and our head. All that we have we receive from Him and with Him we form, as St. Augustine said, the *Christus totus,* the whole Christ. This realization underlies the whole of Christian teaching about the Church.[22]

It is also important to note that Pope John Paul II, in his first encyclical, on March 4, 1979, asked similar questions ("How? How should we proceed? What must be done?") and came to the identical solution: "It is here that a fundamental, essential answer arises and it is this: the only orientation of the spirit, the only guide to the intellect, to will and to the heart for us is this— towards Christ, man's Redeemer, towards Christ, Redeemer of the world. We will look to Him because there is salvation only in Him, Son of God, and declare anew with Peter: Lord, to whom will we go? Yours are the words of eternal life."[23]

What is the Spirit saying? *Jesus.*

[22] Pope Paul VI, "Opening of the Second Session of the Ecumenical Council", September 29, 1963, in *Pope Speaks,* vol. 9 (1963), pp. 125–41. I am indebted to Fr. Avery Dulles, S.J., for drawing this speech to my attention.

[23] Pope John Paul II, Encyclical *Redemptor Hominis* (*Redeemer of Man*), 7.

Chapter Five

The Church, Repentance, and Faith

I was born into a Catholic family and went to a Catholic elementary school, high school, and university. Yet I am not a Catholic simply by accident or by culture or by inertia; I am a Catholic by conviction. I believe that contained within the very act of faith in Jesus is the Church and that it is impossible to have Jesus, in individual isolation, without the Church.

As Vatican II has put it: "All those, who in faith look towards Jesus, the author of salvation and the principle of unity and peace, God has gathered together and established as the Church, that it may be for each and everyone the visible sacrament of this saving unity."[1]

Or as Cardinal Ratzinger has put it recently: "The Church is not an institution which imposes itself upon the faith from outside and creates an organizational framework for the joint activities of the faithful; it belongs to the very act of faith. The 'I believe' is always also a 'we believe'."[2]

I believe what the Catholic Church teaches about herself. I believe that Christ established the Catholic Church and that the fullness of the means of salvation subsists within her. I believe the Catholic Church is biblically based and has been guided by the Holy Spirit in her doctrinal development and that nothing that she officially teaches is in contradiction with Scripture. As Vatican

[1] Constitution on the Church *Lumen Gentium, 9.*
[2] Cardinal Joseph Ratzinger, "What Does the Church Believe?" *Catholic World Report,* March 1993, p. 58.

II puts it: "This is the sole church of Christ which in the Creed we profess to be one, holy, catholic, and apostolic, which our Savior, after his Resurrection, entrusted to Peter's pastoral care (Jn 21:17), commissioning him and the other apostles to extend and rule it (see Mt 28:18), and which he raised up for all ages as 'the pillar and mainstay of the truth' (1 Tim 3:15). This church, constituted and organized as a society in the present world, subsists in the Catholic Church, which is governed by the successor of Peter and by the bishops in communion with him."[3]

I believe also, as the Church teaches, that Catholics who, believing the true Church of Christ subsists in the Catholic Church, nevertheless leave it, place their salvation in jeopardy: "Hence they could not be saved who, knowing that the Catholic Church was founded as necessary by God through Christ, would refuse either to enter it, or to remain in it."[4]

I also believe, as does the Catholic Church, that many of the means of salvation and gifts of the Holy Spirit exist outside the institutional boundaries of the Catholic Church in the many other Christian churches and communions.

As the Second Vatican Council put it: "The Church knows that she is joined in many ways to the baptized who are honored by the name of Christian but who do not however profess the Catholic faith in its entirety or have not preserved unity or communion under the successor of Peter . . . these Christians are indeed in some real way joined to us in the Holy Spirit for, by his gifts and graces, his sanctifying power is also active in them and he has strengthened some of them even to the shedding of their blood."[5]

An even stronger statement is made in the Decree on Ecumenism:

It remains true that all who have been justified by faith in baptism are incorporated into Christ; they therefore have a right to be called Christians, and with good reason are accepted as brothers by the children of the Catholic Church.

[3] Constitution on the Church *Lumen Gentium,* 8.
[4] Ibid., 14.
[5] Ibid., 15.

Moreover, some, even very many, of the most significant elements and endowments which together go to build up and give life to the Church itself, can exist outside the visible boundaries of the Catholic Church: the written Word of God; the life of grace; faith, hope and charity, with the other interior gifts of the Holy Spirit, as well as visible elements. All of these, which come from Christ and lead back to him, belong by right to the one Church of Christ. . . . It follows that the separated Churches and communities as such, though we believe they suffer from the defects already mentioned, have been by no means deprived of significance and importance in the mystery of salvation. For the Spirit of Christ has not refrained from using them as means of salvation which derive their efficacy from the very fullness of grace and truth entrusted to the Catholic Church.[6]

The Council urges us to "acknowledge and esteem" these gifts and workings of the Spirit outside the visible bounds of the Catholic Church: "Catholics must gladly acknowledge and esteem the truly Christian endowments of our common heritage which are to be found among our separated brethren. It is right and salutary to recognize the riches of Christ and virtuous works in the lives of others who are bearing witness to Christ, sometimes even to the shedding of their blood. For God is always wonderful in his works and worthy of all praise.

"Nor should we forget that anything wrought by the grace of the Holy Spirit in the hearts of our separated brethren can contribute to our own edification. Whatever is truly Christian is never contrary to what genuinely belongs to the faith; indeed, it can always bring a more perfect realization of the very mystery of Christ and the Church."[7]

I believe also that many aspects of the Christian message may be better understood and more faithfully practiced in these churches and communions in a given time and place than they are in the Catholic Church at a given time and place. And I believe that the Catholic Church is always in one way or another in need of renewal and reform. *"Ecclesia semper reformanda"* is a principle

---

[6] Decree on Ecumenism *Unitatis Redintegratio,* 3.
[7] Ibid., 4.

embraced by the Catholic Church and not just the churches of the Reformation: "The Church, however, clasping sinners to her bosom, at once holy and always in need of purification, follows constantly the path of penance and renewal."[8]

Or again as the Council states: "Christ summons the Church, as she goes her pilgrim way, to that continual reformation of which she always has need, insofar as she is an institution of men here on earth. Consequently, if, in various times and circumstances, there have been deficiencies in moral conduct or in Church discipline, or even in the way that Church teaching has been formulated—to be carefully distinguished from the deposit of faith itself—these should be set right at the opportune moment and in the proper way."[9]

I believe that the Catholic Church herself has been wounded and impoverished by the disunity of Christians, as have all Christians worldwide been wounded and impoverished by our disunity, and that we have much to learn from each other as the Spirit works to bring us back into communion with each other, as we all, in humility, follow the path of repentance and renewal.

What Father Cantalamessa points out about the Catholic and Orthodox separations can be extended to the whole broken body of Christ:

> Just as in the Trinitarian mystery it was given to the Eastern Church to experience at greater depth the Trinity of the persons and to the Western Church the unity of nature, and as in the mystery of redemption it was given to the Eastern Church to place greater value on the Incarnation and to the Western Church on the Paschal mystery, so within the Paschal mystery itself it was given to the Eastern Church to give greater value to the resurrection and to the Western Church, the Passion. This took place to make us dependent on one another and to give rise to the appeal for ecumenical unity from the very depth of the mystery we celebrate together. For each great mystery it's as if God made two "keys" to be used together, giving one to the Eastern Church and the other to the Western Church so that

[8] Constitution on the Church *Lumen Gentium*, 8.
[9] Decree on Ecumenism *Unitatis Redintegratio*, 5.

neither one nor the other can open to or reach the fulness of truth without the other. As an ancient axiom said: "You cannot reach such a great mystery by one way only."[10]

It is clear from salvation history that even those whom God has specially chosen, called, gifted, and made eternal promises to can stray from his purposes, suffer from self-righteousness, spiritual blindness, hardness of heart, lukewarmness, indifference, pervert what is most holy, and forget him. The history of Israel, the apple of God's eye, is a sobering reminder that being special, called, chosen, commissioned, and gifted does not make one immune to the most wretched of unfaithfulness and idolatry, with its subsequent pitiable consequences, humiliations, chastening, and purification. The history of the Church contains many parallels. But in the history of both Israel and the Church, while unfaithfulness can lead to judgment, judgment can lead to repentance, and repentance can lead to a restoration of blessing, life, and fruitfulness.

As we have seen from our survey of the situation of the Catholic Church in the first several chapters, several things stand out clearly. One is that where Jesus is lifted up and proclaimed with confidence and joy in the power of the Holy Spirit, many are attracted to him and the Church grows. Another is that where the message is not clear, where there is doctrinal and moral confusion, where Jesus is not at the center, where the Holy Spirit is not free to move, hardly anybody comes and many who are already there leave for practical paganism or other churches. Simple lessons but profound ones. This is a message and these are lessons that many of us in the Catholic Church need to understand in a practical and spiritual way, but there are obstacles that stand in the way. Let us take a closer look at some of the obstacles to hearing what the Spirit is saying to the Church today and responding adequately.

[10] Fr. Raniero Cantalamessa, *Life in the Lordship of Christ* (Kansas City, MO.: Sheed and Ward, 1990), p. 89.

Catholic Pride

There is a great mystery of incarnation at the heart of God's plan of creation and redemption. God chose to create and now chooses to redeem through the material, through flesh-and-blood creatures like ourselves. He chooses particular tribes and peoples and individuals and nations at different times in his plan to fulfill his purposes. And because of our fallen natures and our inclinations to selfishness and sin, even after faith and baptism, being chosen, called, gifted, carries with it a spiritual danger to which we all too often succumb: pride. Like mankind at the Tower of Babel, we can use our gifts to "make a name for ourselves" (Gen 11:4) in an expression of corporate and individual pride. What was intended to shine forth to the glory of God in the specificity of his choice is diverted to the glory of the creature, the institution, or the nation. We end up glorifying ourselves rather than him and grasp to ourselves the treasures we have been given rather than giving them to others freely. We use our chosenness as a way of lording it over others and putting them down rather than serving them. We use our institutional identification as a way of feeding our ego. We take to ourselves the achievements of the institution. Not having allowed the grace of God to heal us deeply enough, we deal with our insecurity and need to feel superior and better than others by flaunting the very real gifts God has given us in a way that offends and antagonizes rather than invites others.

A commentator on the work of Cardinal Newman says it well: "Newman also asks questions of us Catholics as well. If we are Catholics because we are basically 'organization men' or because we naturally gravitate towards the 'big battalions', if we indulge in adulation of those in authority, if we are willing to compromise on principle or go along with a majority view to keep the peace, if we are, above all, not serious in laboring to meet God and Christ in prayer, Newman will be, or rather is, a sign of contradiction for us too. *If we use the Church, her sacraments, her organization, her history, or her culture as screens to hide behind and avoid a confrontation with the Living God,* then we, too, need Newman and his writings, *we too need a conversion.*"[11]

There is an awful tendency to believe gradually that somehow we deserve the gifts we have been given or, even worse, that we are the source or cause of them. There is an awful tendency to act gradually as if we control God or possess him, which leads to a terrible narrowness of vision of him and his purposes and a perversion of the called, chosen, gifted individual or institution or nation. We can end up boasting of the very gifts we have truly been given in a way that profoundly offends God, thwarts his plan, and produces in us a terrible self-righteousness and spiritual blindness. Both the Old and New Testaments are full of prophetic and apostolic warnings against this dangerous tendency.

The prophet Jeremiah saw how sick and sad this prideful delusion can be: "Thus says the Lord of hosts, the God of Israel, Amend your ways and your doings, and I will let you dwell in this place. Do not trust in these deceptive words: 'This is the temple of the Lord, the temple of the Lord, the temple of the Lord!' For if you truly amend your ways and your doings, if you truly execute justice with one another, if you do not oppress the alien, the fatherless, or the widow, or shed innocent blood in this place, and if you do not go after other gods to your own hurt, then I will let you dwell in this place, in the land that I gave of old to your fathers for ever" (Jer 7:3–7).

Everything about the temple was a gift from God. It was exactly what he wanted. It was an incredible gift to Israel. Yet rather than respond with gratitude, humility, and a desire to serve and to give—with true holiness—the response in the time of Jeremiah was smug pride. I am sorry to say that I have heard among us Catholics refrains not unsimilar to those in Jeremiah's time: "We're the one true Church, the one true Church, the one true Church"—not simply stating what the Church believes about herself but a smug pride that is both insensitive to others and

[11] Fr. Charles Dilke, C.O., "Canterbury Tales", 30 *Days* (February 1991): 82. Italics mine.

ineffective in communicating the treasures of Christ given to the Catholic Church. A "hyper-Catholicism" can sometimes be masking psychological needs to be part of a rigid system with elitist claims, to be "holier than thou" through membership and association rather than by actual transformation in Christ.

One of the positive developments in recent years has been the revival of Catholic apologetics. Faced with the ignorance of many Catholics about their Faith and the aggressive attacks of some evangelicals, there has been a significant resurgence of Catholic apologetics. Books, magazines, and conferences are all helping Catholics better understand their Faith and defend it when attacked. Along with this has gone major publicity on prominent Protestants who have become Catholics. While I think that this is fundamentally a work of the Holy Spirit, I am concerned at times that the wrong kind of Catholic pride and fear makes its contribution too. I have been grieved to hear sometimes the views of Protestants caricatured and made fun of and Catholic "converts" promoted as trophies as if in a competition. That this of course is how Catholic converts to Protestantism have often been publicized does not mean that we should respond in the same way. This is simply not the Spirit of Christ, nor is it the path the Holy Spirit has set the Church on in Vatican II: "Sacred theology and other branches of knowledge, especially those of a historical nature, must be taught with due regard for the ecumenical point of view, so that they may correspond as exactly as possible with the facts.

"It is important that future pastors and priests should have mastered a theology that has been carefully elaborated in this way and not polemically, especially in what concerns the relations of separated brethren with the Catholic Church."[12]

The Council further calls us to a spirit of repentance, humility, self-denial, and charity in matters that pertain to our disunity as Christians.[13]

Monsignor George Kelly once commented to me that Pope Pius XII was so concerned that the Catholic Church not be

[12] Decree on Ecumenism *Unitatis Redintegratio,* 10.
[13] Ibid., 7–10.

related to as an ideology or an "ism" that in one of his allocutions he recommended that we not use the word *Catholicism*.

Cardinal Groër, Archbishop of Vienna, makes a similar point in regard to the abstraction *Christianity:* "In effect, Christianity does not exist. Christ exists, people exist, men exist who turn to him. . . . It is not to be found outside of that."[14]

While it is difficult in everyday speech to refer consistently to the substance of our Faith, namely, the personal relationship with the Father, Son, and Holy Spirit, it is helpful to do so whenever possible, because words like *Catholicism* and *Christianity* all too easily permit one to entertain images that do not touch on the essence of faith, the personal relationship with God himself. It is all too easy to think of "Catholicism" or "Christianity" as simply a competing ideology or system or institution rather than the expression of an encounter with the living God that it in substance is.

The Apostle Paul saw how other great gifts of God, the law and circumcision, could perversely function to increase pride rather than to produce humility (Rom 2:17-29). As Paul put it another time, "For in Christ Jesus neither circumcision nor uncircumcision is of any avail, but faith working through love" (Gal 5:6).

An Orthodox theologian tells an interesting story that sheds light on what we are trying to understand here: "A holy man was once asked, 'Why is it that people who are very religious—who go to church and light candles and kiss icons—why is it that they become worse instead of better?' The answer is simple, said the holy man: they do not really want God. They want something else—anything from playing a role to being a prophet to having a happy life, to being healthy, wealthy and wise. There is such a thing as spiritual hedonism, spiritual greed, spiritual avarice. We can even want to be holy for the sake of holiness, rather than for the sake of the love of God. And then our desire becomes impure. . . . It is so easy to want something other than God."[15]

<hr />

[14] Cardinal Hans Hermann Groër, "From Values to Reality", 30 *Days,* no. 5 (1993): 62.

[15] Fr. Thomas Hopko, "Continuous Conversion", *Faith and Renewal,* March–April 1992, p. 4.

Of course, these tendencies are rooted deep within human nature, and they express themselves in parallel ways in Protestant and Pentecostal contexts as well.

Having the law justified no one, and yet certain Jews boasted of simply possessing the law, neglecting to notice how they were not keeping it, and indeed could not keep it without the undeserved mercy of God. Others prided themselves on being circumcised, focusing on the outward sign, totally blind to the substance of faith and gift that the sign signified. There is a tendency among us Catholics too to pride ourselves on possessing the fullness of truth within the Catholic Church while neglecting to see how far we are from living it, as well as to focus on the external signs, for example, the sacraments, without being aware of or living what the signs and ceremonies signify. It might be said as Paul said of the Jews, "One is a Catholic inwardly, and being a Catholic is of the heart, in the spirit, not the letter."

Jesus himself had some of his most hostile encounters with those religious leaders who self-righteously and smugly had perverted the religion of which they were the legitimate custodians. The combination of pride with power and hypocrisy is deadly, and yet it is something we all have to guard against: "Then said Jesus to the crowds and to his disciples, 'The scribes and the Pharisees sit on Moses' seat; so practice and observe whatever they tell you, but not what they do; for they preach, but do not practice" (Mt 23:1–3).

"Woe to you, scribes and Pharisees, hypocrites! for you tithe mint and dill and cummin, and have neglected the weightier matters of the law, justice and mercy and faith; these you ought to have done, without neglecting the others. You blind guides, straining out a gnat and swallowing a camel!" (Mt 23:23).

It is very possible in our zeal to focus on secondary things, which while they may be valid overshadow what is primary, to "make a mountain out of a molehill": "Woe to you, scribes and Pharisees, hypocrites! for you cleanse the outside of the cup and of the plate, but inside they are full of extortion and rapacity. You blind Pharisee! first cleanse the inside of the cup and of the plate, that the outside also may be clean" (Mt 23:25–26).

"Woe to you, scribes and Pharisees, hypocrites! for you are like whitewashed tombs, which outwardly appear beautiful, but within they are full of dead men's bones and all uncleanness. So, you also outwardly appear righteous to men, but within you are full of hypocrisy and iniquity" (Mt 23:27–28).

It has become popular to talk about personal change needing to proceed from inside out.[16] There is a real point to it. If the burden of external practices we take upon ourselves outstrips our interior transformation, healing, and freedom, serious distortions of "true religion" can occur. Both the Protestant and Catholic churches have been shocked, and hopefully humbled, by the revelation of serious hypocrisy in high or prominent places.

In his excellent book *Life in the Lordship of Christ,* Father Cantalamessa points out some of the more subtle ways that "piety" can cloak an uncleanness that functions as a form of idolatry.

> The specific accusation the apostle makes against the "pious" is that "they themselves are doing the exact same things" they judge others for. But in what sense? Is it that they materially do the exact same things? this is also sometimes true (cf. Rom 2:21–24); but he is especially talking about the essence which is impiety and idolatry. There is a masked form of idolatry at work in our present world. If it is idolatry "to bow down to the work of our hands" (cf. Is 2:8; Hos 14:4), if it is idolatry "to put the creature in the place of the Creator", then I am idolatrous whenever I put the creature—*my* creature, the work of *my* hands—in the Creator's place. My creature could be the home or the Church I have built, the family I have formed, the child I have given life to (how many mothers, even Christian mothers, unconsciously make a God out of their children, especially out of an only child!); it could be the work I do, the school I direct, the book I write.... Then there is my "self", the prince of idols. In fact, idolatry is always based on autolatry, self-worship, self-love, placing oneself first at the centre of the world, sacrificing everything else to this. The "substance" is always impiety, the non-glorification of God, but always and only one's self. It is even making use of God for our own success and personal

---

[16] Dr. Larry Crabb, *Inside Out* (Colorado Springs: NAVPRESS, 1988); Dr. John White, *Changing on the Inside* (Ann Arbor, Mich.: Servant Publications, 1991).

affirmation. If it is true, in fact, that often those who defend man's rights are actually defending their own rights, it is no less true that often those who defend God's rights and the rights of the Church are really defending themselves and their own interests. This is why even today "the name of God is blasphemed among the Gentiles" (cf. Rom 2:24). The sin St. Paul denounced in the "Jews" throughout the whole Letter [Romans] was that they sought self-justice and self-glory and they did this even in their observance of God's law.[17]

"They love the place of honor at feasts and the best seats in the synagogues, and salutations in the market places, and being called rabbi by men. But you are not to be called rabbi, for you have one teacher, and you are all brethren. And call no man your father on earth, for you have but one Father, who is in heaven. Neither be called master, for you have one master, the Christ. He who is greatest among you shall be your servant; whoever exalts himself will be humbled; and whoever humbles himself will be exalted" (Mt 23:6–12).

There is a danger, which Jesus vividly points out, of the leadership that indeed is God given operating in a way as to block people's access to and relationship with God himself. Leaders are not supposed to get in the way or substitute their relationship with God for the peoples' but rather to help each and every one relate directly and personally to God. In relationship to God himself, leaders and led are together brothers, or as another translation puts it, "all learners", and fellow disciples.[18] This, of course, applies to all levels of leadership, whether clergy or lay, institutional or "charismatic".

Cardinal Ratzinger has some striking comments on the applicability of this text to the way leadership functions in the Church today: "It is clear that the false hierarchism and dignity of office cultivated by the Jews is contrasted with the undifferentiated brotherliness of Christians. And one cannot avoid the serious

---

[17] Cantalamessa, *Life in the Lordship of Christ,* pp. 37–38.

[18] See also the biblical orientation Vatican II's Decree on the Ministry and Life of Priests *Presbyterorum ordinis* gives to the role of priests in relationship to the laity, as "brothers among brothers", especially no. 9.

challenge that this text puts to us: Does not our actual Christian reality resemble more the Jewish hierarchism castigated by Jesus than the picture he gave of Christian brotherhood?"[19]

"But woe to you, scribes and Pharisees, hypocrites! because you lock the kingdom of heaven against men; for you neither enter yourselves, nor allow those who would enter to go in" (Mt 23:13).

"Woe to you, scribes and Pharisees, hypocrites! for you build the tombs of the prophets and adorn the monuments of the righteous, saying, 'If we had lived in the days of our fathers, we would not have taken part with them in shedding the blood of the prophets. Thus you witness against yourselves, that you are the sons of those who murdered the prophets' (Mt 23:29–31).

There are those leaders who sometimes out of complacency, laziness, lukewarmness, pride, jealousy, or fear do not themselves respond to what the Spirit is doing and saying and discourage others or even forbid them from responding themselves. We read in Scripture the shocking words that it was "out of jealousy" that the religious leaders of the day handed over Jesus to be crucified. May God help us so that our own sin, our own pride, jealousy, fear, or lukewarmness will not lead us to oppose what God is doing!

Sometimes leadership can even oppose what God is doing "in the name of God": "They will put you out of the synagogues, indeed, the hour is coming when whoever kills you will think he is offering service to God" (Jn 16:2).

Father Marie-Dominique Philippe, O.P., has some very insightful things to say about both the historical Pharisees and the pharisaical tendencies we all have to guard against:

> Obviously, being people blessed by God isn't easy. . . . And to be blessed people without becoming Pharisees, without becoming possessive and proprietary about it. . . . It's not easy to remain poor! . . . The people of Israel didn't remain poor in their high priests. Ah! The clericalism of the Old Testament is really striking! And we must never forget that we still continue

[19] Cardinal Joseph Ratzinger, *The Meaning of Christian Brotherhood* (San Francisco: Ignatius Press, 1993), pp. 59–60.

to have a bit of nostalgia for this. Clericalism is really something terrible since the priest should be the poorest of all. And
the clericalism of the high priests was so great that it led them
to reject Jesus. They refused to let Jesus "rank ahead of them." . . .
Jealousy leads to homicide. This is why I believe that Jesus was
crucified due to jealousy, a fraternal, priestly, pontifical jealousy —
it can go that far! . . . It was the jealousy of the high priest that
decided everything. The high priest could not accept the fact
that Jesus surpassed him so he had to eliminate at all costs the
One whom he considered his rival . . . priestly jealousy . . . ! . . . In
a certain sense Jerusalem embodies the religious traditions that
are preserved and possessed; it's the authority and religious
power represented by the Sanhedrin — very powerful since it
was the alliance of the political and the religious. . . . Authority
is authority only when it seeks the truth, or, when it's a
question of Christian authority, when it testifies to the faith.
When power has replaced authority, we must always be very
careful not to fall into power's clutches. No one, in fact, has the
right to put himself in a state of dependency with respect to a
power. John the Baptist is well aware of this — he's moved by
the Holy Spirit. . . . He's astute, with the astuteness of hope. . . .
And hope is marvelously astute because it must always pass
between the various powers-that-be to maintain the primacy of
mercy alone. . . . Pride as well as spiritual and intellectual riches
are the mountains that prevent the coming of Christ. . . . The
Pharisee represents anti-poverty; he is someone who is satisfied
with himself and refuses to become poor . . . the great failing of
the people of Israel at the time is self-satisfaction. Here we see
the right of the eldest: they are the ones who have received the
promise. And they are certain that this promise will be fulfilled
for them according to their own conceptions. . . . The Christ is
in their midst — and they cannot see Him! They are so blinded
by their power that they cannot see Him. . . . Adoration purifies
our heart, takes from us all our desire for power, all our rights
as eldest, and gives us the ability to go much further according
to the inspiration of the Holy Spirit. Very often people who
have much to lose don't dare speak the truth. They are held
captive by their power. They are held captive by their possessions.
Ah! We need people like John the Baptist today to shake up
those who confuse authority with power and who want to

dominate.[20] . . . Jesus doesn't go to meet the Levites and the priests. Jesus let the priests and the Levites return home. They are incapable of receiving the truth. They're satisfied, full of themselves. They're tied to the Pharisees. . . . Jesus comes to meet the poor one; he comes to meet John the Baptist, who then receives light. Sometimes we have to enter into very, very profound poverty in order to receive God's light. Basically, only the poor are enlightened by the Holy Spirit. The poor alone. As soon as we love power more than truth, the Holy Spirit can do nothing with us. But it's very difficult to always search for truth more than power![21]

From another part of the Body of Christ, from a Baptist pastor from Texas, comes the same discernment of the relevance of John the Baptist for our times and the danger of the "self-preservationist":

We must also be willing to be nonessential. John the Baptist finally had his head cut off. His ministry was not a long-lived ministry — it was a *transitional* ministry. He was persecuted because he stood for the truth in a world of deceit. His message contradicted the mentality of the day. John kept magnifying Jesus instead of making a name for himself. Individually or as a church we may not have our heads cut off, but we must be willing to be dispensable. If we are not willing to live with a dispensable mentality, when the greater ministry comes, we will end up competing with it, and ultimately persecuting it.

If God says one morning, "O.K., thanks guys, you did a good job but now your job is over", we must have as much fun closing the ministry down as we did building it. Otherwise we

---

[20] Dr. Joyce Little, professor of theology at the University of St. Thomas, in Houston, Texas, made an excellent presentation on the distinction between authority and power at the conference held in Omaha, Nebraska, in July of 1993, to celebrate the 25th anniversary of *Humanae Vitae*. It is available on tape from the Paul VI Institute, 6901 Mercy Road, Omaha, NB 68106. Cardinal Ratzinger has also developed some distinctions between authority and power in "Against the Power of Intellectuals", an essay published in 30 *Days* (March 1991): 68–71.

[21] Fr. Marie-Dominique Philippe, O.P., *Follow the Lamb . . .* (Laredo, Tex.: Congregation of Saint John, 1991), pp. 102, 177–92.

will become self-preservationists with territorial rights which are controlled by territorial spirits.[22]

When "religious hegemony" or dominance is threatened, there is a strong tendency to rely on the arm of the flesh, of force, power, intimidation, or appeals to the secular power, to preserve the religious monopoly of a particular church or institution. In this regard the Catholic Church is having a real struggle finding the gospel approach to dealing with the "sects".

Just using the word *sects* to refer to such established and respected church bodies as, for example, the Assemblies of God is already a way of showing disrespect and disdain. The very use of the term is a "polemical intensifier", as a Catholic observer of the contemporary situation has pointed out.[23]

As Catholic theologian Father Thomas Weinandy puts it: "There is great consternation in Catholic quarters today over the threat of the 'fundamentalist sects', notably in the U.S. and Latin America. Dismissed by this pejorative and indiscriminate label are Christians, especially Pentecostals, who constitute the fastest growing Christian movement in the world today. True, some are anti-Catholic and their message falls short of the entire Christian message, yet they do proclaim the heart of the Gospel. Most of them offer people a living relationship with Jesus.

"The Catholic Church is facing a real problem here, but the crisis is more within the Church than with the 'sects', rightly or wrongly identified, which have merely exposed our own vulnerability and evangelistic ineptitude."[24]

In some ways we in the Catholic Church are in danger of taking the stance of the elder brother in the parable of the prodigal son, unable to humble ourselves and accept the prodigal mercy of the Father in bestowing forgiveness and the outpouring of the Holy Spirit on those "outside the camp".[25]

---

[22] Dudley Hall, *Out of the Comfort Zone: The Church in Transition* (Pineville, N.C.: Morning Star Publications, 1991), p. 44.

[23] Joseph E. Davis, "The Protestant Challenge in Latin America", *America,* January 19, 1991, p. 38.

[24] Fr. Thomas Weinandy, "Why Catholics Find It So Hard to Evangelize", *New Covenant,* October 1993, p. 19.

[25] I am looking forward to the publication of a book by Neil Lozano

I would hope that we as a Church could find a way truer to the Spirit of Jesus to refer to these most recent of "separated brothers", millions of whom love him so much and sacrifice much in his service.

In the past, churches, including the Catholic Church, have sometimes relied on force and power to preserve their dominance, and since this tendency is in our hearts, it is easy for it to be manifest again. A recent statement of the Catholic bishops of El Salvador reveals how contemporary this struggle is. In reflecting on the rise of sects in their country, the bishops made many useful observations about the situation and also direct appeals to the powers that be to block the evangelizing of the sects: "We ask owners of the media to be aware that many of the messages spread by these groups run counter to the interests of the true Christian faith and the religious unity of our people. . . . We urge the authorities to be attentive to the enforcement of article 25 of the Political Constitution which protects freedom of worship but which also requires that the public and the moral order be safeguarded by protecting the tranquility of homes and communities against deafening and insulting broadcasts."[26]

Ironically, the Orthodox Church in the former Soviet Union is facing the same temptation, perhaps driven by a territorial spirit: to rely on the secular power, which has just stopped persecuting her; to preserve her position rather than focus on what is best for the kingdom of God, relying on Christ crucified and the power of the Holy Spirit. The Russian Orthodox Church is on record as supporting legislation that would make it much more difficult for other Christian groups to evangelize in the former Soviet Union.

A Russian Orthodox priest, Father Gleb Yakunin, who has

---

devoted to analyzing the dynamics of the "elder brother" found within all of us. I have read it in draft form and think it is an original and sensitive contribution to the literature of spiritual growth and holiness that will be helpful to many. Its title is not finalized yet, nor is its publisher, but when it is published we will make it available through our newsletter: Renewal Ministries, Box 7712, Ann Arbor, MI 48107.

[26] Bishops of El Salvador, "Offsetting the Proselytism of Sects", *L'Osservatore Romano* (English ed.), August 27, 1990, p. 9.

been a prophetic voice in the Church, described the situation like this: "'The amendment is a new discriminatory law, aimed at creating favorable conditions for the Moscow Patriarchate which is using its lobby in the Supreme Soviet to muzzle all competing organizations in its preaching activities.' . . . But the idea that the church, after 70 years of repression, was asking for renewed state controls, troubled many."[27]

At least this time the President of Russia refused to go along with this religion-inspired repression and offered amendments to the legislation that would blunt its effects, although it would still allow the government to bar religious groups from outside Russia if they were to engage in "coercive" proselytizing or "offend the religious feelings of Russian citizens".

Also, the law still calls for state support of religions that are "traditional" in Russia. But, as Father Yakunin has pointed out, the most traditional of all religions in the land we now call Russia is paganism.[28]

Of course, since this tendency to rely on power or force to maintain one's position is rooted in fallen human nature, it is not just the Catholic and Orthodox churches that manifest this tendency. Protestant churches have also often turned to the secular power to maintain their position, nor are the newer evangelical and Pentecostal churches immune from this tendency. Nevertheless we all must take responsibility for our own situation. It is always easier to see the speck in our brother's eye than the beam in our own: "O Jerusalem, Jerusalem, killing the prophets and stoning those who are sent to you! How often would I have gathered your children together as a hen gathers her brood under her wings, and you would not!" (Mt 23:37).

Leadership can sometimes form and train disciples in the same prejudices, fears, narrownesses, judgmentalism, loveless zeal, self-righteousness, and pride from which leaders themselves suffer. In

[27] Serge Schmemann, "Russians Pass Measure to Restrict Foreign Religious Groups", *New York Times,* July 16, 1993, p. A6.

[28] Alan Cooperman, "Pope Heads for Baltics as Religions Compete", *Ann Arbor News,* September 2, 1993, p. A7.

fact, it is inevitable: "Woe to you, scribes and Pharisees, hypocrites! for you traverse sea and land to make a single proselyte, and when he becomes a proselyte, you make him twice as much a child of hell as yourselves" (Mt 23:15).

That is perhaps why the Apostle warns: "Let not many of you become teachers, my brethren, for you know that we who teach shall be judged with greater strictness" (James 3:1).

Legalism had come to overshadow mercy and compassion; self-glorifying leadership had come to obscure God himself; a mean, self-righteous spirit had come to crush the weak and poor; a spiritual blindness venerated the tombs of prophets past while persecuting prophets of the present day. All of these tendencies to pervert religion are contained within our fallen human natures; all of them have been present in the Church at various ages and times. They make Jesus angry—and sad.

Jesus wants the individuals he has chosen, the institutions he has established, the rituals he has authorized, the teaching he has given all to lead to a deeper, life-giving relationship to him in the power and freedom of the Holy Spirit. They are not ends in themselves; they are pathways and doorways to him or responses to him. When they function as substitutes for personal union with him or as obstacles, it is a grave matter to him.

As Father Dubay puts it in relation to the transforming union with God that John of the Cross and Teresa of Avila speak of:

> Our being filled with God is, of course, the reason for everything else in the economy of salvation ... the transforming union is likewise the purpose of all else in the Church. The Eucharist itself, the Sacrament of all sacraments, is, according to the word of the Lord, aimed at producing eternal life here on earth. Jesus declares that whoever eats His flesh and drinks His Blood *has* eternal life. It is a life that is to be abundant, to the full. The fullness is the transformation; there is no other. In this Mystical Body of Christ we are to find our fulfillment, not something less. Thus all structures in the Church—institutions, priesthood, curias, chancery offices, books and candles and all else—are aimed at producing

this abundance of life, this utter immersion in triune splendor, this transforming union.[29]

John of the Cross in his *Ascent of Mount Carmel* points out that there is a tendency for what mediates God gradually to take the place of God, and in effect lead to an idolatry of persons or things. There must be a purification, or "dark night", that involves everything that is not God himself.

This can be true even in regard to the "values" of the kingdom of God. There is a great tendency to speak only of the values of the kingdom that are most popular with secular society and to remain silent about the crucified and risen King who is the source and guarantor of these values. As Oscar Cullmann, a leading Protestant theologian, has said: "We are emptying the churches by repeating things the world is already saying ... all many theologians do is repeat things that the world is saying on its account and much more effectively."[30]

Even practices of devotion and asceticism can become perverted. As a Russian Orthodox saint puts it: "Those who do not practice ascetical means—fasting, praying, reading the scriptures, standing in church, singing the songs, prostrating, bowing, keeping vigil, keeping quiet—remain animals.... Those who would make these ascetic practices the essence of the faith don't remain animals, they become demons."[31]

The Apostle Paul warns of a similar abuse of devotion and asceticism, the twisting of religious things by the disordered desires of our fallen human natures: "Therefore let no one pass judgment on you in questions of food and drink or with regard to a festival or a new moon or a sabbath. These are only a shadow of what is to come; but the substance belongs to Christ.... If with Christ you died to the elemental spirits of the universe, why do

[29] Fr. Thomas Dubay, S.M., *Fire Within,* (San Francisco: Ignatius Press, 1989), pp. 196–97.

[30] Lucio Brunelli and Alfred Labhart, "Ratzinger and the Son of Luther", 30 *Days,* no. 3 (1993): 9.

[31] St. Ignatius Brianchaninoff, as cited in Hopko, "Continuous Conversion", p. 8.

you live as if you still belonged to the world? Why do you submit to regulations? 'Do not handle, Do not taste, Do not touch!' (referring to things which all perish as they are used), according to human precepts and doctrines? These have indeed an appearance of wisdom in promoting rigor of devotion and self-abasement and severity to the body, but they are of no value in checking the indulgence of the flesh" (Col 2:16–17, 20–23).

Paul goes on to exhort the Colossians to keep their focus on Christ and their asceticism focused on renouncing the disordered tendencies of our fallen natures and growing in Christian virtue (Col 3:1–17).

The Sacred Scriptures are an inestimable gift of God. What life, what insight, what help are contained in the Scriptures! Yet we men, in our perversity and hardness of heart and capacity for self-delusion, can use something as holy and life giving as the Scriptures to hide from personal, life-changing encounter with Jesus: "You search the scriptures, because you think that in them you have eternal life; and it is they that bear witness to me; yet you refuse to come to me that you may have life" (Jn 5:39–40).

In an important talk on the occasion of the anniversaries of key papal documents on biblical studies, Pope John Paul II warned against the very dangers that Scripture itself warns against:

> As the Council well reminded us: "In the sacred books the Father who is in heaven comes lovingly to meet his children, and talks with them. And such is the force and power of the word of God that it can serve the Church as her support and vigour, and the children of the Church as strength for their faith, food for the soul, and a pure and lasting source of spiritual life." (*Dei Verbum,* no. 21) . . . Without this support [a vigorous spiritual life], exegetical research remains incomplete; it loses sight of its main purpose and is confined to secondary tasks. It can even become a sort of escape. Scientific study of the merely human aspects of the texts can make him forget that the word of God invites each person to come out of himself to live in faith and love. . . .
>
> While engaged in the very work of interpretation, one must remain in the presence of God as much as possible . . . they will

avoid becoming lost in the complexities of abstract scientific research which distances them from the true meaning of the Scriptures. Indeed, this meaning is inseparable from their goal, which is to put believers into a personal relationship with God.[32]

Although the Catholic Church has a long and valuable theological and philosophical heritage, there is a danger that she can become lost in a world of thought and documents and not notice the lack of connection with real life and real people. It is like one organ of a human body being overdeveloped and others weak and nearly useless. The "brain" of the Catholic Church is certainly well developed, but sometimes it does not notice that the rest of the body is weak and is not going anywhere and can hardly move. The disconnection of thought from life is a form of "losing touch with reality" that the Catholic Church must guard against.

As Cardinal Suquia puts it:

This means, to point out only one example, overcoming in thought and in life the habits of the idealistic experiment that has permeated European culture everywhere. It means learning again to be concerned for reality, realizing that thought does not precede life, nor legitimate it, but that a lively and true thought can be born and sustained only in a permanent tension toward the truth of the real. Having forgotten this has already cost the world millions of deaths and the physical and moral destruction that we all know, the fruit of ideologies that were imposed on man without confronting reality, and without respect for it. Not having taken this sufficiently into account has cost the Church—excepting the saints, who represent the most consistent and human realism that can be found in history. She has conserved perhaps for her internal use an admirable thought, but has lost man, who does not know what to do with this thought and is no longer at all interested in conforming to it. . . . The gospel is full of these simple, direct questions, asked in the language of real life, and of answers that are no less direct and real. "Master, what must I do to inherit eternal life?"; "Zaccheus, come down, for I must stay in your house today";

[32] Pope John Paul II, "Bible Experts Must Be Guided by Spirit", *L'Osservatore Romano* (English ed.), April 28, 1993, pp. 3–4.

"if you knew the gift of God . . . you would have asked him, and he would have given you living water"; . . . "come and see"; "your sins are forgiven." Unless we Christians can listen, understand, and respond to the questions that the man of today asks himself with this same simplicity and concreteness, in the language . . . of real life, perhaps it would not be opportune to speak too much about the new evangelization. . . . The entire content of the faith of the Church, her dogmas, are not above all a beautiful intellectual edifice. They are the reasoned testimony of the experience of the Church, and the systematic formulation of the conditions for the possibility of this miracle of mercy that has occurred innumerable times since Jesus Christ lived among us in the flesh, and that continues to occur today among us. Thus, if something can happen, if in fact it happens, it is because Christ lives, and lives in the Church, in this frail body that is ourselves. And if Christ lives, it is because he is the Son of God, the redeemer, and the hope of man.[33]

Father Raniero Cantalamessa speaks of the two modes of approaching God, through truth or doctrine and through experience, but also speaks of the possibility of a past lack of balance in our approach as Catholics: "Both ways of approaching the mystery are therefore necessary and precious but we cannot deny that if there was a lack of balance in the past, it was certainly not in favour of reality and experience but of speculation and intellectualism. When we talk of Christian 'reality', we mean, above all, the divine persons in that they give themselves to us and we encounter them in the mysteries: God, who is 'our Father', Jesus Christ who lives in us 'as the hope of glory', the Holy Spirit whose 'first fruits' we savour; then we have faith, hope, love, sonship."[34]

Father Avery Dulles points out that this tendency to narrow God and "put him in a box" is not absent among contemporary theologians either: "Theologians should not so confine themselves to a single school or system that they overlook elements of truth

---

[33] Cardinal Angel Suquia, "The New Evangelization: Some Tasks and Risks of the Present", *Communio*, Winter 1992, pp. 515–40.

[34] Cantalamessa, *Life in the Lordship of Christ*, p. ix.

or value that are more evident from a perspective other than their own. The persistent temptation of systematic theology is to become too self-enclosed. At its worst such theology tends to treat God, Christ and grace as ciphers to be manipulated within a system. Theology needs to nourish itself by a continual return to the sources of faith and piety. If the theologian is in touch with the reality of God through prayer and worship, God will be tacitly perceived as infinitely greater than all our images or concepts."[35]

Cardinal Ratzinger points out that faith is the criterion for everything: "The highly cultured are not the men who determine the truth of the baptismal faith but it is the baptismal faith which determines what is valid in cultured interpretations. The intellectuals do not put the faithful to the test. It is the faithful who put intellectuals to the test. Baptismal faith is not measured by intellectual explanations but, ingenuously literal, it is the baptismal faith which measures all theology. The baptized, he who lives in the faith of baptism, does not need to be instructed. He has received the definitive truth and he carries it with him with the faith."[36]

The above is Cardinal Ratzinger's reformulation of one of the most important passages of the New Testament for making clear the radical nature of the New Covenant: "But the anointing which you received from him abides in you, and you have no need that any one should teach you; as his anointing teaches you about everything, and is true, and is no lie, just as it has taught you, abide in him" (1 Jn 2:27).

Father Marie-Dominique Philippe also has something important to say in this area: "When we read Scripture we need to remind ourselves that the Holy Spirit is thinking about us through this living Word. At this point, it is no longer Scripture but a direct dialogue with God. We are taught directly by God and we understand how faith leads us directly to the school of the Holy Spirit, directly to this hallowed institute. Is there a better professor than the Holy Spirit? All the rest are adjunct professors, but He is

[35] Fr. Avery Dulles, S.J., "From Symbol to System: A Proposal for Theological Method", *Pro Ecclesia* 1, no. 1, p. 43.

[36] Ratzinger, "Against the Power of Intellectuals", pp. 68–69.

the Master who gives us trustworthy teaching. And if we want to be Christians, if we want to live the Christian life in the fullest sense, we must learn from the Holy Spirit and listen to Him, through God's Word, through the living Word."[37]

Paradoxically, just as the Catholic Church is defending herself against evangelical charges that she kept the Bible from the common man during earlier centuries, she is again in danger of removing the Bible from the common man by instilling a fear of "fundamentalistic" interpretation and the lack of proper scientific exegetical knowledge.

Cardinal Ratzinger has strong words to say about this:

> Every Catholic must have the courage to believe that his faith (in communion with that of the Church) surpasses every "new magisterium" of the experts, of the intellectuals. Their hypotheses can be helpful in providing a better understanding of the genesis of the biblical books, but it is a prejudice of evolutionistic provenance if it is asserted that the text is understandable only if its origin and development are studied. The rule of faith, yesterday as today, is not based on the discoveries (be they true or hypothetical) of biblical sources and layers but on the Bible *just as it is,* as it has been read in the Church since the time of the Fathers until now. It is precisely the fidelity to this reading of the Bible that has given us the saints, who were often uneducated and, at any rate, frequently knew nothing about exegetical contexts. Yet they were the ones who understood it best.[38]

The rhythm of the liturgical year, with its objective, balanced unfolding of the great mysteries of the life of Christ, its times of fasting and of celebrating, its periodic focus on self-denial, all can lead in a wonderful way to a deepening union with Christ, if he remains the focus. If not, a form of legalism, almost superstition, can creep in that uses even these holy things and extraliturgical devotions that grow up in an imbalanced way as a screen between us and Christ rather than pathways to encounter with him. We

[37] Philippe, *Follow the Lamb...,* p. 31.
[38] Cardinal Joseph Ratzinger with Vittorio Messori, *The Ratzinger Report* (San Francisco: Ignatius Press, 1991), p. 76.

can relate to these pathways of personal relationship as "things" and miss the Person who is waiting to encounter us through these sacred signs and the living, vital power of his Resurrection that he desires to impart to us through them: "But Jesus answered them, 'You are wrong, because you know neither the scriptures nor the power of God'" (Mt 22:29).

We can be extremely knowledgeable about the Scriptures and yet not know them at all in the way Jesus is talking about, as doorways to relationship with him.

We can be up to our eyeballs with the form of religion yet not know its power to transform us, because we are not really giving ourselves to him and allowing him to do with us what he pleases. We are not really surrendering.

In every case of abuse and distortion cited in the Scripture and tradition, what are lacking are the focus on and the real, living relationship with the Person of Christ. It is the Father's intention that Christ be the center of everything, and when he is not, a distortion occurs.

Let us repent of using the great gifts of God for our own selfish purposes; let us repent of a possessiveness and exclusiveness that has created walls rather than doors; let us repent of a reliance on the things of God rather than on God himself; let us repent of our pride and arrogance, of boasting of anything, except the Cross of Jesus Christ, which alone saves us.

Cardinal O'Connor, in speaking recently of the great trials and purification "by fire" that the Church is going through, spoke of the heartfelt repentance that is needed: "It is long since time to get down on our knees, to beat our breasts, to ask God's mercy."[39]

It has been difficult for the Church as Church to admit that she needs to repent or to acknowledge that she has ever done anything wrong and is in need of forgiveness. Probably out of a fear that if she admits the obvious, she will lose credibility regarding her infallible teaching authority in the area of faith and morals (pride often masquerades as prudence), she has been very slow to

[39] Peter Steinfels, "Inquiries Pledged on Abusive Priests", *New York Times,* July 2, 1993, pp. A1, A7.

admit the obvious. I think our credibility would increase if we acknowledged mistakes and more serious failings when appropriate.

Father Peter Hocken, the British ecumenical theologian, thinks that such repentance is essential if we are to become an evangelizing Church:

> Vatican II intuitively grasped this essential link between renewal of the Church and ecumenism: that each tradition, including the Roman Catholic, needs the witness of the Spirit in other traditions for its own full vitality and vigor.
>
> An essential element in this renewal is repentance for our failings in the past and the present. As a church, we score more highly in modern times for rethinking our theology and adapting our structures than we do on publicly admitting our failures. This has important spiritual repercussions. Because an authentic renewal requires a change of heart before God, becoming an effective evangelizing church may require a corporate humbling before the Lord, along with the confession of our weaknesses and failings in this area.[40]

As Father Benedict Groeschel, C.F.R., director of spiritual development for the Archdiocese of New York, has pointed out, there is a need not just for individual repentance when appropriate but also for institutional repentance: "In addition to the individual, communities in the Church, societies that consider themselves Christian and the whole Church herself must constantly repent and believe again with new fervor the Good News of salvation brought and proclaimed by Our Lord Jesus Christ."[41]

Father Groeschel goes on to speak specifically of the humiliation and embarrassment the Church is going through as a result of the clergy sex abuse scandals: "More than any time in the past 200 years, the Catholic Church in the United States is filled with pain.... Since I believe deeply in the mercy of God, and know that he painfully punishes his children only to correct them, I suspect that the present humiliation may have some beneficial

[40] Fr. Peter Hocken, *Ecumenical Issues in Evangelization* (unpublished ms.).

[41] Fr. Benedict J. Groeschel, C.F.R., *The Reform of Renewal* (San Francisco: Ignatius Press, 1990), p. 28.

effects. It could lead to a real reformation of our moral practice as a Church, and to a thorough examination of our moral teaching, from kindergarten to doctoral studies. . . . We could make better use of all this suffering by putting our house in order."[42]

It is encouraging to see John Paul II, and the Church as a whole, taking responsibility to acknowledge Church failings, not touching on her infallible teaching authority, but significant nonetheless, whether it be mistakes made in the Galileo case, in contributing to the breaking of the unity of Christians, or "dark spots and shadows" in the evangelization of the New World and the treatment of the native Indians or acknowledging Catholic involvement in African slavery.

The Church is human but, unlike her head, Christ, not without sin: "It is in that historical and cultural framework, far removed from our own times, that Galileo's judges, incapable of dissociating faith from an age-old cosmology, believed, quite wrongly, that the adoption of the Copernican revolution, in fact not yet definitively proven, was such as to undermine Catholic tradition, and that it was their duty to forbid its being taught. This subjective error of judgement, so clear to us today, led them to a disciplinary measure from which Galileo 'had much to suffer'. These mistakes must be frankly recognized, as you, Holy Father, have requested."[43]

> In this one and only Church of God from its very beginnings there arose certain rifts, which the Apostle strongly censures as damnable. But in subsequent centuries much more serious dissensions appeared and large communities became separated from full communion with the Catholic Church—for which, often enough, men of both sides were to blame . . . their [the Catholic faithful's] primary duty is to make a careful and honest appraisal of whatever needs to be renewed and done in the Catholic household itself, in order that its life may bear witness more clearly and faithfully to the teachings and

---

[42] Fr. Benedict J. Groeschel, C.F.R., "Making Sense of the Scandal", *Catholic World Report,* November 1993, pp. 43, 46.

[43] Cardinal Paul Poupard, " 'Galileo Case' Is Resolved", *L'Osservatore Romano* (English ed.), November 4, 1992, p. 8.

institutions which have been handed down from Christ through the apostles.

For although the Catholic Church has been endowed with all divinely revealed truth and with all means of grace, yet its members fail to live by them with all the fervor that they should. As a result the radiance of the Church's face shines less brightly in the eyes of our separated brethren and of the world at large, and the growth of God's kingdom is retarded. . . . St. John has testified: "If we say we have not sinned, we make him a liar, and his word is not in us" (1 Jn 1:19). This holds good for sins against unity. Thus, in humble prayer we beg pardon of God and of our separated brethren, just as we forgive them that offend us.[44]

These men, women and children were the victims of a disgraceful trade in which people who were baptized, but who did not live their faith, took part. How can we forget the enormous suffering inflicted, the violation of the most basic human rights, on those people deported from the African continent? How can we forget the human lives destroyed by slavery?

In all truth and humility this sin of man against man, this sin of man against God, must be confessed. . . .

From this African shrine of black sorrow, we implore heaven's forgiveness. We pray that in the future Christ's disciples will be totally faithful to the observance of the commandment of fraternal love which the Master left us.[45]

At the special consistory of cardinals held in June 1994 to prepare for the celebration of the two thousandth year of Christ's birth, Pope John Paul II invited the assembled cardinals to include as part of the preparation repentance for sins of the Church's past that have not been publicly acknowledged.

"As she faces this Great Jubilee, the Church needs *'metanoia'*, *that is, the discernment of her children's historical shortcomings and negligence* with regard to the demands of the Gospel. Only the courageous acknowledgement of faults and omissions, for which

[44] Decree on Ecumenism *Unitatis Redintegratio*, 3, 4, 7.
[45] Pope John Paul II, "From This African Shrine of Sorrow Let Us Implore Heaven's Forgiveness", *L'Osservatore Romano* (English ed.), March 4, 1992, p. 2.

Christians have in some way been responsible, as well as the generous intention to remedy them with the help of God, can give an effective impetus to the new evangelization and make the path to unity easier."[46]

The preparatory document for the Consistory, which had been sent out with the Pope's approval called specifically for a reflection on "the dark sides of the Church's history, evaluating them in the light of the principles of the Gospels.... How can we ignore the many forms of violence that were also perpetrated in the name of faith, such as wars between religions, the Inquisition trials and other forms of violations of the rights of persons?"[47]

The *Catechism of the Catholic Church* also acknowledges these sorry features of our history as a Church:

> In times past, cruel practices were commonly used by legitimate governments to maintain law and order, often without protest from the Pastors of the Church, who themselves adopted in their own tribunals the prescriptions of Roman law concerning torture. Regrettable as these facts are, the Church always taught the duty of clemency and mercy. She forbade clerics to shed blood. In recent times it has become evident that these cruel practices were neither necessary for public order, nor in conformity with the legitimate rights of the human person. On the contrary, these practices led to ones even more degrading. It is necessary to work for their abolition. We must pray for the victims and their tormentors (2298).

The first words Jesus is recorded as having said in his public ministry were "repent, for the kingdom of God is at hand." And down through the centuries, brought to our attention time and time again by the Spirit of God, these words continue to be spoken to us as individuals and as a Church.

---

[46] Pope John Paul II, "Address to Extraordinary Consistory of Cardinals", *L'Osservatore Romano* (English ed.), June 22, 1994, p. 8.

[47] Lisa Palmieri-Billig, "Ecumenism", *Inside the Vatican,* May 1994, p. 20.

Narrowing God

Another tendency of our fallen humanity is to narrow our conception of God and his plan to simply the group or institution that we belong to, to erect walls where God intended for there to be doors and windows. Even though I am a committed Catholic, I do not believe God is limited in his significant actions to the Catholic Church, and I think there is a great danger in this kind of narrowed vision. God is bigger than the visible institutions he establishes and the leadership he anoints. Consider how Moses responded when people with a narrower vision brought their concerns to him.

Because Moses possessed the Spirit of God, he was deluged with pressure from the people to meet their needs. Feeling the burden of leadership, Moses asked, and God responded favorably for others to be given the Spirit to share in leadership. Two of the leaders chosen to receive the Spirit were not where they were supposed to be but received the Spirit anyway and began to prophesy. Moses' response is important: "And a young man ran and told Moses, 'Eldad and Medad are prophesying in the camp.' And Joshua the son of Nun, the minister of Moses, one of his chosen men, said, 'My lord Moses, forbid them.' But Moses said to him, 'Are you jealous for my sake? Would that all the Lord's people were prophets, that the Lord would put his spirit upon them!' " (Nb 11:27–29).

Because Moses' heart was right with God, he was not possessive or jealous of others sharing the Spirit. In fact, his heart's desire was that everyone could share in what he had been given.

Consider also how God used pagan nations to do his will, even to the point of using them to purify his chosen people (2 Kings 24:1–4; Jer 22).

Consider also how Jesus spoke about how if the "chosen, gifted, and called" perversely harden their hearts, others will come and take their place at the wedding feast; others will come from east and west and take their places.

If those who are properly the children of Abraham do not respond to the Lord wholeheartedly, he will raise up new children from the very stones.

Time and time again we discover that what God said through the prophet Isaiah is absolutely true: "My thoughts are not your thoughts, neither are your ways my ways" (Is 55:8).

Many of those who had spent their whole lives "searching the Scriptures" for wisdom about the coming Messiah missed him because they had narrowed their horizons too much and "put God in a box". All of us have a tremendous tendency to "put God in a box" and determine how, when, and through whom he must act. All of us have a tendency to be "in control" of our relationship with God in a way that inevitably limits him.

But God is sovereign. He does what he wants, when he wants, through whom he wants in ways that often surprise us.

Many were not prepared to accept a Messiah who came as a suffering servant; they missed the hour of their visitation with untold catastrophic consequences for them personally and for their nation.

Unfair? No. Jesus made clear time and time again that the words he spoke and the deeds he did, never done by any man before, were more than enough evidence for those whose hearts were genuinely open to God and open to the truth.

The Apostle Peter and the early Church had a terrible struggle opening up to the fact that God wanted to extend his salvation through Jesus to the Gentiles, without first requiring them to become Jews. The Lord had to use dramatic means to convince Peter and the other Jewish Christians to widen their hearts to receive the Gentile Christians as true brothers in Christ.

Father Raniero Cantalamessa points out, in accordance with Scripture (Rom 11) that when God again deals with the Jews as a people, in preparation for his return, and there is some corporate conversion to Christ, as promised in the Scriptures, the Catholic Church will again face a challenge in widening her conception of what God does and how he does it, and widening our hearts as well:

> Can we Christians exclude that what is happening in our day, that is, the return of Israel to the land of its fathers, is not connected in some way, still a mystery to us, to this providential order which concerns the chosen people and which is carried out even through human error and excess as happens in the

Church itself? ... This responsibility of faith requires the Church to love the Jews, to wait for them, to ask, as it already does, their pardon for having in certain times hidden the true Jesus from them, that Jesus who loves them and who is their "glory"; ... If the delay has been so long and painful, it has also undoubtedly been so through the fault of Christians ... it is certain that the rejoining of Israel with the Church will involve a rearrangement in the Church; it will mean a conversion on both sides.[48]

The tendency to become possessive about the religious system that we are a part of and to start serving it as a projection of our own ego and security rather than the living God who "blows where he wills" is strong in all of us.

The bitter history of schism and heresy is also instructive. Catholics, rightly wishing to safeguard the unity and integrity of the one Church that Christ established, have dealt severely with schism and heresy over the centuries. Terrible things have been said and done. Sadly, it is very possible to be theologically right and attitudinally or spiritually wrong, compounding the very real theological divisions with perhaps even greater relationship and personal divisions.

Happily, as a result of Vatican II, Catholics are not only working and praying to solve the theological divisions but also taking responsibility for their role in the bitter personal and relationship divisions.

In retrospect, even though schism and heresy have greatly wounded and weakened the entire Body of Christ, including the Catholic Church, it is clear that God did not abandon his divided people, even when one side was "theologically" in the wrong. Without endorsing what was wrong in the schism or heresy, God continued to endorse what was right, especially when what was right involved genuine devotion to his Son, Jesus.

God's love is always deeper, wider, and wiser than our love, and we will never be done learning from it and repenting as we encounter it.

[48] Fr. Raniero Cantalamessa, *The Mystery of Christmas* (Middlegreen, Slough, U.K.: St. Paul's Publications, 1988), pp. 94–102.

While the Church and her sacraments are the ordinary means of salvation and sanctification, God is not limited even to what he has established in a special way. The whole earth tells us of his glory. He reveals himself to all men in the creation, in the wonder and glory of the universe. He reveals himself to all men in the instinct for right and wrong he has placed within them; he is, indeed, the true light, which enlightens every man coming into the world. In his hands are the rising and falling of nations; in his hands are the judgment, purification, and blessing of the churches; in his hands are the creation and redemption of the entire human race. While using individuals and institutions that he has truly chosen and anointed, he is not limited to them; his kingdom is bigger than us all.

What then might the Spirit be saying to the Catholic Church? A message as old and ever new as the day of Pentecost: Repent, believe, and you too will receive the gift of the Holy Spirit (Acts 2:38).

Let us repent of any ways in which we have narrowed God, or limited him, in our thoughts, words, or actions. Let us repent of any ways we have obscured the central place of Jesus and put secondary things in his place. Let us repent of that "eccclesiocentrism" that puts the Church in the place of Christ. Let us repent of any ways we have grieved the Holy Spirit and through our pride or fear resisted his workings.

Chapter Six

Jesus, Head of the Catholic Church

Catholics sometimes speak of the Pope as being head of the Catholic Church, and he is, in a temporary, limited, representational manner. But the true Head of the Catholic Church is Jesus.

As Vatican II has put it, even though the Pope has been given an important continuing role in the life of the Church in the service of her unity, nevertheless, Christ Jesus himself forever remains "the chief corner-stone and shepherd of our souls":[1] "The Church is . . . a flock, of which God foretold that he would himself be the shepherd (cf. Is 40:11; Ex 34:11f.), and whose sheep, although watched over by human shepherds, are nevertheless at all times led and brought to pasture by Christ himself, the Good Shepherd and prince of shepherds (cf. Jn 10:11; 1 Pet 5:4), who gave his life for his sheep (cf. Jn 10:11-16). . . . The head of this body is Christ."[2]

And the Holy Spirit himself is the primary principle of unity of the Church and also, in a real sense, her ruler: "It is the Holy Spirit dwelling in those who believe, and pervading and ruling over the entire Church, who brings about that wonderful communion of the faithful and joins them together so intimately in Christ that he is the principle of the Church's unity. By distributing various kinds of spiritual gifts and ministries, he enriches the Church of Jesus Christ with different

[1] Decree on Ecumenism *Unitatis Redintegratio,* 2.
[2] Constitution on the Church *Lumen Gentium,* 6, 7.

ictions 'in order to equip the saints for the work of service, so as to build up the body of Christ' (Eph 4:12)."[3]

And as Cardinal Ratzinger has put it: "We still have not touched upon the decisive point: as a living organism, the Church is, in Paul's words, both head and body. A body without a head is no longer a body: it is a corpse. The head of the Church is Christ. This is the most profound element and intimate essence of the Church as the Body of Christ and regardless of any public opinion poll, it must be represented. Without it, the Church and humanity would be the corpse."[4]

But Jesus is far more than Head of the Catholic Church; he is the Head of all who comprise his Body, far beyond the visible, institutional bounds of the Catholic Church; he is indeed Lord of all creation, of the entire universe: "He is the image of the invisible God, the first-born of all creation; for in him all things were created, in heaven and on earth, visible and invisible, whether thrones or dominions or principalities or authorities—all things were created through him and for him. He is before all things, and in him all things hold together. He is the head of the body, the church; he is the beginning, the first-born from the dead, that in everything he might be pre-eminent. For in him all the fulness of God was pleased to dwell, and through him to reconcile to himself all things, whether on earth or in heaven, making peace by the blood of his cross" (Col 1:15–20).

Jesus is not "added on" to the world, to the universe, to the church, to humanity: he is the source and sustainer of the world, the universe, the Church, humanity. Everything that is, including all of us, was created through him and for him. We have come from him, and we have been created to find our meaning and purpose only in him. There is no fulfillment for the universe, for creation, for any creature, for any of us apart from him. There is no way for any man or any organization or institution to reach its destiny, achieve its purpose, apart from him.

---

[3] Decree on Ecumenism *Unitatis Redintegratio,* 2.

[4] Cardinal Joseph Ratzinger, "Against the Power of Intellectuals", 30 *Days* (March 1991): 70.

As regards the Church, she has no meaning or purpose apart from Jesus. He is the founder of the Church, the inspirer of the Church, the sustainer of the Church, the guide of the Church. Even more, the Church is in her deepest identity his Body; he is the Head of the Body. Everything in the Church, everything that the Church does has ultimately one purpose: to glorify God the Father, in and through Jesus Christ, in the power of the Holy Spirit.

Sometimes this is not clear, in either the minds or the experiences of many Catholics, or in the witness that the Catholic Church gives to those who are not Catholic. It is important that those who are members of the Catholic Church, as well as those who are not, understand how profoundly Christ-centered she is. It is beyond the scope of this book to provide a complete catechesis or apologetics for the various features of Catholic life, but I would like to single out three elements—the Eucharist, Mary, and the hierarchy—three of the most difficult elements for both Catholics and non-Catholics properly to understand, and I will attempt to illumine their intrinsic Christ-centeredness.

The Eucharist

The Eucharist or the Mass is at heart worshipping God the Father, in union with Jesus, in the power of the Holy Spirit. It is also, both in its actions and in its words, a powerful proclamation of the gospel. The Eucharist, which simply means thanksgiving, is a response of obedience to Jesus, doing what he asked us to do: "And he took bread, and when he had given thanks he broke it and gave it to them, saying, 'This is my body which is given for you. Do this in remembrance of me.' And likewise the cup after supper, saying, 'This cup which is poured out for you is the new covenant in my blood' " (Lk 22:19–20).

The reality of the encounter with the Lord in the Eucharist was clearly witnessed to in the early Church and in the writings of the Fathers:

"For I received from the Lord what I also delivered to you, that the Lord Jesus on the night when he was betrayed took bread, and when he had given thanks, he broke it, and said, 'This is my body which is for you. Do this in remembrance of me.' In the same way also the cup, after supper, saying, 'This cup is the new covenant in my blood. Do this, as often as you drink it, in remembrance of me.' For as often as you eat this bread and drink the cup, you proclaim the Lord's death until he comes.

Whoever, therefore, eats the bread or drinks the cup of the Lord in an unworthy manner will be guilty of profaning the body and blood of the Lord.... For any one who eats and drinks without discerning the body eats and drinks judgment on himself. That is why many of you are weak and ill, and some have died" (1 Cor 11:23–30).

The remembering (anamnesis) of the Eucharist is not simply an intellectual remembering or a nostalgic remembering or an empty ritual remembering; it is a remembering that makes present what it remembers, because Jesus promised it would, and allows us more deeply to participate in, thank God for, and be nourished and sustained by the great once and for all sacrifice of Jesus for us on the Cross. The Eucharist does not "sacrifice Jesus again" but makes present to us and allows us to participate in the once and for all sacrifice that remains eternally fruitful and powerful and that Jesus wants to be accessible to all generations. One of the most extraordinary ways he has made it present is in the Eucharist.

The central place the Catholic Church gives to the Eucharist is a way in which she fulfills the scriptural injunction "to know nothing among you except Jesus Christ and him crucified" (1 Cor 2:2).[5]

As John Paul II said in his first encyclical:

The Church never ceases to relive his death on the cross and his Resurrection, which constitute the content of the Church's daily life. Indeed, it is by the command of Christ himself, her

---

[5] All the sacraments of the Catholic Church are profoundly rooted in the Scriptures. An important book that explicates the profound interconnection between the Scriptures and the liturgy is that by Jean Daniélou, S.J., *The Bible and the Liturgy* (Ann Arbor, Mich.: Servant Books, 1979).

Master, that the Church unceasingly celebrates the Eucharist, finding in it the "fountain of life and holiness", the efficacious sign of grace and reconciliation with God and the pledge of eternal life. The Church lives his mystery, draws unwearyingly from it and continually seeks ways of bringing this mystery of her Master and Lord to humanity—to the peoples, the nations, the succeeding generations, and every individual human being— as if she were ever repeating, as the Apostle did: "For I decided to know nothing among you except Jesus Christ and him crucified." The Church stays within the sphere of the mystery of the Redemption, which has become the fundamental principle of her life and mission.[6]

The fact that when Jesus spoke of the need to eat his body and drink his blood disciples drew back and no longer followed (Jn 6) and he did nothing to "reinterpret" what he had just said but instead let them go is one of the reasons the Catholic Church has always believed that Jesus intended truly to be present in a special way, under the appearance of the bread and wine of the Eucharist. Also, as the churches that the apostles personally founded taught and expanded on the apostolic teaching, it was clear that their understanding was the same. The Catholic Church believes, with good reason in my opinion, that her understanding of the Eucharist is firmly grounded in the Scripture, in the words of Jesus, in the teaching of the apostles, in the practice and teaching of the apostolic churches, from the beginning.

Not that God cannot act in marvelous ways outside of the liturgy, in the life of Catholics, or in the life of Christians in other Christian bodies, but the liturgy is a special and God-established way of him acting.

As Dietrich von Hildebrand states in his important work *Liturgy and Personality:*

> It is precisely in the Liturgy that there are presented to us, in the deepest and most organic form, the fruits of the divine life received by us in baptism, and that the man who is entirely formed by the spirit of the Liturgy is most like unto Christ. Not

---

[6] John Paul II, Encyclical *Redemptor Hominis* (*Redeemer of Man*), 7.

that this formation can be achieved only through the Liturgy! God is able to raise up out of stones children of Abraham. He may give this spirit to a man who has but scant familiarity with the Liturgy and prays little according to the forms of the Liturgy. But in each saint, in whom the image of Christ shines anew, the spirit of the Liturgy lives. Perhaps it cannot always be found in his teachings or in the forms of devotion introduced by him, but it is there in his sanctity, in the fact of his being a saint. It still remains true that the Liturgy, in its organic relation to inner prayer and asceticism, is the God-given path for growth in Christ. Toward those for whom this fact is still hidden, our hearts must always echo with the words already quoted: "If Thou didst know the gift of God!"[7]

At the heart of the Mass is a holy remembering (anamnesis) of the great sacrifice Jesus made for us on the Cross as he gave his own body and blood for the remission of sins and the salvation of the world, and a participation in the power and grace released through that sacrifice.

As the Council of Trent said: "In the sacrifice of the Mass, Christ's Sacrifice on the Cross is made present, its memory is celebrated, and its saving power is applied, . . . as in the Sacrifice of the Cross, the sacrificial gift (Christ) and the primary sacrificing priest (Christ) are the same; only the nature and the mode of the offering are different."[8]

The Mass also includes a remembrance of the whole creation and the whole family of God. It preserves, respects, and transmits the incarnational risk that God himself has taken in creating the universe and mankind. It honors what and who God honors, without fear of taking honor away from God. It in fact honors God and glorifies him by honoring what he honors. It briefly but meaningfully remembers Mary and some of the great saints, it prays for the living and the dead, but most of all it attempts to open up all who participate to a deeper appreciation and awareness

[7] Dietrich von Hildebrand, *Liturgy and Personality* (Manchester, N.H.: Sophia Institute Press, 1986), pp. 9–10.

[8] Denzinger, 938, 940.

of what Jesus has done for us and gives glory to the Father in and through and with Jesus, in the power of the Holy Spirit.

Sometimes, because we simply need words to refer to more complex realities in a shortcut way, what the Mass is really all about can be obscured. Words like the Mass and the Eucharist, rooted in Latin and Greek words that not many understand, do not really indicate what is going on to the average person today. It can sometimes seem that the Mass and the other sacraments are talked about as if they are simply things, or ceremonies, or obligations, rather than primarily Christ-centered encounters with the living God in the power of the Holy Spirit.

But while the Second Vatican Council spoke of the Eucharist as the "summit" of worship, focusing as it does in such a special way on the key person and action of all history, a Catholic's focus on Jesus is not supposed to be limited to the Eucharist. The purpose of the special focus that the Eucharist brings is to enable those who participate in it to live more fully in the presence of Christ and have him more as the center of their lives twenty-four hours a day, giving their whole lives more fully to God.

As Vatican II put it: "The spiritual life . . . is not limited solely to participation in the liturgy. The Christian is indeed called to pray with others, but he must also enter into his bedroom to pray to his Father in secret (Mt 6:6); furthermore, according to the teaching of the apostle, he must pray without ceasing (1 Th 5:17). We also learn from the same apostle that we must always carry around in our bodies the dying of Jesus, so that the life also of Jesus may be made manifest in our mortal flesh. That is why we beg the Lord in the Sacrifice of the Mass that 'receiving the offering of the Spiritual Victim,' he may fashion us for himself 'as an eternal gift.' "9

The last words spoken at the Eucharist express this well: "The Mass is ended; go in peace to love and serve the Lord."

Paul spoke of the great holiness of the Eucharist and its power as a privileged place of prayer and encounter with Jesus: he also

---

9 Constitution on the Sacred Liturgy *Sacrosanctum Concilium,* 12.

spoke, and frequently, of the need to pray always, to give thanks always, to rejoice always, to bless always.

The Eucharist is intended to open us to a whole world of prayer and praise and thanksgiving. It is not intended to restrict our relationship to God or exhaust that relationship to the time we spend in church at Mass. Sometimes Catholics can talk and act as if the Mass were the only place where real prayer takes place or Jesus is truly encountered and lived with. This is seriously to distort the meaning and place of the Mass in the life of a Catholic.

Jesus is present always and everywhere and wants us to be aware of his presence and commune with him always and everywhere. He wants us to abide with him continually.

Sometimes, out of an insecurity, or perhaps an impoverishment of life with God, the form of the Mass can be focused on or clung to, almost as a substitute for a wider and more continually personal relationship with God.

Contemporary liturgical scholarship is increasingly recognizing that since the liturgy is fundamentally a deep, personal, and corporate encounter with Christ, what goes on outside the Eucharist in the life of individual Christians and the Christian community is critical for the true flowering of the Eucharist itself.[10]

Mary

The Catholic Church pays special honor to Mary, the Mother of Jesus. She does so in what she believes to be obedience to the

[10] Paul Bernier, S.S.S., *Eucharist: Celebrating Its Rhythms in Our Lives* (Notre Dame, Ind.: Ave Maria Press, 1993); Robert Taft, "What Does Liturgy Do?" *Worship* 66, no. 3 (May 1992); Jerome Murphy-O'Connor, "Eucharist and Community in First Corinthians", *Living Bread, Saving Cup,* ed. R. Kevin Seasoltz, O.S.B. (Collegeville, Minn.: Liturgical Press, 1982), pp. 1–29; Christopher Kiesling, "The Formative Influence of Liturgy", *Studies in Formative Spirituality* 3, no. 3 (November 1982): 377–86; Regis A. Duffy, "Formative Experience and Intentional Liturgy", *Studies in Formative Spirituality* 3, no. 3 (November 1982): 351–62; Jennifer Glen, C.C.V.I., "Twenty Years Later: A Reflection on the Liturgical Act", *Assembly: Notre Dame Center for Pastoral Liturgy* 12, no. 4 (April 1986): 325–28.

Scriptures and the leading of the Holy Spirit. God chose Mary, she surrendered to the offer of the angel, the Holy Spirit overshadowed her, and the Son of God became man in her womb.

Mary had the inexpressible privilege of carrying within her the Word become flesh for nine months. Along with Joseph, she nurtured and raised Jesus. She was prophesied to by Simeon regarding her role of sharing in the sufferings of Jesus. Jesus did his first miracle in response to her request. Mary was there at the Cross, and Jesus spoke some of his last words to her as he commended her to John, and John to her, in an action that the early Church viewed as having wider significance than for just the two of them, but was rather the sharing of his Mother with those who are his disciples. Mary was there at Pentecost.

As the angel said to Mary, "Hail, full of grace, the Lord is with you!" (Lk 1:28). And as Mary said, inspired by the Holy Spirit:

> My soul magnifies the Lord,
> and my spirit rejoices in God my Savior,
> for he has regarded the low estate of his handmaiden.
> For behold, henceforth all generations will call me blessed;
> for he who is mighty has done great things for me,
> and holy is his name (Lk 1:46–49).

In the plan of God, Mary is to be honored; all generations are supposed to call her blessed. God has done something in Mary that he wants to be seen, understood, and honored. He is honored when we honor those he honors. In Mary he has chosen a woman to be blessed specially and specially used to advance the salvation of man. He is saying something by his choice that he wants noticed and honored.

For a long time I have noticed that women, in general, seem to be more responsive to the Lord and more generally loving, faithful, and self-sacrificing. Holier, if you will. Almost everywhere there are more of them in church.

Even when you discount various sociological reasons and critique an overly feminine approach to church, there still seems to be something intrinsically holier about women. I never was able to determine whether there was anything to this observation until someone recently gave me a book by the founder of a new French religious order, Father Marie-Dominique Philippe, O.P., of the Congregation of St. John. In it he gave an exegesis of the creation narratives in Genesis that made sense to me in connection with what I had been observing.

Guided by a principle of St. Thomas Aquinas, that what is first in the order of intention is last in the order of execution, Father Philippe sees the creation of woman, as God's last act of creation, as God's masterpiece: "Following God's intention woman is clearly the masterpiece of creation: she is last; she is the ultimate. . . . God's final mystery is contained in man and woman—we cannot separate them too much—still woman comes last . . . she is the masterpiece. . . . Saint Augustine, thinking of Mary in particular, has expressed this beautifully. The masterpiece of creation is woman and the Woman par excellence is Mary."[11]

Father Philippe goes on to say: "God created woman to be the mediatrix of love. She carries the secret of love and she must help man to love, to rise above his work, above his toil, above his desire to dominate. She must teach him to love."[12]

This theme is also reflected in the teaching of John Paul II when he speaks of the woman having a certain "precedence over the man".[13]

The mysteries and secrets of God must be approached with reverence. There is more. There is always more. And this "more" yields itself not to impatient demands or arrogant intellects but only to humble reflection with truly open hearts. This prayerful reflection over the centuries has unlocked some of God's secrets for the Church, secrets hidden in the Scriptures and in his heart: "Many things greater than these lie hidden, for we have seen but few of his works" (Sir 43:32).

"But there are also many other things which Jesus did; were every one of them to be written, I suppose that the world itself could not contain the books that would be written" (Jn 21:25).

[11] Fr. Marie-Dominique Philippe, O.P., *"Follow the Lamb . . .* (Laredo, Tex.: Congregation of St. John, 1991), p. 68.

[12] Ibid., p. 69

[13] John Paul II, Apostolic Letter *Mulieris Dignitatem* (*On the Dignity and Vocation of Women*), 19.

Mary is one of the great Secrets of God. She is not a wall between us and Christ, but a window that opens onto incredible depths of the Father's love and plan for man, and in a particular way for woman.

Many of the leading Protestant reformers had a high regard for Mary and a strong devotion to her, including Luther: "I believe that there is no one among us who would not leave his own mother to become a son of Mary. And that you can do, all the more because that has been offered as a choice to you, and it is an even greater joy than if you embraced your mother with real embraces. . . . Mary is the mother of Jesus and the mother of us all. If Christ is ours, we must be where he is, and where he is, we must be also, and all that he has must be ours, and his mother therefore also is ours."[14]

Yes, sometimes Catholics speak of Mary and relate to her in a way that seems more central than how they relate to Christ. That is not God's plan or intention or the teaching of the Catholic Church, and it is something that even the most devoted of Marian scholars are aware of and warn against.

Some might ask: What about the Immaculate Conception and the Assumption? Are these in the Bible? Not directly. But they do not contradict what is in the Bible and make a lot of sense when you consider their true meaning in light of what is in the Bible.

If John the Baptist was filled with the Holy Spirit in Elizabeth's womb when she encountered Mary, who was carrying Jesus in her womb, why could the Holy Spirit not have been with Mary from the moment of her conception, in anticipation of what Jesus would do on the Cross (which is what the Immaculate Conception means)? Would there not be something fitting about God preserving Mary from original sin, not by her own merits but by the choice of God in light of the sacrifice of Christ and her role in carrying and nurturing the only begotten Son of God?

As Vatican II put it: "The Father of mercies willed that the Incarnation should be preceded by assent on the part of the predestined mother, so that just as a woman had a share in bringing

---

[14] Martin Luther, Christmas homilies of 1523 and 1529, cited in Fr. Mateo, "CRI's attack on Mary", *This Rock*, October 1992, p. 15.

about death, so also a woman should contribute to life. This is preeminently true of the Mother of Jesus, who gave to the world the Life that renews all things, and who was enriched by God with gifts appropriate to such a role. It is no wonder then that it was customary for the Fathers to refer to the Mother of God as all holy and free from every stain of sin, as though fashioned by the Holy Spirit and formed as a new creature."[15]

And the Assumption. If Enoch and Elijah were taken up by God from the earth without their bodies seeing corruption, would it not be even more fitting that the vessel that bore the Son of God be taken up into heaven without seeing corruption? God is glorified in his saints. What God has done in Mary brings glory to him. Honoring Mary for what God has done in her and through her does not take honor away from God. Honoring Mary is part of the normal Christian life as presented in the New Testament, lived by the early Church, and guided by the Holy Spirit throughout the ages.

It is not honoring Mary or God to exaggerate her role or let it overshadow the role of Christ in our devotional expressions. That would be, as Paul complained to the Jews, to bring the things of God into disrepute, to place obstacles to perceiving the true place of Mary in God's plan.

The Father gave Mary a role in bringing forth Jesus, and the Father has entrusted to her a role through her intercession, through her holiness, in bringing forth the sons and daughters of God:

> In the words of the apostle there is but one mediator: "for there is but one God and one mediator of God and men, the man Christ Jesus, who gave himself a redemption for all" (1 Tim 2:5-6). But Mary's function as mother of men in no way obscures or diminishes this unique mediation of Christ, but rather shows its power.... It does not hinder in any way the immediate union of the faithful with Christ but on the contrary fosters it.... For, taken up into heaven, she did not lay aside this saving role, but by her manifold acts of intercession continues to win for us gifts of eternal salvation. By her maternal charity,

---

[15] Constitution on the Church *Lumen Gentium,* 56.

Mary cares for the brethren of her Son who still journey on earth surrounded by dangers and difficulties, until they are led to their happy fatherland. Therefore the Blessed Virgin is invoked by the Church under the titles of Advocate, Auxiliatrix, Adjutrix, and Mediatrix. *These, however, are to be understood so that they neither take away from nor add anything to the dignity and efficacy of Christ the one Mediator.* [16]

In the richness of God's plan, God in some sense does everything himself. In another sense he richly shares the work of salvation with those who are joined to him. There is one mediator between God and man, Jesus Christ, but Jesus Christ now entrusts a share in his work of mediation to Mary. He has entrusted a share in the work of mediation to the apostles and to all who become disciples of Jesus Christ. We become mediators of the grace of God to others. It is a part of the incarnational principle of God's plan that the Catholic Church has kept clear all these years. God is not robbed of honor and glory by the honor and glory he gives to creatures; God is glorified in his creatures.

As the Council puts it: "No creature could ever be counted along with the Incarnate Word and Redeemer; but just as the priesthood of Christ is shared in various ways both by his ministers and the faithful, and as the one goodness of God is radiated in different ways among his creatures, so also the unique mediation of the Redeemer does not exclude but rather gives rise to a manifold cooperation which is but a sharing in this one source.

"The church does not hesitate to profess this subordinate role of Mary, which it constantly experiences and recommends to the heartfelt attention of the faithful, so that encouraged by this maternal help they may the more closely adhere to the Mediator and Redeemer."[17]

What about Marian apparitions? If God permitted Moses and Elijah to appear to accomplish his purposes at a certain point, why could he not permit Mary to appear for the accomplishment of his purposes? He is the God of the living, not of the dead. Let us take

16 Ibid., 60, 62. Italics mine.
17 Ibid., 62.

a look at a few of the Marian apparitions to see if we can perceive the purposes of God.

With growing frequency in the past several centuries it appears that God has sent Mary as a prophetic/evangelistic messenger to highlight the urgency of the times and the need to turn to the Lord and believe the gospel.

Mary at Guadalupe

In 1531 Mary appeared to a poor Mexican Indian, Juan Diego. God was using an extraordinary means to herald an extraordinary action he was about to take. At the time, a single diocese had been established in the Americas, the Diocese of Mexico City. It was the beachhead of the gospel of Jesus Christ in the whole New World, but the missionaries were not making much headway.

God sent Mary on an evangelistic mission. She manifested herself to Juan Diego with a few simple words. She called him by diminutive expressions such as "my little Juan" and "my dear little Juan Diego". She showed him motherly tenderness and left an image of herself on his cloak. The composition of that picture has defied scientific analysis and time itself, remaining as bright today as the day it was given. It hangs for all to see in the Basilica of Our Lady of Guadalupe in Mexico City.

The image was successful in communicating to millions of Indians God's love for them—the love that would move him to send the Mother of the Savior. In the course of seven years eight million Indians were baptized; extraordinary evangelistic fruitfulness flowed from Mary's mission and intercession.

My wife, Anne, and I have a picture of our Lady of Guadalupe in our bedroom. Often, before going to bed, I will look at it for a while. I believe that as I have reflected on that icon, God has shown me that the fruitfulness of Mary's intercession is directly related to her holiness. She is a sign of the enormous power he releases into the world through holiness.

Mary at Lourdes

In 1858 Mary appeared to a French girl, Bernadette, at Lourdes in France. She said, "I am the Immaculate Conception." Four years earlier the Church had given formal definition to the teaching of Mary's conception without any mark of sin.

I read Father René Laurentin's book on Lourdes a few years ago and I kept saying, "Where's the message?" Mary did not say very much. What really stands out is, "I am the Immaculate Conception." My personal view is that the main message of Lourdes was Mary herself. God was saying, "Look at someone who has given herself to me unreservedly, with perfect purity of heart. Look at my masterpiece!" The message of Lourdes is to look at the grace and holiness of Christ in Mary, become converted, and be healed. It is a call to Christ, a call to enter fully into the fruit of his redemption.

Bernadette was another part of the message of Lourdes—simple Bernadette. She was not educated; she could not explain things very well. She was despised by the world. But she had purity of heart. It was a purity of heart that came through beholding the Virgin Mother of God. This purity of heart opened her up to receive the grace of the Holy Spirit and to experience the fruits of redemption in Jesus Christ. Thus, she became a saint.

To whom does Mary appear? Does she tell us something by those to whom she appears? Incredible healings and conversions have flowed from Lourdes over the last century. Many of them have been well documented by medical experts. Millions of people have turned more deeply to Jesus because of the simple message, "I am the Immaculate Conception", and the response of Bernadette, who in simplicity of heart said, "I know what I saw."

Indeed, as the twentieth century draws to a conclusion, the crowds coming to Lourdes and other Marian shrines are increasing. Over 5.5 million pilgrims came to Lourdes in 1992, 1.5 million more than in 1983: "At a time when church attendance has sharply declined throughout Europe, growing numbers of people are also flocking to other shrines across the continent. . . . Some shrines, or places of special devotion, report that they have twice as many visitors as a decade ago. . . . 'We have no sure answers but we all talk about this', said Father de Roton, whose office looks out over the busy Lourdes esplanade. 'Perhaps people find religious life too monotonous and want something more intense, more festive, more emotional. Perhaps the form our religion has taken today does not respond to people's needs.' "[18]

Mary's appearance and Bernadette's response are a picture of what it means to love God with our whole heart, mind, soul, and strength and to love our neighbor as ourself. It is a visible expression of purity of heart that calls us to respond to Jesus in the only appropriate way, which is, "Be it done unto me completely and fully according to your word. Accomplish in my life fully what you want to accomplish."

Mary at Fatima

In 1917 at Fatima in Portugal, Mary appeared to three children. There was a message this time—a significant message. Mary allowed the children to see hell, and they were stunned to see people going down into it. Mary said, "You have seen hell, where the souls of poor sinners go. To save them, God wants to establish in the world the devotion to my Immaculate Heart." Devotion to the Immaculate Heart of Mary is devotion to purity of heart, to holiness, to a fullhearted response to the work and Person of Christ.

Mary also said to the children, "If people will do as I shall tell you, many souls will be saved and there will be peace." Holiness has to do not just with personal piety; holiness has to do with the history of the world. Holiness has to do with the destiny of nations. Holiness has to do with war and peace.

Furthermore, Mary told the children about some future events: "The war [World War I] is going to end, but if people do not stop offending God, another and worse one will begin in the reign of Pius XI. When you see a night illuminated by an unknown light, know that this is the great sign that God is giving you that he is going to punish the world for its crimes by means of war and famine, and persecution of the Church and of the Holy Father." In the last year of Pius XI's pontificate, World War II broke out. Shortly before it broke out, strange lights appeared in northern Europe, Canada, and the United States. The strange display of

---

[18] Marlise Simons, "Pilgrims Crowding Europe's Catholic Shrines", *New York Times,* October 12, 1993, pp. A1, A6.

lights was talked about in the newspapers, and some people wondered, "What is the meaning of this?" The sign that Mary predicted was given.

"To prevent this", Mary said, "I shall come to ask for the consecration of Russia to my Immaculate Heart, and for communions of reparation on the first Saturdays. If they heed my request, Russia will be converted and there will be peace. If not, she shall spread her errors throughout the world, promoting wars and persecution of the Church. The good will be martyred, the Holy Father will have much to suffer, various nations will be annihilated."

How hard it would have been for people in 1917 to believe that Russia would ever spread her errors throughout the world because a civil war was going on then in Russia and the Communists had not even consolidated their hold over the Russian people. The extraordinary thing in 1917 was not the promise of Russia's conversion; the extraordinary thing was the prediction of the spread of Marxism.

Mary went on to say: "In the end, my Immaculate Heart will triumph. The Holy Father will consecrate Russia to me, she will be converted, and a certain period of grace will be granted to the world."

A number of years ago, I was in Rome for an international conference of leaders from the Catholic charismatic renewal. In conjunction with the conference I was able to see the Pope. As I was flying back to the United States, Pope John Paul II was shot. It was on the feast of our Lady of Fatima, who, he believed, was instrumental in the intercession that saved his life. When he went to Fatima, he made an oblique consecration of Russia to the Immaculate Heart of Mary, in the name of all the bishops. Lucy, the last survivor of the three children who saw the apparitions at Fatima, was asked whether this counted. She said, "It counted, but it's late. There is still going to be much suffering." A few years later, in 1984, Pope John Paul II, joined by most of the bishops of the world in their own dioceses, again consecrated the world to Mary, especially those nations in special need. In 1985 Gorbachev came to power and the dismantling of communism began.

A few days after Mary spoke that message to the children, she appeared again and said: "Many souls are going to hell because nobody is praying and sacrificing for them." I think that one of the reasons for the apparitions of Mary at Fatima is to recall to us that Christianity is real. It has consequences. A spiritual struggle is going on, and what is at stake is the eternal destiny of everyone on the face of the earth.

Our action, our prayer, our holiness of life have been given a place in God's plan. God has entrusted something to us, and something really depends on it. How we live, what we say, and what we do really make a difference, and the difference is heaven or hell. Fatima is the message that Christianity is not a game, that the gospel is true, and that eternal life and eternal punishment are at stake.

But even the most convinced of Fatima scholars recognize the dangers of exaggeration and imbalanced emphasis:

> First of all, there is a tendency, especially among those not well catechized in the faith, to become too absorbed in the external phenomena of the Fatima apparitions—absorption, for instance, in the details of the apparitions.
>
> The visions of Our Lady, her Immaculate Heart surrounded by thorns, the harrowing sight of hell, the miracle of the sun should lead to and not distract from the core and nucleus of the message: the call of Jesus to faith and conversion.
>
> Related to this is the danger of isolating the Blessed Virgin from Jesus and the sum of his salvific teachings. It certainly is possible to speak of Our Lady in such a way that non-believers might think that she is the object of our worship and the sole director of world events.[19]

John Paul II stated this concern very directly on his first visit to Fatima in 1982: "If the Church has accepted the message of Fatima, it is above all because that message contains a truth and a call whose basic content is the truth and the call of the Gospel itself. 'Repent and believe in the Gospel' (Mk 1:15). These are the first words the Messiah addressed to humanity. The message of

---

[19] Fr. Frederick L. Miller, "The Mystery of Fatima", *Fatima Family Messenger*, January–March 1993, p. 28.

Fatima is in its basic nucleus, a call to conversion and repentance, as in the Gospel."[20]

In a further message to a gathering at Fatima, in 1992, Pope John Paul II spelled out very clearly how love for Mary and the experience of her maternal love, leads to Jesus: "Fatima is revealed as an oasis of God, where a Mother's Heart points and leads men to the fountains of Life eternal! Truly, how many men and women, won over by Maternal affections, find there the grace which overcomes their human respect, renews their spiritual life, and transforms them into true apostles.

"Thus, everything leads me to entrust to your pilgrim hearts a pressing appeal: on returning to your countries and to your daily lives, be witnesses of how much you saw and heard here. Heaven and earth have need of new and courageous witnesses of Jesus Christ!"[21]

The comments of one of the visionaries of one of the most significant contemporary reported apparitions, that of Medjugorje, also bear out this point: "We discovered a new life with the Blessed Mother. For example, in the beginning she permitted us to fall in love with her. And then through her messages she permitted us to go deeper and deeper into living what is written in the Holy Scriptures. The Blessed Mother said, 'All those messages I'm giving you now are nothing new.' For that reason, she has invited us to put the Holy Bible in a visible place in our house. She has invited us to walk the right path. When we were fully in love with the Blessed Mother, she put like a veil over herself and she said, 'I am not important. The important one is Jesus.' "[22]

Recent public messages from Medjugorje pick up the same theme: "Dear Children! I want you to understand that I am your Mother, that I want to help you and call you to prayer. Only by prayer can you understand and accept my messages and practice them in your life. Read Sacred Scripture, live it, and pray to

---

[20] Ibid., p. 25.

[21] Pope John Paul II, "Fatima — An Oasis of God", *Fatima Family Messenger*, January–March 1993, p. 43.

[22] "A Message from Marija Pavlovic", *Marian Update: The World Report*, Pittsburgh Center for Peace, 1992. See also *Medjugorje Star*, February 1992, p. 2.

understand the signs of the time. This is a special time. Therefore, I am with you to draw you close to my heart and the Heart of my Son, Jesus. Dear little children, I want you to be children of the light and not of the darkness. Therefore, live what I am telling you. Thank you for having responded to my call."[23]

"Dear Children, Today I rejoice in my heart in seeing you all present here. I bless you and I call you all to decide to live my messages which I give you here. I desire, little children, to guide you all to Jesus because *He is your salvation.* Therefore, little children, the more you pray the more you will be mine and of my Son Jesus. I bless you all with my motherly blessing, and I thank you for having responded to my call."[24]

The Second Vatican Council itself spoke of the need to correct abuses that have developed in relationship to devotion to Mary and the saints:

> [This council] . . . strongly urges theologians and preachers of the word of God to be careful to refrain as much from all false exaggeration as from too summary an attitude in considering the special dignity of the Mother of God. Following the study of Sacred Scripture, the Fathers, the doctors and liturgy of the Church, and under the guidance of the Church's magisterium, let them rightly illustrate the duties and privileges of the Blessed Virgin which always refer to Christ, the source of all truth, sanctity and devotion. Let them carefully refrain from whatever might by word or deed lead the separated brethren or any others whatsoever into error about the true doctrine of the Church. . . . This council urges all concerned to remove or correct any abuses, excesses or defects which may have crept in here or there, and so restore all things that Christ and God be more fully praised. Let us teach the faithful therefore, that the authentic cult of the saints does not consist so much in a multiplicity of external acts, but rather in a more intense practice of our love, whereby, for our own greater good and that of

[23] The message of August 25, 1993. Published in *The Blue Letter,* August 1993, p. 1.

[24] The message of June 25, 1994. Published in *The Blue Letter,* June 1994, p. 1.

the Church, we seek from the saints 'example in their way of life, fellowship in their communion, and the help of their intercession'. On the other hand, let the faithful be taught that our communion with these in heaven, provided that it is understood in the full light of faith, in no way diminishes the worship of adoration given to God the Father, through Christ, in the Spirit; on the contrary, it greatly enriches it.[25]

There is a message not only in what Mary says but also in to whom she appears. This message is found in the words of Jesus: "In that same hour he rejoiced in the Holy Spirit and said, 'I thank thee, Father, Lord of heaven and earth, that thou hast hidden these things from the wise and understanding and revealed them to babes; yea, Father, for such was thy gracious will' " (Lk 10:21–22).

Those of us who are educated, who are in professions, who have authority and influence, run a tremendous hazard. We are in danger of having the things of God hidden from us as we become confused in a false complexity and lose the path that leads to life. Straight and narrow is the way that leads to life, and few there are who follow it—and the way is through fear of the Lord, humility, and purity of heart. Broad and wide is the way that leads to destruction, and many there are who are following it—and the way is filled with false sophistication, artificial complexity, and servile fear.

God has chosen Mary to underline this truth. He has given her to us as an image of the holiness and the purity of heart that lead to eternal life. Indeed, how fitting it is that we join in the fulfillment of the prophetic message that all generations will call her blessed. Blessed is she among women, and even more blessed is the fruit of her womb, Jesus!

As the twentieth century has unfolded and draws to a close, the number of purported appearances of Mary in countries throughout the world has mushroomed. In recent years there has been a veritable explosion in reports of Mary's prophetic intervention, whether it be apparitions, visions, or locutions. By one recent

[25] Constitution on the Church *Lumen Gentuim,* 67, 51.

count, there have been 232 reports of such events in thirty-two separate countries.[26]

The messages are strikingly similar: a time of chastisement is coming to the world; God is showing mercy in sending his Mother and offering time for repentance and conversion; prayer, holiness, and love are keys to extending God's mercy to the world. While undoubtedly not all of these purported apparitions are on the same level of importance or validity as Guadalupe, Lourdes, or Fatima, there can be no question that something extraordinary is happening by way of divine warning. Mary continues in so many different ways to point to Jesus and tell us: Do whatever he tells you. The Father continues to tell the world in so many different ways, including through his handmaiden, Mary: This is my beloved Son, in whom I am well pleased, listen to him. The Holy Spirit continues to speak through his servants, the prophets, including through Mary, Queen of prophets.

Some believe that just as God used Mary in a special way to prepare for the first coming of his Son, he is currently using Mary to prepare for the Second Coming of Jesus. In the early eighteenth century St. Louis De Montfort prophesied: "It was through Mary that the salvation of the world was begun, and it is through Mary that it must be consummated."[27]

Could the tears of Mary, witnessed to in so many contemporary accounts, be a participation in the tears of Jesus as he wept over the city of Jerusalem, foreseeing its impending destruction? Is Jesus now weeping over the cities of our world? Are we in danger of missing the hour of our visitation?

The Hierarchy

There is a stereotype of the hierarchy of Church leadership—bishops, priests, and deacons—common in films and other media

[26] Fr. Michael Scanlan, "The Marian Movement", *New Covenant,* March 1993, p. 23.

[27] St. Louis De Montfort, *True Devotion to Mary* (Rockford, Ill.: Tan Publishers, 1985) p. 28, II, 3, 49.

as well as in some anti-Catholic publications that goes like this: priests and bishops in particular are relatively old men, removed from the realities of life, who perform strange ceremonies, walk in meaningless processions, and block direct access to God on the part of the people by claiming to be necessary mediators between God and man. Is there any truth to this stereotype? Yes, certainly. At various times and places, various Church leaders have certainly not functioned in a Christ-honoring or Christ-centered manner. Is there anything intrinsic to these offices of leadership that requires that this happen? No. And there have been multitudes of holy bishops, priests, and deacons who have nobly and courageously served the cause of Christ in their ministry of leadership and are doing so today.

Christ himself established offices of authority and leadership among his people. He called and commissioned the apostles. He gave Peter a primary leadership role among the apostles. The apostles themselves established deacons (servants), presbyters (elders), and bishops (overseers) among the early Christian communities. And while there is much scholarly debate over what role and function these different offices took and the differences in different churches and the exact manner in which these roles evolved and are still evolving, there can be no doubt that Christ established an authoritative leadership in his Church and expected it to be present in each generation of Christians.

However, Christ made it very clear that he wanted leadership in the Church to function very differently from leadership in the world. In that great leadership-training chapter of the twenty-third chapter of Matthew's Gospel, Jesus spells out very clearly how not to carry out leadership in the Church. He makes a special point of indicating that leaders are not to get in the way of a direct relationship of Jesus and his Father with his people. In the same chapter and elsewhere Jesus explains the spirit of humble service that is to characterize leadership in the Church.

The same is to characterize the role of the Pope (father) in his relations with the other leadership of the Church and with the people. The Pope is not to lord it over either the other bishops or the people. He, like Peter, is to encourage and strengthen the brethren and point them toward Jesus. He has real authority and important responsibilities, but they are limited and to be exercised so that Christ can increase among the Church, so that holiness, love, prayer, and zeal for the gospel may increase, and so that the whole Church may be more equipped for a life of holiness and service. It is a tough responsibility, and any Pope, just like the rest of us, is only partly successful in carrying out the duties of his office.

During the short time that John Paul I was Pope, he confided to a cardinal: "The Pope is a man. . . . From the beginning of October you will have to take over most of these 'papers'. . . . I don't want to see any more briefcases on my desk. I wasn't elected Pope to be a penpusher. This is not how Christ imagined his Church. Reform of the Curia is urgent, just as reform of Canon Law is urgent. . . . The pope is infallible as far as the conditions sanctioned by dogma are concerned but he is not all-knowing, he is not the wisest of all, he is not armored against imprudence or immune to it. He is a man. I will tell you that in all sincerity I am first and foremost a priest. I'm the Pope, too, now but I want to be a Pastor, not some bureaucratic official or other. . . . Primarily I am the Bishop of Rome, then Pope."[28]

Cardinal Ratzinger, in commenting on Pope John Paul II's authoritative reaffirmation of priestly ordination of men alone, *Ordinatio Sacerdotalis,* points out the limits of the Pope's and Church's authority. "With the new document, the Pope does not wish to impose his own opinion but precisely to verify the fact that the Church cannot do whatever she wants and that he, indeed precisely he, cannot do so. Here it is not a question of hierarchy opposed to democracy, but of obedience opposed to autocracy. In matters of faith and the sacraments, the Church cannot do whatever she wants . . . instead, she can only hand on in respectful fidelity what she has received."[29]

While participating in a private study session for bishops in the winter of 1994, I had occasion to hear a story in a conversation

[28] Andrea Tornielli, "A Curate on Peter's Throne", 30 *Days,* no. 9 (1993): 48.

[29] Cardinal Joseph Ratzinger, "The Limits of Church Authority", *L'Osservatore Romano* (English ed.), June 29, 1994, p. 6.

with the Bishop of Little Rock, Arkansas, which relates to what we are discussing here.

On his *ad limina* visit to Rome recently, the Bishop of Little Rock, upon meeting with the Pope, said, "Holy Father, I am the little rock and you are the big rock." In response the Pope said, "Jesus is the big rock."

Have the Pope and bishops sometimes appeared to be lording it over others and in fact actually done so? Yes, I am sure it has happened and happens, just as I am sure that any leadership pattern, or no leadership pattern, will in practice end up being abused because of the tendency of all of us to selfishness, self-glorification, laziness, lukewarmness, and infidelity. There is no magic system of government that can eliminate human sin or guarantee that its office holders will be both competent and holy. At times during the Catholic Church's history the "imperial" aspect of the papacy and episcopacy has often been accented. When the Roman Empire collapsed and the Church became perhaps the only stable transnational institution left standing, there was a tendency for the leaders of the Catholic Church headquartered in Rome to take on many of the trappings of the defunct empire as well as many of its material and temporal responsibilities: "The celebration (of the Eucharist) became increasingly full, deriving its modes of expression from the customs of secular society, even as the bishops became officials of the Constantinian state and, like the priests of ancient paganism, received the same honors as magistrates."[30]

Up until the second half of the nineteenth century the Pope was still the temporal sovereign of large amounts of territory called the papal states. Up until the end of the reign of Pius IX, in 1879, the Pope still had a minister of war.[31] Did this dual responsibility, temporal and spiritual, sometimes give off confusing signals and conflict with a pure gospel witness? It certainly did.

When one walks through Rome, one is struck by the still-imposing presence of the ancient Roman Empire and how elements

---

[30] Robert Cabie, *The Eucharist,* vol. 2, *The Church at Prayer,* ed. A. G. Martimort (Collegeville, Minn.: Liturgical Press, 1986), p. 43.

[31] Charles R. Morris, "The Three Ages of the Catholic Church", *Harpers,* July 1991, p. 110.

of that imperial legacy were carried on in the style of the Roman papacy. One of the Pope's traditional titles is *Pontifex Maximus*, which is a priestly and kingly title, literally meaning something like "greatest bridge builder", which was the title the Roman Emperor used to take in his office of head of the state and head of the imperial religion. This title is chiseled and engraved in Church property throughout the city. The popes were rulers of the papal states, including the city of Rome for many centuries, as well as leaders of the Church, and it is clear that the simplicity, radicalness, and purity of the gospel were often obscured. Are these difficulties intrinsic to the office of Pope? No. And many popes throughout the centuries, even many of those who led in the midst of the imperial pomp, led lives of holiness and provided wonderful leadership to the cause of Christ.

In our century we have seen a remarkable purification of the papacy and the episcopal office. Many of the temporal and imperial trappings have been repudiated, and a gospel model of leadership has more clearly been embraced. Vatican II makes clear that the bishops are to function as servants of the purposes of the Lord in the Church, "administering it under the guidance of the Lord".[32] Pope Paul VI was the last Pope to wear the papal tiara, and the style of leadership of the recent popes has more clearly manifested a gospel style. Another traditional papal title has come to the fore: servant of the servants of the most high.

In the course of my work I have had the opportunity to be in Rome many times, sometimes for very significant events, like the funeral of Paul VI and the conclave that elected John Paul I as well as the conclave that elected John Paul II. While I worked in Belgium with Cardinal Suenens, he very generously invited me to many important events and introduced me to key leaders in the Church, allowing me to get an "inside view" that not many have the opportunity of having, including significant contact with both Paul VI and John Paul II. I have also had the opportunity to meet many bishops all over the world and work closely with some of them. I must say that both in Rome and "in the field" I have

---

[32] Constitution on the Church *Lumen Gentium*, 19.

been very impressed by the personal dedication, humility, and holiness of many of the bishops I have met and their efforts to follow and serve Christ and their people sincerely. The same is true of many of the priests I have met all over the world. While I and others have been saddened and angered by the infidelity and cowardice of some who remain silent or become accomplices in undermining the faith and morality of many, I am profoundly grateful for the heroic sacrifices so many in "holy orders" are making in the gift of themselves to Christ and the Church in celibacy and service so that the Body may be built up and Christ glorified. I have sensed the hand of Christ upon both bishops and priests, the "mark" of the sacrament of holy orders, and have thanked God for his presence among us in the leadership he has ordained for his Church. I have experienced, as I believe many have, that it is Christ himself who is often at work through the bishops guiding the Church and promulgating the gospel.

As Vatican II has put it: "Chosen to shepherd the Lord's flock, these pastors are servants of Christ and stewards of the mysteries of God (cf. 1 Cor 4:1), to whom is entrusted the duty of affirming the Gospel of the grace of God (cf. Rom 15:16; Acts 20:24), and of gloriously promulgating the Spirit and proclaiming justification (cf. 2 Cor 3:8–9)."[33]

Or as a recent papal document has put it: "Although the Church possesses a 'hierarchical' structure, nevertheless this structure is toally ordered to the holiness of Christ's members. And holiness is measured according to the 'great mystery' in which the Bride responds with the gift of love to the gift of the Bridegroom. She does this 'in the Holy Spirit', since 'God's love has been poured into our hearts through the Holy Spirit who has been given to us' (Rom 5:5)."[34]

But the purpose of this all is that Jesus may be lifted up and so, as he prophesied, draw all men to himself. The liturgy, Mary, the Pope and the hierarchy, and the other elements of the Catholic

---

[33] Ibid., 21.

[34] John Paul II, Apostolic Letter *Mulieris Dignitatem* (*On the Dignity and Vocation of Women*), 27.

Church that we have not considered here are all intended in God's plan to be windows and pathways to the divine, to Christ himself, to the Father, Son, and Holy Spirit. When the windows in a house are dirty and are blocking the view, the solution is not to break them but to clean them.

As one bishop recently told me, "Since the end of the Vatican Council II, with all the stress on the Church and her internal affairs, it sometimes seemed to me that Jesus had gotten lost again in the temple."

The need for such cleansing and purification is acknowledged by the highest level of Church leadership. As John Paul II has stated, the role of the prophetic function in the Church holds a place of special importance:

> Among the various gifts, St. Paul holds that of prophecy in such high esteem, as we noted, that he recommends: "Strive eagerly for the spiritual gifts, above all that you may prophesy" (1 Cor 14:1). It appears from the history of the Church and particularly from the lives of the saints that frequently the Holy Spirit inspires prophetic words meant to foster the development or the reform of the Christian community's life. Sometimes these words are addressed especially to those who wield authority, as in the case of St. Catherine of Siena, who intervened with the Pope to obtain his return from Avignon to Rome. There are many faithful and, above all, many saints who have given Popes and other Pastors of the Church the light and strength necessary for fulfilling their mission, especially at difficult times for the Church.[35]

Understanding better how the prophetic ministry and the other "ministry gifts" described in the New Testament (Eph 4:1; 1 Cor 12; Rom 12; etc.) can be encouraged and function properly in the Church today is a task still awaiting Catholic theologians and pastoral leaders, although the foundations for such work have clearly been established in the work of the Second Vatican Council and in the experience of renewal movements since: "Guiding

---

[35] John Paul II, "Charisms Have Role in Church's Life", *L'Osservatore Romano* (English ed.), July 1, 1992, p. 11.

the Church in the way of all truth (cf. Jn 16:13) and unifying her in communion and in the works of ministry, he bestows upon her varied hierarchic and charismatic gifts, and in this way directs her; and he adorns her with his fruits (cf. Eph 4:11–12; 1 Cor 12:4; Gal 5:22). By the power of the Gospel he permits the Church to keep the freshness of youth. Constantly he renews her and leads her to perfect union with her Spouse. For the Spirit and the Bride both say to Jesus, the Lord: 'Come!' (cf. Rev 22:17)."[36]

As Pope John Paul II has recently pointed out: "Dear brothers, the new evangelization awaits its prophets and apostles."[37]

Perhaps these prophets and apostles will be those prophesied by St. Louis de Montfort in the eighteenth century that will appear in the midst of an age of Mary and an age of the Holy Spirit: "They shall be the true apostles of the latter times, to whom the Lord of Hosts shall give the words and the might to work marvels and to carry off with glory the spoils of His enemies. . . . They shall be like clouds thundering and flying through the air at the least breath of the Holy Spirit; who, detaching themselves from everything and troubling themselves about nothing, shall shower forth the rain of the Word of God and of life eternal . . . all those to whom they shall be sent on the part of the Most High."[38]

In addition to the prophetic function properly speaking, there also can be a prophetic element in constructive criticism, which is also useful for the Church.

John Paul II goes on to say:

This fact shows the possibility and usefulness of freedom of speech in the Church: a freedom which can also appear in the form of constructive criticism. The important thing is that what is said truly expresses a prophetic inspiration coming from the Spirit. As St. Paul says, "where the Spirit of the Lord is, there is freedom" (2 Cor 3:17). The Holy Spirit fosters in the faithful a manner of acting characterized by sincerity and mutual

---

[36] Constitution on the Church *Lumen Gentium,* 4.

[37] Pope John Paul II, "Lights and Shadows Mark the Life of the Church in Portugal", *L'Osservatore Romano* (English ed.), December 9, 1992, p. 3.

[38] De Montfort, *True Devotion to Mary,* pp. 28–35.

trust (cf. Eph 4:25) and enables them "to admonish one another" (Rom 15:14; cf. Col 1:16).

Criticism is useful in the community, which must always be reformed and must try to correct its own imperfections. In many cases it helps the community to take a new step forward. But if it comes from the Holy Spirit, criticism must be animated by the desire to advance in truth and love.[39]

In the eighth century there were zealous Christians who saw how the outward signs rather than opening up to the divine realities were tending to be related to as ends in themselves. They wanted the icons, the images of sacred realities painted by Church artists to be destroyed and outlawed, as they thought it a violation of the Commandment that forbade graven images and, perhaps even more, on the pastoral level were appalled by what appeared to be superstitious, idolatrous use of icons. The Church at that time gave these concerns serious consideration and after much prayer and discussion, under the guidance of the Spirit, decided that just because something can be abused does not mean it should be abolished (Second Council of Nicea, 787). The tendency to idolatry is in our hearts and cannot be safeguarded against by eliminating created things or holy images that can legitimately be used as aids to prayer, aids to contact with Christ, rather than as ends in themselves or objects of superstitious veneration.

The Catholic Church is a sacramental Church, and what it means to be a sacrament is to be a sign that points beyond itself to a mystery, a hidden, invisible reality. While for a long time the institutional dimension of the Church's existence predominated, recent years have seen increasing attention paid to the reality of the Church as communion, a communion or community of God and the redeemed: "The initial working document prepared prior to the [Second Vatican] Council approached the question of the Church primarily as a visible society, defining it in juridical terms. Such an approach has a venerable history in the West, but the bishops felt that before elaborating the structure of the Church, it was important to describe its inner spiritual dynamic. One of the

---

[39] Pope John Paul II, "Lights and Shadows Mark the Life of the Church in Portugal", p. 3.

bishops at the time explained, 'Before, the Church was defined above all as an institution; today it is seen more clearly as a communion.' This concept of 'communion' lies at the heart of the Church's whole self-understanding."[40]

This focus on the Church as a visible society and an institution, a "perfect society", as it were, also had its influence on the approach to obedience and the lack of openness to the here-and-now interventions of God in the life of the Church:

> Going through the New Testament, trying to find out what the duty of obedience consists in, it is surprising to discover that obedience is almost always obedience to God. All the other forms of obedience are certainly mentioned: obedience to parents, masters, superiors, governing powers, "to every human institution" (1 Pet 2:13), but much less so and much less solemnly. The noun "obedience" (*hypakoe*)—which is the strongest term in the Greek New Testament—is used always and only to indicate obedience to God or, at the most, to instances connected with God, except in one passage in the Epistle to Philemon, where it indicates obedience to the Apostle. St. Paul speaks of obedience to *faith* (Rom 1:5; 16:26), of obedience to the *teaching* (Rom 6:17), of obedience to the *Gospel* (Rom 10:16; 2 Th 1:8), of obedience to *truth* (Gal 5:7), of obedience to *Christ* (2 Cor 10:5). . . .
>
> But is it still possible and meaningful to talk of obedience to God, after the living will of God, manifested in Christ, has been completely expressed and objectified in a series of laws and hierarchies? Is it permissible to think that, after all this, there are still new "free" manifestations of God's will to be accepted and fulfilled? If the living will of God could be captured and thoroughly and definitely expressed in a series of laws, norms and institutions, that is in an "order" instituted and defined once and for all, the Church would end up paralysed. The rediscovery of the importance of obedience to God is a natural consequence of the rediscovery, started by Vatican Council II, of the charismatic and spiritual dimension, along with the hierarchical dimension, of the Church . . . and of the supremacy of the Word of God in the Church. . . .

[40] Fr. Milton T. Walsh, "Shepherds in Christ's Church: Vatican II on the Bishops", *Lay Witness,* November 1992, p. 2.

Obedience to God and the Gospel was necessarily put a little in the shade when the Church was thought of above all in terms of an institution, as a "perfect society", furnished from the beginning with all the means, powers and structures required to lead men to salvation without the need of any other specific and timely intervention by God. From the moment when the Church is again clearly seen as "mystery and institution" together, obedience returns again to being, as it was for St. Paul, not only obedience to the institution but also to the Spirit, not only to men, but also and first of all to God.[41]

Building on the work of Henri de Lubac and Hans Urs von Balthasar, Cardinal Ratzinger and Pope John Paul II have frequently drawn our attention to the theme of the Church as communion. It has also played a role in the ecumenical dialogue that the Catholic Church is carrying on with other churches.[42] I believe this is a development led by the Holy Spirit that highlights that aspect of the Church's reality that is most necessary in our time. The fundamentals can no longer be presupposed; we must begin again with the encounter with God.

It was this concern that led Pope John Paul II to appeal to the bishops and priests present for the World Youth Day of 1993: "In this interior advancement of grace, we bishops and priests have a great responsibility. Are we always ready to help young people discover the transcendent elements of the Christian life? From our words and actions do they conclude that the Church is indeed a

[41] Cantalamessa, *Life in the Lordship of Christ,* pp. 227–29. See also Fr. Raniero Cantalamessa, *Obedience* (Middlegreen, Slough, U.K.: St. Paul Publications, 1989).

[42] Cardinal Joseph Ratzinger, "Letter to the Bishops of the Catholic Church on Some Aspects of the Church Understood as Communion", *L'Osservatore Romano* (English ed.), June 17, 1992, pp. 8–9. Pope John Paul II, "The Church Is a 'Communio' of Love", *L'Osservatore Romano* (English ed.), January 22, 1992, p. 11. Pope John Paul II, "The Church: A 'Communio' of Prayer", *L'Osservatore Romano* (English ed.), February 5, 1992, p. 11. Pope John Paul II, "Church Lives in Mystery of 'Communio' ", *L'Osservatore Romano* (English ed.), February 12, 1992, p. 11. "Anglican-Roman Catholic International Commission (ARCIS II): The Church as Communion", Documentation Supplement, Secretariat for Christian Unity.

mystery of communion with the Blessed Trinity, and not just a human institution with temporal aims?"[43]

The Church herself in that sense is a sacrament, and the mystery she points to is Christ himself. The mystery of the Catholic Church is Christ himself, dwelling in her, ruling over her, guiding, correcting, disciplining, forgiving, encouraging, protecting. While for many centuries the institutional model of the Church perhaps predominated, our century has seen a blossoming of biblical studies and theology that has greatly enriched the contemporary Catholic's possibilities of discovering the richness of the mystery of the Church. The Church is not just structures and rules; she is a people, won for God by Christ; she is a temple where God himself dwells; she is, most profoundly perhaps, the very Body of Christ. Christ is the Head, and the Church is his Body. The union between Christ and the Church is so great that the union between a man and his wife in marriage is but an earthly sign of the greater reality of the union of Christ and the Church.

Some first discover Christ's Body, the Church, and are convinced by her history or theology or structure that she is indeed Christ's Body, but these people need to go on and discover the Head of the Body they have encountered, the source of her life, history, structures, theology, all of which are but servants of his, Christ himself.

As Hans Urs von Balthasar has said: "It is not through communion with the members of the Church that the Christian enters into communion with Christ, but vice versa: it is in the individual's personal profession of faith and relationship to Christ that he enters into the communion of his mystical body."[44]

There are others who discover the Person of Christ and are won by his glory, his truth, his power, his radiance. These people need to go on to discover Christ's Body, the Church, and learn to

---

[43] Pope John Paul II, "Be Ready to Help Youth Discover the Transcendent Elements of Christian Life", *L'Osservatore Romano* (English ed.), August 25, 1993, p. 5.

[44] Hans Urs von Balthasar, *Theodramatik,* II, 2 (Einsiedeln, 1978), p. 414, cited in Bishop Paul Cordes, *Charisms and New Evangelization* (Middlegreen, Slough, U.K.: St. Paul Publications, 1992), p. 101.

love her and abide in her as Christ loves and abides in her. Christ has identified himself with his Body in a remarkable way: "And he fell to the ground and heard a voice saying to him, 'Saul, Saul, why do you persecute me?' . . . 'I am Jesus, whom you are persecuting' " (Acts 9:4–5).

"I say to you, as you did it to one of the least of these my brethren, you did it to me . . . as you did it not to one of the least of these, you did it not to me" (Mt 25:40, 45).

But perhaps the most special of all windows onto this hidden reality, this mystery, is the mystery of the bride and the bridegroom. The most special, intimate, and tender of human relationships is given to us by the Holy Spirit as the image that perhaps most specially reveals the heart of the relationship between Christ and the Church. We, the Church, are the Bride; Christ is the Bridegroom.

As a historical institution the Church is simply a means, but in her identity as Bride she is an end. Henri de Lubac expresses it well:

> From yet another point of view, she is either a historic institution or else she is the very city of God. In the first case, as a society founded by Christ for the salvation of men, she labors to bring them to it; she is then a means, and we can say with Pius XI: "Men, were not made for the Church, but the Church was made for men: *propter nos homines et propter nostram salutem*" [for us men and for our salvation]. A necessary means, a divine means, but provisional as means always are. Whereas in the second case, since the Bride is henceforward but one with the Bridegroom, she is that mysterious structure which will become fully a reality only at the end of time: no longer is she a means to unite humanity in God, but she is herself the end, that is to say, that union in its consummation. *Christus propter ecclesiam venit* [Christ came on account of the Church].[45]

As the Scripture scholar Father Francis Martin has said: "The church is a bride, and she shows to the world that her spouse is

[45] Henri de Lubac, *Catholicism: Christ and the Common Destiny of Man* (San Francisco: Ignatius Press, 1988), p. 70.

alive by living by his power and receiving life from him. There is a danger in our day that the church will look more like a widow, alone and without resources except those possessed by any human organization. If we yield to what the Lord has poured out upon us—his Spirit—the world will know that the church is truly the spouse of a living Lord."[46]

There is something odd, almost ugly, about the bride bragging about her own beauty and specialness, pointing to her own uniqueness or special relationship with the bridegroom. It should really be the bridegroom that speaks of his beloved, the Church, and he does, and he will. The Church, the Bride, should be speaking of her beloved, the Bridegroom: about how wonderful he is, about how she owes everything to him, about how good he is and how truthful and faithful and powerful and glorious. The Church, when she is most true to her nature as Bride, will be pointing to the Bridegroom and drawing attention to him, not to herself; it is the Bridegroom who in due time and in his inimitable way will point to his beloved, the Church. We, the Church, can safely leave that in his hands.

What is true on the individual level is also true on the corporate level. He who exalts himself will be humbled; he who humbles himself will be exalted: "God opposes the proud, but gives grace to the humble. . . . Humble yourselves before the Lord and he will exalt you" (James 4:6, 10).

An extraordinary session of the world Synod of Bishops expressed the same truth: "The church makes herself more credible if she speaks less of herself and ever more preaches Christ crucified (cf. 1 Cor 2:2) and witnesses with her own life. In this way the church is sacrament, that is, sign and instrument of communion with God and also of communion and reconciliation of men with one another. The message of the church, as described in the Second Vatican Council, is Trinitarian and Christocentric."[47]

And as John Paul II has put it: "The Church's fundamental

---

[46] Fr. Francis Martin, "The Grace of This Century", *Faith and Renewal*, January–February 1994, p. 11.

[47] Synod of Bishops, "The Final Report", *Origins*, December 19, 1985, p. 446, II.A.I.2.

function in every age, and particularly in ours, is to direct man's gaze, to point the awareness and experience of the whole of humanity toward the mystery of Christ."[48]

We are all, as the Apostle says, to fix our eyes on Jesus (cf. Heb 12:1–2).

This is a call not just to the Church as a whole but to each and every one of us. Our *personal* response to Jesus, to what the Spirit is saying, is very important. We may not be in a position directly to influence the difficult situation the Church is facing on the national or international level. We may not be able significantly to influence the situation of our parish or diocese. But if all of us who "have eyes to see, and ears to hear" would give ourselves to God more and more fully and do what he inspires us to do in the way of prayer and action in the circumstances of our lives, great things will come to pass.

Our efforts to turn from sin and give ourselves more fully to Christ; to persevere in prayer; to intercede for family, friends, relatives, and others; to do works of mercy and kindness; to share the gospel in informal conversations, in service in our parish, in teaching CCD, or in helping with RCIA or marriage preparation programs; to live lives of faithfulness, forgiveness, and mercy in our most immediate relationships will all, over time, make a great difference. As Jesus continues to say to us, "If you believe, you will see the glory of God."

In the remaining chapters of this book I would like to consider how we can root and ground ourselves more deeply in God, through faith, hope, and love, and so bear the fruit that will remain, that will make a difference. I will not be providing an action plan for the situation we face, since there are many good plans and programs, organizations and movements in place in which we could participate, other than the action plan of Mary, the action plan of the gospel: "Do whatever he tells you."

---

[48] John Paul II, Encyclical *Redemptor Hominis* (*Redeemer of Man*), 10.

PART TWO

Our Personal Response

Chapter One

Personal Surrender

There is a tendency for all of us to think of God as primarily a principle, a force, a law, or a power, impersonal. Even if we think of him as personal, there is a tendency to think of him as rather distant and aloof, not really aware of or concerned about someone as insignificant as ourselves. This is why we need continually to deepen and renew our understanding and experience of the incredibly personal nature of God and the relationship he wants to have with us. Only as we more deeply surrender to the Father, Son, and Holy Spirit can the Church be what she is called to be and we participate as friends, not just servants, in what God is unfolding as we approach a new millennium.

Recently, while talking to a group of American bishops, Pope John Paul II stressed this point: "Sometimes even Catholics have lost or have never had the chance to experience Christ personally: not Christ as a mere 'paradigm' or 'value', but the living Lord: 'the way, and the truth, and the life' (Jn 14:6)."[1]

The recognition that many Catholics are impoverished in terms of a personal relationship with and knowledge of Jesus is more and more being acknowledged by prominent Church leaders.

Cardinal Godfried Danneels, Cardinal Suenens' successor as Primate of the Catholic Church in Belgium, in commenting

---

[1] John Paul II, "New Catechism Will Promote National Recatechizing Effort", *L'Osservatore Romano* (English ed.), March 24, 1993, p. 3.

recently on the inroads of the New Age movement among Catholics, pointed out how an imbalanced emphasis on other aspects of the Church, other than the personal encounter with God, has made Catholics vulnerable to such deception:

> There may well be some truth in the accusations of New Age against Christianity with respect to the lack of lived experience, the fear of mysticism, the endless moral exhortations and the exaggerated insistence on the orthodoxy of doctrine. In recent years especially, Christianity has practically been reduced to a moral system. The creed, as a doctrine of life and source of religious and mystical experience, has been neglected. Many have become disenchanted with this kind of obstinate moralism and have gone to seek peace elsewhere. But did Christ not say: "Come to me, all you who labour and are overburdened, and I will give you rest. Shoulder my yoke and learn from me, for I am gentle and humble in heart, and you will find rest for your souls! Yes, my yoke is easy and my burden light" (Mt 11:28–30)?[2]

In addressing the need for a new evangelization of Europe, Cardinal Danneels again pointed out the tendency to speak of the values of Christianity but to neglect the living Person of Christ:

> Many of our faithful, in our parishes, schools and movements, are strongly attached to the values of the Gospel, especially those that we have for the most part in common with all men of good will: justice, peace, solidarity, respect for creation. But this cult of values is separated from the cult of the living person of Christ: from prayer, adoration, and sacramental practice.
>
> Christ, then, is relegated in speech to the third person: he said this, he showed that by his example. In such speech, there is a curious absence of referring explicitly to prayer and of meeting him in the sacraments: "You are my Saviour. I adore you. . . . " Such a Christianity, reduced to an ethic, can not subsist for long . . . an ethic without mysticism, a morality cut off from prayer and the sacramental life, even if they still resemble a

[2] Cardinal Godfried Danneels, *Christ or Aquarius? Exploring the New Age Movement* (Dublin: Veritas Publications, 1992), pp. 27–28.

living body, are only mummies, destined to ashes, when one looks at them more closely.[3]

And Father Giussani, founder of the Communion and Liberation Movement, pointed out how as long as Christianity stays on the level of "values", modern secular society will give it a place, but as soon as it truly witnesses to the Person of Christ and his claims on man, it will have no real place: "As long as Christianity sustains Christian values . . . it will be given room and a welcome everywhere. But when Christianity is the annunciation in everyday, social, historical reality of the permanent Presence of God who became One among us—Jesus Christ present in His Church—the object of experience like the presence of a friend, of a father, of a mother, one total horizon shaping life, ultimate love, the core of the way we see, conceive and deal with the whole of reality, the meaning and spark of every action, then it has no dwelling place."[4]

Cardinal Groër, the Archbishop of Vienna, Austria, uses even stronger language: "It is a grave error for churches to talk mainly of values. In the Gospel, the concept of 'value' never appears. . . . When he speaks of the treasures of heaven Christ is not referring to 'values' but to the 'Supreme Good': God himself as a personal reality."[5]

In discussing the increasing emphasis on evangelization in the Church today, Cardinal Arinze of Nigeria, currently president of the Pontifical Council for Inter-Religious Dialogue, stressed the "supreme value of knowing Jesus Christ": "Evangelisation aims at helping the individual to know Jesus Christ personally. Every person who is evangelised should not just know about Jesus Christ or be informed about him from books. He should know the Son of God made man personally as the Person whom he meets in faith, in hope and in love."[6]

---

[3] Cardinal Godfried Danneels, "Intervention at the Special Synod of Bishops: December 1991", Archdiocese of Malines, Brussels, January 1993, *Pastoralia,* p. 5, translated from the French by Gary Seromik.

[4] Massimo Borghesi, "A New Beginning", 30 *Days,* no. 12 (1993): 68.

[5] Cardinal Hans Hermann Groër, "From Values to Reality", 30 *Days,* no. 5 (1993), 62.

[6] Cardinal Francis Arinze, *The Essence of Evangelisation: The Supreme Value of Knowing Jesus Christ* (Dublin: Veritas Publications, 1990), sec. III.

And Cardinal Ratzinger, Prefect of the Congregation for the Doctrine of the Faith, continually stresses the encounter with the living God as the heart of our Faith and the center of the Church's life: "The Christian faith is, in its essence, an encounter with the living God."[7]

As I read the Scriptures, I am profoundly struck by how insistent Jesus is that we come to him personally, and not stop short, or be stopped short, by anything or anyone else, even "religious" things or people. Jesus wants everyone to come to him personally, even those who are regarded as insignificant or unworthy: "And they were bringing children to him, that he might touch them; and the disciples rebuked them. But when Jesus saw it he was indignant, and said to them, 'Let the children come to me, do not hinder them; for to such belongs the kingdom of God. Truly, I say to you, whoever does not receive the kingdom of God like a child shall not enter it.' And he took them in his arms and blessed them, laying his hands upon them" (Mk 10:13–16).

"All that the Father gives me will *come to me;* and him who comes to me I will not cast out" (Jn 6:37).

"You search the scriptures, because you think that in them you have eternal life; and it is they that bear witness to me; yet you refuse to *come to me* that you may have life" (Jn 5:39–40).

"I am the bread of life; he who *comes to me* shall not hunger, and he who *believes in me* shall never thirst" (Jn 6:35).

"On the last day of the feast, the great day, Jesus stood up and proclaimed, 'If any one thirst, let him *come to me* and drink. He who *believes in me,* as the scripture has said, 'Out of his heart shall flow rivers of living water'" (Jn 7:37–38).

"*Come to me,* all who labor and are heavy laden, and *I will give you rest.* Take my yoke upon you and *learn from me;* for I am gentle and lowly in heart, and you will find rest for your souls. For my yoke is easy, and my burden is light" (Mt 11:28–30).

Jesus, quite simply, wants us to come to him. He wants nothing else but us and him simply being together. But as we come to him

---

[7] Cardinal Joseph Ratzinger, "What Does the Church Believe?" *Catholic World Report,* March 1993, p. 27.

we discover even more wonderful things about how personal the whole plan of God for man is, how personal God himself is. As we come to Jesus, he introduces us to the Father; indeed, we discover that it was the Father himself who sent Jesus to us and revealed Jesus to us. We discover, as it were, that "behind" Jesus stands the Father, from whom all fatherhood in heaven and on earth receives its name and nature: "I am the way, and the truth, and the life; no one comes to the Father, but by me. If you had known me, you would have known my Father also; henceforth you know him and have seen him. . . . He who has seen me has seen the Father . . . I am in the Father and the Father in me. The words I say to you I do not speak on my own authority; but the Father who dwells in me does his works" (Jn 14:6–7, 9–10).

"For this is the will of my Father, that every one who sees the Son and believes in him should have eternal life; and I will raise him up at the last day. . . . No one can come to me unless the Father who sent me draws him; and I will raise him up at the last day" (Jn 6:40, 44).

"He said to them, 'But who do you say that I am?' Simon Peter replied, 'You are the Christ, the Son of the living God.' And Jesus answered him, 'Blessed are you, Simon Bar-Jona! For flesh and blood has not revealed this to you, but my Father who is in heaven' " (Mt 16:15–17).

At the heart of Jesus' desire for his friends is the desire that they come to know God as their Father. In the last days of his earthly life, in fact, he spoke urgently and clearly of the relationship his disciples were to have to God as their Father, similar to the relationship that Jesus himself has with the Father.

When we first think of in what way Jesus reveals who God is to us, we think of his mercy and compassion in forgiving sin and healing the sick and conclude from these, rightly, that Jesus reveals to us the mercy and compassion of God. But Jesus is intent on revealing not just the characteristics or attributes of God but also the identity of the Persons of God, the astounding fact that God is a union of three Persons and that it is into that union that he invites his disciples.

In the Gospel of John alone Jesus speaks of his Father more than a hundred times, and the picture that emerges of the relationship is one in which there is an utterly profound commitment of love between the Father and the Son and a total self-giving of one to the other.

Jesus time and time again clearly indicates that he is fully obedient to the Father (Jn 8:28–29), does nothing on his own authority and does only what pleases the Father, and is set on doing not his own will but "the will of him who sent me" (Jn 6:38). Jesus indicates again and again that he teaches and speaks only what the Father gives to him to teach and speak (Jn 8:26–29) and indeed that "the Son can do nothing of his own accord, but only what he sees the Father doing; for whatever he does, that the Son does likewise" (Jn 5:19). Jesus even states that what he lives or subsists on, what is food to him, is "to do the will of him who sent me, and to accomplish his work" (Jn 4:34).

Just as Jesus does everything to please the Father and gives his whole life in service of the Father, so too does the Father give everything to Jesus and totally commits himself to an absolute support. Just as Jesus honors the Father, so too does the Father honor the Son. The Father gives the Spirit to Jesus "without reserve". This phrase characterizes their whole relationship; they give themselves to each other "without reserve". They share a profound intimacy. Only to the Son, who abides in the heart of the Father, has the Father shown himself fully (Jn 1:18). And because of the nature of the relationship, it is through the Son that the Father gives himself to others. He has entrusted to Jesus the work of reconciling the world to the Father and has chosen to put all things into his hands. He never leaves Jesus alone but is always with him (Jn 16:32). Just as Jesus abides in the heart of the Father, the Father abides within Jesus, and accompanies him, works with him, in all that he says and does, so much so that Jesus can say, "The Father and I are one."

The total commitment that the Father and Son have to one another is finally and vividly expressed as Jesus gives himself up to suffering, crucifixion, and death, as the fullest possible act of abandonment in trust of the Father possible to a man. And the Father receives Jesus and raises him up from the dead and establishes him at his right hand, restoring Jesus to the glory he had before the world began. Jesus and the Father glorify one another, honor one another, raise one another up, out of a staggeringly profound and complete love, union, and self-giving, out of a relationship that gives them a remarkable joy, peace, confidence, and security.

The Father reveals Jesus to us and focuses our attention on Jesus: "This is my beloved Son, with whom I am well pleased; listen to him . . . when they lifted up their eyes, they saw no one but Jesus only" (Mt 17:5–8).

As we give ourselves to Jesus, center our lives on him, become his disciples, servants, and friends, he shows us the Father.

Then the Father and the Son send the Holy Spirit to us, so we can be in a continuing close personal relationship with them: "And I will pray the Father, and he will give you another Counselor, to be with you for ever, even the Spirit of truth. . . . I will not leave you desolate; I will come to you. . . . In that day you will know that I am in my Father, and you in me, and I in you. . . . If a man loves me, he will keep my word, and my Father will love him, and we will come to him and make our home with him" (Jn 14:16–23).

In these verses and many others, Jesus makes it clear that those who come to him and put their trust and faith in him also come into a direct relationship with God the Father, that he is a Father to the followers of Jesus just as he is to Jesus. Jesus also makes clear that those who come to him are "born of water and the Spirit" (Jn 3:5) and in the process made "partakers of the divine nature" (2 Pet 1:4), sons of God, with Jesus, sharing in a direct relationship with the Father, partaking of all the possibilities and responsibilities of sonship. We are not just called sons and daughters, we are.

Unfortunately, one of the works of the evil one in our time has been to insinuate lies and deceptive feelings about the Father that are intended to keep us from coming to him and experiencing the love and security that come from being his son or daughter.

Father Cantalamessa expresses it like this:

There exists a tragic "father complex" and the very people that introduced this idea have often been victims of such a complex without realizing it. It consists in the inability to accept oneself as "son" at a deeper and more general level than the physical one, that is as being generated by someone, as being a dependent creature and, as a consequence, the inability to accept a Father who is the origin of one's existence and freedom and in whom the last meaning of things is placed. The refusal of the Father which exists in our day, and which psychoanalysis emphasizes, has the same basis mentioned by St. Paul when speaking of the refusal of God in general, and that is, impiety. This is man's will to be himself God, his own origin or at least to be able himself to build his own God to which he can submit himself, calling "god" the work of his own hands or his own "invention".[8]

In a certain sense as we live in the time between the first and second comings of Jesus, we could be said to be living in that time in God's plan where Jesus and the Spirit are playing the central roles. This is now the age where the main task at hand is the reconciliation of the human race through Jesus. The Father himself is pointing to Jesus now and asking us to pay attention to and listen to and obey his beloved Son. There is a sense also in which even in the eternal plan of God, the primacy or preeminence in all things properly belongs to Jesus and has been given to him for all eternity by the Father: "He is the head of the body, the church; he is the beginning, the first-born of the dead, that in everything he might be pre-eminent" (Col 1:18).

As we have seen, though, as we give Jesus the central place, as we acknowledge him as our Lord and Head of the Church, his Body, as we give him preeminence in all things, he shows us the Father, and the Father himself comes and dwells with us, even in this age. But there is another age coming, in which an even greater fullness of relationship with the Father is coming. When the work of Christ is finally fully done, when the kingdoms of this world have become the kingdom of God and of his Christ, when all things have become fully subject to Jesus, then he will present everything to the Father, and the Father finally will be all

[8] Fr. Raniero Cantalamessa, *Life in the Lordship of Christ* (Kansas City, Mo.: Sheed and Ward, 1990), p. 114.

in all, everything to everyone: "When all things are subjected to him, then the Son himself will also be subjected to him who put all things under him, that God may be everything to every one" (1 Cor 15:28).

In the meantime what is the most useful thing we can do to bring about the reign of Christ over all the earth?

Give ourselves more fully to him.

And for that there needs to be an ongoing breaking of pride.

Chapter Two

Faith and the Breaking of Pride

The original "paradise" between God and man depended on the loving trust between the creature and his Creator. When the first man and woman took back that faith and trust and decided to strike out on their own to "be like Gods" (Gen 3:5), all manner of evil flooded in and life on earth became in substance a "vale of tears". Pride was at the root of this tragic fall. The threefold temptation of Genesis 3:6 is articulated in 1 John 2:16, the familiar translation of which is "lust of the flesh and the lust of the eyes and the pride of life". The "clincher" is pride of life, that infernal, diabolical desire to be independent from God, to be autonomous, to be self-sufficient, to need no one and no thing, to be as gods.

A striking statement of how this primordial pride and this rebellion expressed themselves with devastating effects on the entire twentieth century is contained in the words of one of the original Communist leaders, Trotsky: "Man will become immeasurably stronger, wiser and subtler; his body will become more harmonized, his movements more rhythmic, his voice more musical. The forms of life will become dynamically dramatic. The average human type will rise to the heights of an Aristotle, a Goethe or a Marx. And above this ridge new peaks will rise."[1]

It is incredible now to review these words, just some of many speaking of the "new" Soviet man that communism would produce, and survey the incredible human wreckage this demonically driven

[1] Quoted in Philip Yancey, "Disappointment with Trotsky", *Christianity Today*, February 10, 1992, p. 104.

effort to "be as gods" has produced. And yet the same pride, the same desire to "be as gods" apart from God, is in us all—and, to the extent that we yield to it, it produces the same miserable results.

This pride needs to be broken, and the profound wound in our being it caused healed, before union with God can be restored as it was "in the beginning". God has so ordered his plan for saving man that *salvation cannot happen without pride being broken. Faith is the simple but powerful key that breaks pride and releases salvation:* "Since all have sinned and fall short of the glory of God, they are justified by his grace as a gift, through the redemption which is in Christ Jesus, whom God put forward as an expiation by his blood, to be received by faith. . . . Then what becomes of our *boasting?* It is excluded" (Rom 3:23–27).

A lot is said in these few verses, and the themes treated here are developed throughout the Bible. In short: everybody is cut off from God; everybody is undeservedly offered a gift by God of redemption through the sacrifice of Christ; the gift is received through believing in Jesus and what he did for us on the Cross. If we truly understand our situation and how undeserving we are of salvation, how much it is a pure gift of God, we have nothing to boast of—except the Cross of Christ and our weakness and need.

In order for pride to be broken, God arranged that salvation be purely his gift, a gift that no man deserves. We have to receive, not achieve, in order to be saved. There is nothing we can do to merit or earn or deserve salvation. It is purely an extraordinary gift from God that comes to us from our believing in Jesus. Properly understood, this is profoundly humbling. It is supposed to be:

> For Christ did not send me to baptize, but to preach the gospel, and not with eloquent wisdom, lest the cross of Christ be emptied of its power. . . . For since, in the wisdom of God, the world did not know God through wisdom, it pleased God through the folly of what we preach to save those who believe. For Jews demand signs and Greeks seek wisdom but we preach Christ crucified, a stumbling block to Jews and folly to Gentiles, but to those who are called, both Jews and Greeks, Christ the power of God and the wisdom of God. For the foolishness of God is wiser than men, and the weakness of God is stronger

than men. . . . God chose what is foolish in the world to shame the wise, God chose what is weak in the world to shame the strong, God chose what is low and despised in the world, even things that are not, to bring to nothing things that are, so that no human being might boast in the presence of God. . . . "Let him who boasts, boast of the Lord" (1 Cor 1:17–31).

Father Cantalamessa says it well:

However, St. Paul strongly insists on one thing: all this comes about "gratuitously" (*dorean*), through grace, as a gift; he comes back to this point numerous times using different terms. And we wonder why God is so determined on this point! It's because he wants to exclude from the new creation the canker that ruined the first creation: man's boasting. . . . Man hides in his heart the innate tendency to "pay God his price". But "no man can ransom himself or give to God the price of his life" (Ps 49:8). To want to pay God his price through our own merits is another form of the never ending effort to be autonomous and independent of God, and not just autonomous and independent but actually God's creditors because "to one who works, his wages are not reckoned as a gift but as his due" (Rom 4:4).[2]

There is a tremendous danger in our response to Christ to erect structures and establish customs and expectations that over time can come to overshadow the Cross of Christ and its supreme place in our lives, the life of the Church, and the life of the world. It is all too easy to begin to think it is our customs, our patterns, our leadership, our teachings, our longevity, our virtue, our faithfulness, our character, our history, on which the salvation of the world and our own salvation depend, rather than purely and simply on the unmerited grace won for us on Calvary to which we have access simply through believing. The Cross of Christ can become for us a stumbling block, not only initially but also gradually over time, as we transfer our trust and confidence to things other than the Cross of Christ and end up placing our

[2] Fr. Raniero Cantalamessa, *Life in the Lordship of Christ* (Kansas City, Mo.: Sheed and Ward, 1990), pp. 45–46.

confidence in the works of our own hands or the deeds of our own flesh. It is *essential* for those of us who think we are something to be reduced to nothing so that we have no grounds of boasting before God. That also is humbling: "To thee shall all flesh come on account of sins. When our transgressions prevail over us, thou dost forgive them" (Ps 65:3–4).

A proud person always thinks he is right. Humility is being able to say, "I'm wrong; you're right", to both God and others.

I know in my own life God has regularly had to humble me to draw me back to a clearer focus on Jesus Christ and him crucified. Over the past few years in particular God in his mercy has shown us how in our local Christian community we had come to rely too much on our community way of life, our teachings, our approach to things, in a way that overshadowed the Cross of Christ. It has been very hard, but the purification and humbling were very necessary, and the lessons learned are priceless.[3]

Of course pride can also cloak itself in a so-called "personal" or "spiritual" approach to God that does not submit to the divinely established structures and authorities that are established as a safeguard against deception and an expression of the corporate and hierarchical order of the plan of salvation. Only in a balance of the institutional and charismatic can the goal be reached.

In one of his books, Bishop Cordes, while pointing out the great value of the new renewal movements for the Church, speaks of the dangers that these movements face with temptations to exaggerate their own importance, an excessive self-preoccupation or focus, even a "group egoism", and a desire for control, domination, or "hegemony". As he strikingly puts it: "It is inconceivable, for instance, to imagine a St. Francis who contemplated 'Franciscanism', and not Jesus Christ alone: Jesus who in his poverty is the source of all wealth that comes from God."[4]

Cardinal Suquia, of Spain, speaks of the Church's tendency to rely on things other than Christ himself:

[3] Ralph Martin, "Community: A Work in Progress", *Faith and Renewal,* January–February 1993, pp. 3–8.

[4] Bishop Paul Cordes, *Charisms and New Evangelization* (Middlegreen, Slough, U.K.: St. Paul Publications, 1992), pp. 153–56.

The Church must cease to be afraid of her own truth; she must be brave enough to recover the consciousness of her identity and to dare to be simply and transparently herself. . . . The Church should again learn to recognize and to live in the daylight of the mystery that is in her, not to cloak it with foreign trappings as if only they could give it strength and credibility. She must stop understanding herself in ways that convert her into an appendix to the ideology in fashion, and that reduce her to the role of the moralizing instrument of society and of the state, or of a charitable institution to shelter the disinherited that this society produces tirelessly, thus helping, in passing, to sustain her self-love and her irresponsibility. She must renounce every effort to legitimate herself through her social initiatives, or through what is called at times her "specific contribution" to society, and which converts the Church into one more competitor in the multicolored market of humanitarian and social services, with her own interests in that market. The more efforts that are made to understand the Church or to make her understood in this way, the more she empties herself of her own substance, and makes herself more incapable of even this contribution in the social sphere. . . . The new evangelization cannot elude the explicit proclamation of the person of Jesus Christ. What happens is that that proclamation, direct, very concrete—"God loves you, Christ has come for you"—can have no other form than that of a testimony and an invitation. . . . The experience of the Redemption of Jesus Christ, fervently and joyfully lived in the Church, and witnessed to in the world, contains in itself an answer to some of the most profound questions that men raise today.[5]

Father Cantalamessa makes a similar point: "In the measure we decide to want no other security or argument with which to face the world than Jesus Christ crucified, the power of God comes to our help working, even today, 'signs, wonders and miracles'. . . . The Church came into being from the kerygma preached 'in Spirit and power' and also today it would seem evident that a Church renewed in its apostolic strength can only spring from a new

[5] Cardinal Angel Suquia, "The New Evangelization: Some Tasks and Risks of the Present", *Communio*, Winter 1992.

proclamation of the Gospel which is the 'power of God for salvation to everyone who has faith'."[6]

One of the great battles the Lord called the Apostle Paul to fight was to keep clear what was new about the New Covenant. Paul continually faced the tendency both within and without the Church to drift back into depending on religious externals or self-effort rather than on the saving Person and deeds of Jesus: "For by grace you have been saved through faith; and this is not your own doing, it is the gift of God—not because of works, lest any man should boast. For we are his workmanship, created in Christ Jesus for good works, which God prepared beforehand, that we should walk in them" (Eph 2:8–10).

"For who sees anything different in you? What have you that you did not receive? If then you received it, why do you boast as if it were not a gift?" (1 Cor 4:7).

"That is why it depends on faith, in order that the promise may rest on grace" (Rom 4:16).

The tendency to want to save ourselves, not to have to depend utterly on God, is very strong in all of us today. Yves Congar, the great French theologian, warns of this also: "With the constant progress of science, man has gradually lost the awareness that he depends on another. Yet salvation essentially consists in this awareness of dependence. Man cannot save himself by his own efforts. Another saves us. Catholics also are running this risk."[7]

For the sake of the world, for our own sakes, and for the sake of God, we desperately need, as individuals and as a Church, not to behave as if what we have in the way of spiritual or material goods is due to our own merit or a result of our own will or strength rather than the pure grace of God.

However, it is not genuine faith if it does not express itself progressively in a life of morality, prayer, and love for others. But even here, of course, it is God's grace that enables us to live in such a way as to please God. We owe him thanks even for the good deeds that he has prepared for us in advance to carry out: "For we

---

[6] Cantalamessa, *Life in the Lordship of Christ,* pp. x–xi.
[7] Yves Congar, "The Pope Also Obeys", 30 *Days,* no. 3 (1993): 29.

are his workmanship, created in Christ Jesus for good works, which God prepared beforehand" (Eph 2:10).

"For God is at work in you both to will and to work for his good pleasure" (Phil 2:13).

And make no mistake about it; if we have genuine faith, God will be inspiring us to live a righteous life, of morality, prayer, good deeds. A test of the genuineness of our faith is how we live our life.

Saving faith is a faith that issues in works. Saving faith is not just an inner act or disposition but the expression of that inner act or disposition in deeds (Gal 5:6; 6:15; 1 Cor 7:19; 1 Jn 2:3; Jn 14:15). The final judgment is based not just on our interior faith alone but on actions we take in our life that flow from that faith (Rev 22:12; Mt 16:26–27; 25:31–46; Rom 2:5–11; 1 Cor 3:10–15; 2 Cor 5:10).

The Apostle James puts it very directly: "What does it profit, my brethren, if a man says he has faith but has not works? Can his faith save him? . . . You believe that God is one; you do well. Even the demons believe—and shudder. Do you want to be shown, you foolish fellow, that faith apart from works is barren? . . . You see that a man is justified by works and not by faith alone" (James 2:14, 19–20, 24).

But it is the grace that comes through faith that empowers us to do the works. In that sense we are dependent on the grace of God and his working in us even for the works: "For this I toil, striving with all the energy which he mightily inspires within me" (Col 1:29).

There is no conflict between grace and law, or faith and works, properly understood, as Father Cantalamessa expresses so well:

> In the new economy there is no contrast or incompatibility between the interior law of the Spirit and the written external law; on the contrary there is full collaboration; the one is given to guard the other: "Law was given so that we might seek grace and grace was given so that we might observe the law" (St. Augustine, *De Spir. Litt.* 19, 34). The observance of the commandments and, in fact, obedience, is the proof of love; it is the sign that shows whether we are living "according to the Spirit" or "according to the flesh". . . . The law doesn't therefore

suddenly become a giver of life; it remains exactly what it was, that through which the will of God is shown and nothing more. The difference is, though, that now, after the coming of the Spirit, its limited function is openly recognized and therefore it is positive, whereas before, when it was expected to give life, it was misleading and only encouraged the pride of man and sin. The very "letter" is, in other words, only safe in the Spirit.[8]

A fundamental purpose in how God arranged the plan of salvation is that no one would have any grounds for boasting in a self-glorifying way. The very root of sin is pride, and it needs to be broken if God's grace is to triumph. Having to give up our efforts to defend ourselves, explain ourselves, justify ourselves, rationalize ourselves and simply expose our desperate need to Christ's saving love is an essential component of the nature of salvation. Self-delusion and self-righteousness are characteristic of us fallen creatures. The awesome truth is that we are all in desperate need of God, of his forgiveness, of his love, of his Holy Spirit, and all of us need to abandon our pride, admit our need, and come to the foot of the Cross to receive mercy and forgiveness.

As Father Benedict Groeschel has pointed out, the admission of need and helplessness expressed in the twelve steps of Alcoholics Anonymous, now utilized by various other groups, gets to the heart of the gospel: "If you have not given sufficient thought in your own life to the complete destitution and helplessness of the person symbolized by the prodigal son, you should review the twelve steps of Alcoholics Anonymous. . . . Many spiritual writers rightly assume that the utter destitution that these steps reflect is actually the spiritual state of all men. . . . Jesus requires that his followers repent in such a way that they admit their powerlessness over sin and their inability to save themselves."[9]

My name is Ralph, and I am a sinner.

One inspiring expression of this dependence on God is con-

---

[8] Cantalamessa, *Life in the Lordship of Christ,* pp. 146–47.

[9] Fr. Benedict J. Groeschel, C.F.R., *The Reform of Renewal* (San Francisco: Ignatius Press, 1990), p. 44.

tained in Vatican II's Decree on Ecumenism: "This sacred Council firmly hopes that the initiatives of the sons of the Catholic Church, joined with those of the separated brethren, will go forward, without obstructing the ways of divine Providence, and without prejudging the future inspirations of the Holy Spirit. Further, this Council declares that it realizes that this holy objective—the reconciliation of all Christians in the unity of the one and only Church of Christ—transcends human powers and gifts. It therefore places its hope entirely in the prayer of Christ for the Church, in the love of the Father for us and in the power of the Holy Spirit."[10]

And Father Cantalamessa points out another reason why God has chosen faith as the gateway to the kingdom: "If you had been told: the door to the Kingdom is innocence, the door is the strict observance of the commandments, the door is this or that virtue, you could have found excuses and said: It's not for me! I'm not innocent, I haven't got that virtue. But you are being told: the door is faith. Believe! This is not something above or beyond you, it is not so far removed from you."[11]

Recently someone asked me why Southern Baptists were so eager to share the good news with others, in comparison to the average Catholic's total disinterest. As I thought about it several reasons came to mind. The chief reason is that most Baptists have a clear understanding of the heart of the gospel message, namely, that we are saved by grace through faith, and a personal appreciation for what Jesus has done for them. They also believe that it makes a real difference whether someone believes or not and that there really are a heaven and a hell. Unfortunately most Catholics do not seem to have a clear understanding of the basic gospel message or an appreciation of what Jesus has done for them or an understanding of the eternal consequences, at least not enough to motivate them to share the good news with others. Despite all the years of Catholic education and other catechesis, there seem to be some astounding gaps.

---

[10] Decree on Ecumenism *Unitatis Redintegratio*, 24.
[11] Cantalamessa, *Life in the Lordship of Christ*, p. 45.

Dr. Peter Kreeft, professor of philosophy at Boston College, has made similar observations through contact with his predominantly Catholic students:

> The life of God comes into us by faith, through us by hope, and out of us by the works of love.
>
> That is clearly the biblical view, and when Protestants and Catholics who know the Bible discuss the issue sincerely, it's amazing how quickly they come to agree with each other on this, the fundamental point.
>
> But many Catholics still have not learned this thoroughly Catholic and biblical doctrine. They think we're saved by good intentions, or being nice, or sincere, or trying a little harder, or doing a sufficient number of good deeds. Over the past 25 years I've asked hundreds of Catholic college students the question: If you should die tonight and God asks you why he should let you into heaven, what would you answer?
>
> The vast majority of them simply don't know the right answer to this, the most important of all questions, the very essence of Christianity. They usually don't even mention Jesus!
>
> Until we Catholics know the foundation, Protestants are not going to listen to us when we try to teach them about the upper storeys of the building. Perhaps God allows the Protestant-Catholic division to persist not only because Protestants have abandoned some precious truths taught by the Church but also because many Catholics have never been taught the most precious truth of all: that salvation is a free gift of grace, accepted by faith.[12]

Three years later Doctor Kreeft returned to the same theme and stated the awesome truth of the situation even more bluntly: "Most Catholics in America simply do not know how to get to heaven, how to be saved. This may sound like an extreme or exaggerated statement, but I know it's true from years of teaching experience. . . . Most Catholic students do not even mention Christ when they answer the question of how they expect to get to heaven. They think they'll get in if they are good enough. This means, quite simply, that the single most fundamental lesson of

[12] Peter Kreeft, "Luther, Faith and Good Works", *National Catholic Register,* November 10, 1991, p. 8.

the entire Christian religion, the most important thing anyone can ever know on earth, they don't know. They may well get to Heaven after all, but if they do it will not be as Christians but as good pagans. . . . And this is not simply a lesson it would be nice for us to learn; it's a lesson absolutely necessary for us to learn. Eternity is at stake."[13]

In a recent talk to a group of American bishops John Paul II warned against straying too far from focusing on Jesus Christ, and him crucified: "Sometimes even Catholics have lost or have never had the chance to experience Christ personally: not Christ as a mere 'paradigm' or 'value', but the living Lord: 'the way, and the truth, and the life' (Jn 14:6). In addressing this need we, like Saint Paul, must never drift far from the core of the message: 'Christ crucified . . . Christ, the power of God and the wisdom of God' (1 Cor 1:23–24)."[14]

On another occasion he spoke of the essence of salvation as "clinging" to Christ, the type of surrender in faith, admitting our need, that breaks pride: "Whoever wants to be saved has only to cling to Christ."[15]

This is reminiscent of what St. Cyril of Jerusalem had to say about salvation: "O the wonderful goodness of God towards men! The just men of the Old Testament were acceptable to God for the fatigue of many years; but what they managed to obtain through a long and heroic service acceptable to God, is granted to you by Jesus in a brief space of time. For, if you believe that Jesus Christ is Lord and that God raised him from the dead, you will be saved and led into Paradise by him who led the good thief there."[16]

And Cardinal Danneels has pointed out how profound the tendency is in us to resist the truth that we cannot save ourselves, even partly: "Today, the doctrine of grace is no doubt the most neglected concept in theology and in practical Christian life. The

[13] Peter Kreeft, "Protestants Bring Personal Touch to the Life of Faith", *National Catholic Register,* April 24, 1994, pp. 1, 7.

[14] John Paul II, "New Catechism Will Promote National Recatechizing Effort", *L'Osservatore Romano* (English ed.), March 24, 1993, p. 3.

[15] John Paul II, "Christ Reopens the Way to God for Us", *L'Osservatore Romano* (English ed.), March 10, 1993, p. 2.

[16] Cited in Cantalamessa, *Life in the Lordship of Christ,* p. 49.

fact that we are not able to save ourselves, even partly—that we are entirely dependent on the gift of grace from God—is a stumbling block for many. They find it difficult to understand that grace does not eliminate our freedom and our autonomy; on the contrary, it is their very foundation. The dream of a person who is self-sufficient is apparently ineradicable. However, the very essence of faith is to accept the idea of our dependence on God."[17]

In order to avoid the danger of a Pelagian moralism, the new *Catechism of the Catholic Church* emphasizes strongly, in its introduction to Catholic moral teaching, the absolute need to depend on the grace of God in order to live the moral teaching of the Church.

Archbishop Jean Honoré, Archbishop of Tours, France, closely connected to the development of this Catechism, frankly admits that an earlier draft of the catechism was justifiably criticized for not making clear that Christian morality was not just a matter of "virtuous conformity" but required a radical dependence on the grace of God:

> Indeed, while the Catechism succeeded in expressing the call to follow the Gospel and aim at perfection, it did not show (or at least not sufficiently) that this quest can only be accomplished by the baptized with the help of the gratuitous grace that heals and absolves them from sin and supports them along the way. In brief, because it had not been stated fully or with sufficient clarity, it was not immediately obvious that whatever Christians do in the order of salvation and holiness, they do not do alone, but only with divine assistance. In their effort to grow in virtue, all Christians, even the greatest saints, are justified and saved sinners.
>
> By failing to emphasize the prevenient action of the Lord's grace and the inner presence of the Spirit, the Catechism was in danger of omitting one of the most basic conditions of moral action according to the Gospel. A

[17] Cardinal Godfried Danneels, *Christ or Aquarius? Exploring the New Age Movement* (Dublin: Veritas Publications, 1992), pp. 38–39.

conscious effort had been made to avoid the trap of casuistry. That of moralism was narrowly avoided. The draft could be said to have retained a Pelagian tone that still had to be corrected.[18]

As Cardinal Ratzinger put it when speaking of the new Catechism's treatment of moral teaching: "This section of the text is not a list of sins but is aimed at illustrating how moral living is constituted within a Christian perspective. Morality thus becomes a very simple thing; it is friendship with the Lord, it is living and journeying with Him."[19]

Carl Anderson, dean of the John Paul II Institute for Studies on Marriage and Family in Washington, D.C., at a recent private study seminar for bishops from North America, in which I also participated, pointed out the significance of this growing focus on the Person of Jesus:

In the new evangelization the Holy Father has provided us two texts that are essential sources, the *Catechism of the Catholic Church* and *Vertitatis Splendor*. The question may be asked: In what way may these documents escape the difficulties which have affected *Humanae Vitae*? I would suggest that the answer may be found in the documents' explicit Christocentricism. Both are clearly centered on the person of Jesus Christ and both identify the Christian life as one which flows from an encounter with the person of Christ. They reaffirm that the Christian faith has as its center and point of departure the acknowledgement of the living presence of Christ in the lives of his followers. The Christian life is not primarily a morality; it is not a philosophy; it is not a sociology; it is not a politics. Certainly, this was presupposed in the official teachings of the Church prior to these documents; however, in many cases it was not sufficiently explicit. As a result, the Christian proposal has too often been subjected in our culture to a form of reductionism

[18] Archbishop Jean Honoré, "Catechism Presents Morality as a Lived Experience of Faith in Christ", *L'Osservatore Romano* (English ed.), May 12, 1993, p. 10.

[19] Cardinal Ratzinger and Andrea Tornielli, "Testimonies in the Pagan Age", 30 *Days*, no. 11 (1992): 29.

which has attempted to make it primarily a morality or a sociology or a philosophy or a politics.[20]

Dean Anderson points out that what was sometimes presupposed in the previous teaching of the Church, namely, that the foundation of everything is the Person of Jesus, must now be made explicit in our new cultural situation in order for our teaching to be comprehensible.

Father Cantalamessa points out from his extensive experience with religious life and the history of the Church how important the emphasis on grace is:

> The newness of the Christian message becomes clouded when preaching, catechesis, spiritual guidance and all other formative activities of faith unilaterally insist on duties, virtues, vices, punishment and, in general, on what man "should do", presenting grace as an aid that comes to man in the course of his commitment to make up for what he is not able to do alone and not, on the contrary, as something that comes before these efforts and which makes them possible; when "duty" is created by the law and not by grace and when duty is consequently not conceived as our debt of gratitude to God but rather as something that creates, if we accomplish it, a debt of gratitude on God's part towards us; when, in other words, morals become separated from the *kerygma*. In a stricter sphere, the religious life is similarly clouded when in the formation given to young people and novices, in retreats and on other occasions, more time is spent on talking about the charism, traditions, rules and constitutions and the particular spirituality of the order (often very poor and inconsistent) than talking of Christ the Lord and his Holy Spirit. The center of attention imperceptibly moves from God to man and from grace to the law.[21]

Father Thomas Weinandy points out that this tendency has also been present in traditional Catholic missionary work: "In the past,

---

[20] Carl Anderson, "Realistic Catechesis on the Family", text to be published in a collection of the proceedings by the John XXIII Institute in Brighton, Massachusetts.

[21] Cantalamessa, *Life in the Lordship of Christ,* pp. 152–53.

Catholic evangelization in the Third World, and even in Western societies, too often took the form of merely advocating a moral life. Clearly, we must teach people Christian morality, but such a limited approach is not only Pelagian—for it neglects the necessity of faith in Jesus—but also can easily carry the cultural baggage of the evangelist."[22]

Of course this is a problem in the present also.

There is an increasing sensitivity on all levels of the Church to the need to stress the grace of God:

> When St. Paul speaks of the grace which frees from the law, while his principal, direct thoughts are with Mosaic Law, he also seems more or less implicitly to be pondering over all that the concept of law contains, including, perhaps, the Gospel precepts. St. Thomas picked up on the Pauline expression "the letter kills" when he wrote: "By letter we must mean any written law external to man, even moral precepts such as those contained in the Gospel. Therefore, even the letter of the Gospel would kill if there were not the interior presence of the healing grace of the faith (gratia fidei sanans)" (*Summa theologica,* I–II q. 106, a. 2).
>
> Without the grace of the faith that heals the heart of evil, Christian obedience to all the Lord commanded . . . would not only be impossible to practice but would also generate enslavement and alienation.[23]

And as Cardinal Tarancon, former Archbishop of Toledo, Spain, said: "It would be wrong for the Church today to think about imposing Catholic morality on the world. Without the grace of God there is no way anyone can live Catholic morality let alone accept it."[24]

And Bishop Christoph Schönborn, O.P., Auxiliary Bishop of Vienna, Austria, who was secretary of the editorial committee for

---

[22] Fr. Thomas Weinandy, "Why Catholics Find It So Hard to Evangelize", *New Covenant,* October 1993, p. 19.

[23] Editorial, 30 *Days,* no. 5 (1993): 3.

[24] Cardinal Vicente Enrique Y Tarancon and Andrea Tornielli, "Morality and Grace", 30 *Days,* no. 5 (1993): 8.

the new Catechism, speaks of how the Catechism highlights "the primacy of grace".[25]

There is something in us that rebels against the kind of trusting faith that alone saves. There is something in us that would at least like to help God out in saving us, and while we can cooperate with God, thanks to his grace, the initial, primary, saving grace is entirely undeserved and unmerited. Yes, it means that we are entirely in God's debt. Yes, it means that every single one of us is in need of being forgiven much.

And it is only the one who is forgiven much who loves much (see Lk 7:47).

Another name for all of this is mercy. God is rich in mercy, and the Lord has used Sr. Faustina, a Polish nun of this century, to emphasize the mercy of God, just as he used Margaret Mary in the seventeenth century. Recognizing the Divine Mercy is to recognize the heart of the gospel.

Whether we have been obvious sinners or not, all of us have been forgiven much. To refuse to admit our need for forgiveness, that we indeed are sinners, or to acknowledge the forgiveness that is being offered is to run the risk of suicide, as did Judas, or the risk of plunging deeper into our sin, as did Lenin: "In the face of his own sin, of his own crime, of his own error, man, from Cain to Lenin as others have also observed, does not know how to forgive himself, cannot forgive himself. *It's all over.* In Zurich, Lenin himself used Cain's words: 'My evil is too great and cannot be forgiven.' But just that is the supreme paradox of the Christian message: *sin is forgiven. . . .* This is the surprise, the experience of compassion which anyone can have in the relationship with Christ."[26]

As the world is engulfed in ethnic and racial tension and violence, it is more important than ever to realize that it is only through the power and work of the Cross of Christ that the pride and fear that are at the heart of racism and ethnic hostility can be

[25] Christoph Schönborn, O.P., "The Divine Economy Interwoven through New Catechetical Work", *L'Osservatore Romano* (English ed.), March 17, 1993, p. 4.

[26] Msgr. Luigi Giussani, "Reflection: By Grace, Always", 30 *Days,* no. 3 (1993): 71.

removed and replaced with humility, security, love, and forgiveness: "From now on, therefore, we regard no one from a human point of view; even though we once regarded Christ from a human point of view, we regard him thus no longer. Therefore, if any one is in Christ, he is a new creation; the old has passed away, behold, the new has come" (2 Cor 5:16–17).

Admitting our need for Christ, in humility and honesty, is essential for our relationship with him: "Two men went up into the temple to pray, one a Pharisee and the other a tax collector. The Pharisee stood and prayed thus with himself, 'God, I thank thee that I am not like other men, extortioners, unjust, adulterers, or even like this tax collector. I fast twice a week, I give tithes of all that I get.' But the tax collector, standing far off, would not even lift up his eyes to heaven, but beat his breast, saying, 'God, be merciful to me a sinner.' I tell you, this man went down to his house justified rather than the other" (Lk 18:10–14).

Our tendency toward lukewarmness, self-righteousness, and self-satisfaction needs constantly to be challenged by what the Spirit continues to say to the Church and to all of us: "For you say, I am rich, I have prospered, and I need nothing; not knowing that you are wretched, pitiable, poor, blind, and naked. Therefore I counsel you to buy from me gold refined by fire, that you may be rich, and white garments to clothe you and to keep the shame of your nakedness from being seen, and salve to anoint your eyes, that you may see. Those whom I love, I reprove and chasten; so be zealous and repent" (Rev 3:17–19).

What we have to boast of is what Jesus Christ did for us on the Cross, and that is precisely the prayer of Paul: "But far be it from me to glory except in the cross of our Lord Jesus Christ, by which the world has been crucified to me, and I to the world" (Gal 6:14).

"Therefore, since we are justified by faith, we have peace with God through our Lord Jesus Christ. Through him we have obtained access to this grace in which we stand, and we rejoice in our hope of sharing the glory of God" (Rom 5:1–2).

Paul goes on to say that we can also boast of our afflictions and our weakness, as this too gives glory to God: "More than that, we rejoice in our sufferings, knowing that suffering produces endurance, and endurance produces character, and character produces hope, and hope does not disappoint us, because God's love has been poured into our hearts through the Holy Spirit who has been given to us" (Rom 5:3–5).

It is useful to note that when God gives great blessings and revelations, he also gives the circumstances to help keep us from getting proud: "But I refrain from it, so that no one may think more of me than he sees in me or hears from me. And to keep me from being too elated by the abundance of revelations, a thorn was given me in the flesh, a messenger of Satan, to harass me, to keep me from being too elated. Three times I besought the Lord about this, that it should leave me; but he said to me, 'My grace is sufficient for you, for my power is made perfect in weakness.' I will all the more gladly boast of my weaknesses, that the power of Christ may rest upon me. For the sake of Christ, then, I am content with weaknesses, insults, hardships, persecutions, and calamities; for when I am weak, then I am strong" (2 Cor 12:6–10).

It is not just at the beginning of a Christian life that pride must be broken, but all along the way. We have a tendency to attribute to ourselves, our own efforts, our own intelligence, our own hard work, our own virtues what should properly be attributed to the grace of God. What have we that we have not received? We can do this as individuals or as part of the various corporate bodies of which we are a part. Individual pride and corporate pride can both become serious obstacles to the Father's plan of revealing Christ to the world. We need to get out of the way and join with the Father in pointing to Jesus. We do this not only in our initial surrender to Christ but also in an ongoing life of faith, lived daily, in dependence upon the Son of God.

Chapter Three

Living in Faith

A great deal of research has been done to determine why the mainline Protestant churches are experiencing such a decline in numbers, while biblically conservative nondenominational Christian fellowships are growing so quickly, not in rural Appalachia but in major metropolitan centers. All of these studies point in a similar direction. As one recent study summarized its conclusions: "In our study, the single best predictor of church participation turned out to be *belief* — orthodox Christian belief, and especially the teaching that a person can be saved only through Jesus Christ.[1] . . . The underlying problem of the mainline churches cannot be solved by new programs of church development alone. That problem is the weakening of the spiritual conviction required to generate the enthusiasm and energy needed to sustain a vigorous

[1] The Catholic Church's position on the necessity of Jesus for salvation is spelled out clearly in Vatican Council II's Constitution on the Church *Lumen Gentium*, 16. In summary, the Church believes that salvation is impossible apart from Jesus, but that those who "through no fault of their own" have never heard the good news will be judged on the basis of the light God has given them in creation and in conscience (Rom 1–2). It makes clear though that despite this possibility, we should not be lax in preaching the gospel, since "very often, deceived by the Evil One, men have become vain in their reasonings, have exchanged the truth of God for a lie and served the world rather than the Creator (cf. Rom 1:21, 25). Or else, living and dying in this world without God, they are exposed to ultimate despair. Hence to procure the glory of God and the salvation of all these, the Church mindful of the Lord's command, 'preach the Gospel to every creature' (Mk 16:16) takes zealous care to foster the missions" (Constitution on the Church *Lumen Gentium*, 16).

communal life. Somehow, in the course of the past century, these churches lost the will or the ability to teach the Christian faith and what it requires to a succession of younger cohorts in such a way as to command their allegiance."[2]

Other studies show that a vigorous faith correlates with mental health: "Followers of 'that old time religion', a favorite target of comics, may have the last laugh: Their faith gives them a strong mental health edge.... [They] are far more optimistic than followers of moderate or liberal religions, a new study suggests.

" 'We know optimistic people are less vulnerable to depression, and optimism correlates with high achievement', says psychologist Sheena Sethi of Stanford University."[3]

In the Catholic Church, a great deal of effort is being expended today to "professionalize" those who are working in the Church. Degree and certificate programs are proliferating, and it is getting harder to serve in the Church without such qualifications. While such training can obviously be very useful, what is absolutely critical to the success of the life and mission of the Church is faith. Recently, a board member of the Chicago-based National Center for the Laity vividly pointed this out: "He emphasized that no matter how many modern business and administrative techniques the Church adopts, if there's no faith, little progress will occur.

"He cited the story of a Brooklyn, N.Y., black evangelical congregation which has made a substantial impact on its largely impoverished community. Although that congregation . . . has few professional people, what comes through strongly is that the congregation has faith.

" 'This is sometimes what we've lost.... We get at *religion* at times, but we're not good at faith, and sometimes that catches up to us. We don't present the person of Jesus in a compelling way.' "[4]

John Paul II has urgently pointed out the crucial need for a

<hr />

[2] Benton Johnson, Dean R. Hoge, and Donald A. Luidens, "Mainline Churches: The Real Reason for Decline", *First Things,* March 1993, pp. 13–18.

[3] "Strict Religious Faith Lifts Mind as Well as Spirit," *USA Today,* August 2, 1993, p. D1.

[4] Peter Feuerherd, "A Loss of Church Heart?" *National Catholic Register,* March 28, 1993, p. 6.

turning to God in faith, given the circumstances of the world today:

> The whole of humanity, which is at a very difficult time, has great need of it. How, in fact, could we remain silent in the face of the sad spectacle of rape and indescribable cruelty which seems to drive individuals and whole populations onto the brink of the abyss?
>
> How can it happen that in our century, a century of science and technology capable of penetrating the mysteries of outer space, we find ourselves helpless bystanders before the *horrifying violations of human dignity? . . . It is time to return to God! . . .* Please allow me to shout it aloud: *"It is time to return to God!"* The person who does not yet have the joy of the faith is asked for the courage to seek it with confidence, perseverance and openness. Whoever has the grace of possessing it is asked to value it as the most treasured possession of his life, living it thoroughly and witnessing to it with passion. Our world hungers for faith, for an authentic and deep faith, because God alone can fully satisfy the desires of the human heart.[5]

Cardinal König, the retired Archbishop of Vienna, speaks of the growing bureaucracy of the Church as a substitute for conversion: "In the last few days a German cardinal came to see me here in Vienna and he said: 'They're bringing out too much printed matter, I can't manage to read it all. I weigh them to see if the freight charges increase. . . .' But the real danger is that of bureaucracy, a tendency that repeats itself in dioceses and parishes. To avoid one's own conversion one creates bureaucracy."[6]

Bishop Paul Cordes makes a similar point:

> Nonetheless, it has to be recognised that the proclamation of the Gospel runs into a limitation as soon as institutional and professional forces, i.e. mere expertise, gain the upper hand. Professionalism develops a technique which provides a convenient shield against the person's animating impulses. Careerism,

[5] John Paul II, "It Is Time to Return to God!" *L'Osservatore Romano* (English ed.), March 10, 1993, p. 1.

[6] Cardinal König and Andrea Tornielli, "Openness to the World Was Not Enough . . . ", 30 *Days,* no. 10 (1992): 17.

both in thought and action, takes the place of more authentic motivations. The capacity to bear witness is stunted. . . .

It is certainly not by chance that the development of the ordained ministry in the early Church was only accomplished very slowly, and that its New Testament traces were only discovered with a great deal of effort. The importance of the sacrament of Holy Orders, ever more clearly apparent under the breath of the Spirit, undoubtedly led also to the risk of the members of the Church being unjustifiably and detrimentally exonerated from their responsibility for the Church's mission—a fact that in no way diminishes the ministry's biblical and dogmatic legitimacy. . . .

The proclamation of the Gospel through the imitation of Christ makes it absurd to rely exclusively on the formulation of programmes and concepts, the establishment of institutes and the drawing up of curricula in the pursuit of evangelization . . . evangelization is not a social process, to be prepared and implemented according to bureaucratic models; it must spring from people's hearts.[7]

What then is faith?

Faith is a way of knowing and seeing realities that are presently invisible but are of even more importance than the realities we can see with our biological eyes.

If one were so inclined, a very good case could be made that perhaps the central theme of the Bible is faith: "Now faith is the assurance of things hoped for, the conviction of things not seen. For by it the men of old received divine approval. By faith we understand that the world was created by the word of God, so that what is seen was made out of things which do not appear" (Heb 11:1–3).

And how does faith come?

It is a gift of God that he offers to all people. Faith normally comes from hearing the truth of the gospel preached, seeing or hearing of signs and evidence that confirm its truth, and a direct working of the Holy Spirit in the soul (Rom 10:8–15; 2 Cor 3:16–18; Jn 14:10–11; 1 Th 5:9; etc.). Scripture invests the concept of faith with several different meanings.

[7] Bishop Paul Joseph Cordes, *Charisms and New Evangelization* (Middlegreen, Slough, U.K.: St. Paul Publications, 1992), pp. 106–7.

One meaning of the Scripture's teaching on faith is faith as in the "deposit of faith" (2 Tim 1:13–14; 2:2; Jude 3), that body of truths revealed by God. A primary meaning of faith in this sense is faith as a knowledge of truth. This is the meaning of faith we have primarily in mind when we talk about passing on "the Faith" or teaching "the Faith". Obviously, as essential as "propositional" faith is, it is not enough. "Even the demons believe" (James 2:19) but are lacking both obedience and trust.

Another meaning given by Scripture to faith is faith as in "the obedience of faith" (Rom 1:5; 16:26). Faith in this sense is that knowledge of truth that has implicit or explicit in it a call to obedience. Another well-known formulation of this would be "faith by itself, if it has no works, is dead" (James 2:17). Or, as Jesus said, "If you continue in my word, you are truly my disciples, and you will know the truth, and the truth will make you free" (Jn 8:31–32). There is a clear implication of the scriptural teaching that it is indeed obedience to the truth that is revealed that unfolds a deeper understanding of that very truth.

A third and perhaps most common use of the word *faith* in Scripture is faith as trust: "Blessed is she who believed that there would be a fulfilment of what was spoken to her from the Lord" (Lk 1:45).

The basic thrust of Jesus' whole message is to *trust* in him, and in the Father: "But if God so clothes the grass which is alive in the field today and tomorrow is thrown into the oven, how much more will he clothe you, O men of little faith! And do not seek what you are to eat and what you are to drink, nor be of anxious mind. For all the nations of the world seek these things; and your Father knows that you need them. Instead, seek his kingdom, and these things shall be yours as well" (Lk 12:28–31).

The kind of faith that Jesus is calling us to is faith in the goodness of God, the power of God, the truthfulness of God, and most of all the personal love of God for each one of us in every aspect of our lives and needs. He is calling us to the kind of surrender and abandonment (conversion) that are possible only when we know who God is.

It is the kind of faith that Job had when he was able to

say that he would trust in God even if "he will slay me" (Job 13:15).[8]

Sometimes all three meanings are implied when Scripture refers to faith: "For this is the will of my Father, that every one who sees the Son and believes in him should have eternal life" (Jn 6:40).

A fourth dimension of faith that Scripture talks about is what might be called charismatic faith: faith that works wonders, moves mountains, releases the power of God in signs and wonders.

In any event, faith is clearly presented in Scriptures as our lifeline to God. Faith is what inaugurates, sustains, and deepens our relationship with God. As vital as the oxygen line is to the deep-sea diver, so is faith to our life with God. Because this is so important, I am going to let the actual words of Scripture speak for themselves frequently in this chapter. The strength, frequency, and clarity of what the Scripture says about faith is quite extraordinary. Perhaps some of you might find it useful to reflect on the Scripture passages in this chapter and the next two chapters in times of prayer or study.

"Without faith it is impossible to please him. For whoever would draw near to God must believe that he exists and that he rewards those who seek him" (Heb 11:6).

"My righteous one shall live by faith, and if he shrinks back, my soul has no pleasure in him. But we are not of those who shrink back and are destroyed, but of those who have faith and keep their souls" (Heb 10:38–39).

"With whom was he provoked forty years? Was it not with those who sinned, whose bodies fell in the wilderness? And to whom did he swear that they should never enter his rest, but to those who were disobedient? So we see that they were unable to enter because of unbelief" (Heb 3:17–19).

Just as it was unbelief that kept the people of Israel from

---

[8] "In the fifties and sixties, historical and systematic reflection on the foundations of theology helped theologians to see the whole of ecclesial and theological Tradition in new ways and to rediscover the distinct normative power of Sacred Scripture." Siegfried Widenhofer, "The Main Forms of Contemporary Theology of Original Sin", *Communio,* Winter 1991, p. 515.

entering the promised land thousands of years ago, so too is it unbelief today that makes Jesus, the cornerstone of a whole new creation, function for some as a stumbling stone that makes them fall: "What shall we say, then? That Gentiles who did not pursue righteousness have attained it, that is, righteousness through faith; but that Israel who pursued the righteousness which is based on law did not succeed in fulfilling that law. Why? Because they did not pursue it through faith, but as if it were based on works. They have stumbled over the stumbling stone, as it is written, 'Behold, I am laying in Zion a stone that will make men stumble, a rock that will make them fall; and he who believes in him will not be put to shame'" (Rom 9:30–33).

Faith opens us up to the glory of life with God, sustains us along the way, and brings us to the glorious conclusion awaiting us when Jesus Christ returns:

> Blessed be the God and Father of our Lord Jesus Christ! By his great mercy we have been born anew to a living hope through the resurrection of Jesus Christ from the dead, and to an inheritance which is imperishable, undefiled, and unfading, kept in heaven for you, who by God's power are guarded through faith for a salvation ready to be revealed in the last time. In this you rejoice, though now for a little while you may have to suffer various trials, so that the genuineness of your faith, more precious than gold which though perishable is tested by fire, may redound to praise and glory and honor at the revelation of Jesus Christ. Without having seen him you love him; though you do not now see him you believe in him and rejoice with unutterable and exalted joy. As the outcome of your faith you obtain the salvation of your souls (1 Pet 1:3–9).

Faith is the pathway by which power is released into our lives and into the world. Time after time we see Jesus in the Gospels commenting on how it was people's faith in him and his Father that enabled him to work miracles for them: "And they brought to him a paralytic, lying on his bed; and when *Jesus saw their faith* he said to the paralytic, 'Take heart, my son; your sins are forgiven'" (Mt 9:2).

"Jesus turned, and seeing her he said, 'Take heart, daughter; your faith has made you well.' And instantly the woman was made well" (Mt 9:22).

"Then he touched their eyes, saying, 'According to your faith be it done to you' " (Mt 9:29).

"Jesus said to him, 'If you can! All things are possible to him who believes' " (Mk 9:23).

"When Jesus saw their faith, he said to the paralytic, 'My son, your sins are forgiven' " (Mk 2:5).

Sometimes Jesus made clear that it was lack of faith in him that prevented him from working miracles in a particular locality or for particular people: "And he did not do many mighty works there, because of their unbelief" (Mt 13:58).

At the same time he made it clear that a relatively small amount of faith was able to release significant amounts of power: "I say to you, if you have faith as a grain of mustard seed, you will say to this mountain, 'Move hence to yonder place,' and it will move; and nothing will be impossible to you" (Mt 17:20).

Jesus was not interested in their rearranging the geography of Palestine. He himself would be doing that when he returned in glory! He was interested in letting his disciples know that a relatively small amount of faith—the mustard seed is a very small seed—when utilized in loving prayer and action can produce significant results.

One of the most moving chapters in Scripture is chapter eleven of Hebrews, which is a hymn to the many men and women of the Old Covenant who lived by faith, and because of this "through faith conquered kingdoms, enforced justice, received promises, stopped the mouths of lions, quenched raging fire, escaped the edge of the sword, won strength out of weakness, became mighty in war, put foreign armies to flight. Women received their dead by resurrection. Some were tortured, refusing to accept release, that they might rise again to a better life" (Heb 11:33–35).

And as the Apostle John puts it: "Whatever is born of God overcomes the world; and this is the victory that overcomes the world, our faith" (1 Jn 5:4).

Faith is a key to the promises of God coming to pass: "And

blessed is she who believed that there would be a fulfilment of what was spoken to her from the Lord" (Lk 1:45).

"For through the spirit, by faith, we wait for the hope of righteousness. For in Christ Jesus neither circumcision nor uncircumcision is of any avail, but faith working through love" (Gal 5:5–6).

"For this is the will of my Father, that every one who sees the Son and believes in him should have eternal life; and I will raise him up at the last day" (Jn 6:40).

Faith is also an antidote to fear and anxiety: "Let not your hearts be troubled; believe in God; believe also in me" (Jn 14:1).

"But Jesus on hearing this answered him, 'Do not fear; only believe, and she shall be well' " (Lk 8:50).

"He said to them, 'Why are you afraid? Have you no faith?' " (Mk 4:40).

Scripture also makes clear that this fundamental faith and trust in God is important not just at the beginning or renewal points of our Christian lives but is intended to function in a daily way that makes the life of a Christian different, even in the midst of difficulties. One of my favorite Scripture passages expresses this quite well: "I have been crucified with Christ; it is no longer I who live, but Christ who lives in me; and the life I now live in the flesh I live by faith in the Son of God, who loved me and gave himself for me. I do not nullify the grace of God; for if justification were through the law, then Christ died to no purpose" (Gal 2:20–21).

We *have* been crucified with Christ. In baptism, appropriated by faith, a profound transaction has occurred. We have shared in Christ's crucifixion so we can begin to share in his Resurrection, now. Christ himself is now dwelling in us! Talk about an answer to self-esteem, self-worth, human dignity questions! What incredible dignity has been bestowed on us. Christ himself, the Son of God, is living in us!

We still share fully in the human condition; we are not taken out of this fallen, sinful, unjust world. We still share in the suffering, disappointments, and tragedies of life, but with one big difference. We now can live daily a life of faith in the Son of God, who loved me and gave himself for me.

What an incredible source of strength this is. I cannot tell you how much I appreciate being able to get up in the morning with faith in the Son of God, who loved me and gave himself for me. I cannot tell you how much I appreciate that as a husband and father of six children, exposed to all the pressures and temptations that all of us are, I can rely on Christ, who loved me and gave himself for me, for my wife, for my children, and for every single one of us. I continually receive strength, energy, hope, and courage to go on from him, through faith, in a day-by-day way.

Daily faith in the Son of God, remembering his love, his sacrifice and covenant commitment to us, is the way of life of the Christian. What a difference it makes to live in this world, to go through this life with daily faith in the Son of God, who loved me and gave himself for me.

Of course, it is in the Eucharist, when we "do this in memory of me", that we in a special way remember the one who loved me and gave himself for me and receive strength, nourishment, and food for the journey in a special way.

Because faith is so critical to all that God desires to come to pass for us, it is understandable that our "enemies"—the world, the flesh, and the devil—would particularly conspire together to destroy our faith, the faith of others, the faith of the Church.

Because our fallen human natures, even after we are redeemed, still have a strong inclination to self-righteousness and self-reliance, the strong words of Paul to the Galatians are important for us regularly to recall:

> O foolish Galatians! Who has bewitched you, before whose eyes Jesus Christ was publicly portrayed as crucified? Let me ask you only this: Did you receive the Spirit by works of the law, or by hearing with faith? Are you so foolish? Having begun with the Spirit, are you now ending with the flesh? Did you experience so many things in vain?—if it really is in vain. Does he who supplies the Spirit to you and works miracles among you do so by works of the law, or by hearing with faith? . . . So then, those who are men of faith are blessed with Abraham who had faith. For all who rely on works of the law are under a curse (Gal 3:1–10).

This is an extraordinarily important passage for us and for the whole Church. The Spirit is lavished on those who have faith in the Cross of Christ. The Spirit works wonders in the midst of those who have faith in the saving work of Christ. There is a deep-seated tendency in us, and in the Church, to begin in faith, in the Spirit, and then gradually, over time, to drift into relying on external forms, worked out systems and programs, our own strength, intelligence, and hard work. It is *very easy* to drift into reliance on something other than Jesus Christ himself. We need to help each other not to do so, because those who depend on something other than Jesus himself "are under a curse". If we are experiencing a lack of the power of the Holy Spirit in our life or in our corner of the Church, it may be because like the Galatians we have drifted away from simple faith in Jesus Christ and all he has done for us and the world through his surpassing sacrifice on the Cross. Or perhaps some of us may never have surrendered ourselves to Jesus in simple and wholehearted faith to begin with.

As Father Cantalamessa puts it:

It is also possible to imperceptibly fall back under the law even after experiencing freedom of the Spirit and grace. St. Paul had to fight two big battles in his apostolic life, that of urging Judaism to pass from the law to grace, from the old to the new covenant and that of preventing entire communities who had made the passage to turn back and allow themselves to be swallowed up again by the law and by works. . . . He shows us that we can fall away from grace in other ways as well as by sinning . . . (Gal 5:4). We know of only one way to fall away from grace and that is precisely by mortal sin because we have impoverished the meaning of the word "grace" and made it just a "thing". We can fall away from grace by legalism, by seeking our own justice and by fear. That's why St. Paul warns the Romans by saying to them: *"You did not receive the spirit of slavery to fall back into fear"* (Rom 8:15).

The danger of "ending with the flesh" and of falling back to the Old Testament with the mind and heart didn't end with Paul's death; it has always existed and will always exist and we must fight against it and avoid it just as Paul did in his time. To live in the new covenant is like swimming against the current. Origen wrote: "Don't think that the renewal of life that came about once and for all at the beginning is enough; it is necessary to continually renew the newness every day."[9]

We can fall into the sin of unbelief by hardening our hearts in face of the words and deeds of Jesus: "Therefore, as the Holy Spirit says, 'Today, when you hear his voice, do not harden your hearts as in the rebellion, on the day of testing in the wilderness, when your fathers put me to the test and saw my works for forty years. Therefore I was provoked with that generation.... And I swore in my wrath, "They shall never enter my rest." ' Take care, brethren, lest there be in any of you an evil, unbelieving heart, leading you to fall away from the living God. But exhort one another every day, as long as it is called 'today,' that none of you may be hardened by the deceitfulness of sin.... So we see that they were unable to enter because of unbelief" (Heb 3:7–13, 19).

It is shockingly possible to have experienced the Lord and his works and yet harden our hearts. God have mercy on us! "When the Lord heard, he was full of wrath; a fire was kindled against Jacob, his anger mounted against Israel; because they had no faith in God, and did not trust his saving power.... And they ate and were well filled, for he gave them what they craved. But before they had sated their craving, while the food was still in their mouths, the anger of God rose against them and he slew the strongest of them, and laid low the picked men of Israel. In spite of all this they still sinned; despite his wonders they did not believe" (Ps 78:21–22, 29–32).

"I told you that you would die for your sins, for you will die in your sins unless you believe that I am he" (Jn 8:24).

While we have a strong tendency to drift from faith, urged on by a world environment that mocks faith and operates almost exclusively on what it can see with biological eyes, the tempter himself, Satan, is most interested in weakening and, if possible, destroying our faith in Christ. It has been his strategy from the beginning. In the garden he began his diabolical plot to destroy

---

[9] Fr. Raniero Cantalamessa, *Life in the Lordship of Christ* (Kansas City, Mo.: Sheed and Ward, 1990), p. 151.

mankind and mock God by trying to insinuate doubt into our first parents' knowledge of God's Word and the intention of God's heart in relation to them: " 'Did God say, "You shall not eat of any tree in the garden"?' And the woman said to the serpent, 'We may eat of the fruit of the trees in the garden; but God said, "You shall not eat of the fruit of the tree which is in the midst of the garden, neither shall you touch it, lest you die." But the serpent said to the woman, 'You will not die. For God knows that when you eat of it your eyes will be opened, and you will be like God, knowing good and evil' " (Gen 3:1–5).

Jesus and the apostles are very aware that "your adversary the devil prowls around like a roaring lion, seeking some one to devour" (1 Pet 5:8).

Jesus specifically warned Peter of the impending satanic assault: "Simon, Simon, behold, Satan demanded to have you, that he might sift you like wheat, but I have prayed for you that your faith may not fail; and when you have turned again, strengthen your brothers" (Lk 22:31–32).

Jesus was so concerned about the massive assault on faith that was to unfold that he makes this sobering statement: "When the Son of Man comes, will he find faith on earth?" (Lk 18:8).

Paul also expresses great concern: "For this reason, when I could bear it no longer, I sent that I might know your faith, for fear that somehow the tempter had tempted you and that our labor would be in vain" (1 Th 3:5).

Sometimes the devil can use extreme subtlety and ungodly complexity to lure us away from the wholehearted trust in Christ that is the key of a fruitful Christian life: "But I am afraid that as the serpent deceived Eve by his cunning, your thoughts will be led astray from a sincere and pure devotion to Christ" (2 Cor 11:3).

But Jesus and the apostles not only point out the problem of the attack on faith but also give us specific advice on how to counter it: "Submit yourselves therefore to God. Resist the devil and he will flee from you" (James 4:7).

"Resist him, firm in your faith, knowing that the same experience of suffering is required of your brotherhood throughout the world" (1 Pet 5:9).

" . . . above all taking the shield of faith, with which you can quench all the flaming darts of the evil one" (Eph 6:16).

As I speak on these topics in different places, I sometimes ask for a show of hands on how many are experiencing an attack on their faith. Most often the majority of those there, and this some-times includes audiences of many thousands, indicate they feel that their faith is under attack. I assume that this is true also of many of you who are reading this right now. If so, I would like to suggest that you stop and pray before we go any farther and do what the apostles have just advised us to do. Let us pray now, holding onto our faith, submitting to God, resisting the devil, and commending ourselves into God's hands, asking his help in with-standing and overcoming this attack. Let us again renounce Satan and all his works and pomps, as we did in baptism and in the annual renewal of our baptismal promises, and reaffirm our faith in Christ and his sufficiency. If we submit to God and resist the devil, he *will* take flight.

> *Lord Jesus, I submit myself to you and the Father again. I want to be under your rule and your protection. I believe in you. I trust you. You are my only hope. I do not accept the lies of the devil. I do not want to yield to his temptations. Help me with your great power. Give me grace to resist him and stand firm in the Faith.*
>
> *I renounce Satan and all his works and all his tempting lies. I belong to Jesus and am under his protection.*

As negative and tormenting as these assaults on faith can be, God arranges for them to play a positive role in the maturing and purification of our faith: "Count it all joy, my brethren, when you meet various trials, for you know that the testing of your faith produces steadfastness. And let steadfastness have its full effect, that you may be perfect and complete, lacking in nothing" (James 1:2–4).

"Now for a little while you may have to suffer various trials, so that the genuineness of your faith, more precious than gold which though perishable is tested by fire, may redound to praise and glory and honor at the revelation of Jesus Christ" (1 Pet 1:6–7).

When we are going through the "many trials", it is very helpful to remember that God has his hands on us, is permitting these trials, and is using the very force of the trials to draw us closer to himself and deepen in us that purity of heart without which we cannot see God. During these times, as always, it is particularly helpful to keep our eyes fixed on Jesus: "Therefore, since we are surrounded by so great a cloud of witnesses, let us also lay aside every weight, and sin which clings so closely, and let us run with perseverance the race that is set before us, looking to Jesus the pioneer and perfecter of our faith, who for the joy that was set before him endured the cross, despising the shame, and is seated at the right hand of the throne of God. Consider him who endured from sinners such hostility against himself, so that you may not grow weary or fainthearted" (Heb 12:1–3).

Jesus inspires our faith; Jesus sustains our faith; Jesus perfects our faith. Just being with Jesus, becoming familiar with his words, remembering who he is and what he has done for us, being with him in prayer, in Christian fellowship (where two or three gather in his name, he is there!) and especially in the Eucharist; all this helps our faith in him, our relationship with him, grow and develop. Paul explicitly spells out in a remarkably logical way how faith comes to us and singles out in particular the role that "hearing" the word of God has in this process. What is true of how faith initially comes to us is also true about how it can grow:

> The word is near you, on your lips and in your heart (that is, the word of faith which we preach); because, if you confess with your lips that Jesus is Lord and believe in your heart that God raised him from the dead, you will be saved. For man believes with his heart and so is justified, and he confesses with his lips and so is saved. The scripture says, "No one who believes in him will be put to shame." For there is no distinction between Jew and Greek; the same Lord is Lord of all and bestows his riches upon all who call upon him. For, "every one who calls upon the name of the Lord will be saved." But how are men to call upon him in whom they have not believed? And how are they to believe in him of whom they have never heard? And how are they to hear without a preacher? And how can

men preach unless they are sent? As it is written, "How beautiful are the feet of those who bring good news!" (Rom 10:8–15).

How important that we hear and read the word of God! How important that we nourish ourselves on his word, as well as his Body and Blood! His word is truly life to our soul, health to our body, hope and strength to our spirit. How important also that we look for opportunities to help others to hear his word as well. What clarity of thought: everyone who calls on the name of the Lord will be saved. But how can they call on him in whom they have not believed? And how can they believe in him of whom they have not heard?

If you have never opened your heart to him before, do so now. He wants to take away your hopelessness and give you real and genuine hope that will not be disappointed. If you have never really surrendered your life to him, do so now. He wants to receive your life back as a gift and care for you tenderly. If you have never given him your hurt, pain, and disappointment, your anger, bitterness, and resentments, do so now. He wants to bring you the freedom that comes from the power to forgive. He will give you that power, and you will gain that freedom. If you have never given him your biggest worries and greatest fears and most profound anxieties, do so now. He wants to give you the peace and assurance that he is with you and for you and is working even now, for all things work out for the good for those who trust him.

Perhaps this prayer will express something of what is in your heart:

Lord Jesus, I come to you weary and burdened, guilty and fearful, hopeless even. I surrender. I give my life back to you. I put my trust in you, the true and only Savior of the world and my Savior. Forgive me my sins. Make me clean again so that the hope of eternal life may arise in my heart. Send me your Spirit, pour out your love into my heart, so I may begin again, believing, hoping, and loving, each day, until we are united forever in heaven.

Maybe some of you who are reading this already believe and have committed your lives to Christ but have drifted away or have grown more distant in your relationship with him—perhaps as a result of pressure, or disappointment, or troubles or disillusionment, or just plain laziness. He wants you back. He wants you close. He died so you could be close to him forever.

Perhaps this prayer will express something of what is in your heart.

Dear Jesus, I want to come back. I want to walk closely with you again. Please forgive me my sin. I believe; help my unbelief. My spirit is willing, but my flesh is weak. Give me the grace so I can be faithful in a daily way and walk closely with you each day. I want again to place everything in your hands. I surrender to you all my concerns and place my trust anew in you.

Those of us who are Catholics have the great opportunity of giving expression to our repentance in the sacrament of reconciliation and of receiving the graces of forgiveness, peace, and healing from Christ in the person of the priest. For those of us who are Catholics, if we are coming back from serious sin, we *need* to avail ourselves of this opportunity so we can be fully reconciled with Christ in his body, the Church.

As we put our faith in Christ, something truly wonderful and powerful is born in our hearts: hope. The great gift of authentic Christian hope is vital today for us both as individuals and as a Church. Let us examine now what Scripture tells us of hope.

Chapter Four

The Birth of Hope

Sometimes just the daily disappointments of life and work cause a feeling of hopelessness to rise in us. Never being able to get ahead financially. Another car repair at an inopportune time. More serious trouble or deep disappointment with a child. Locked in a marriage whose moments of beauty are few and far between. Trapped in a job that is "not going anywhere". Fired. Again. Unable to find a job. Another medical problem. Isolation. Loneliness. Growing older, our body deteriorating. Arguments. Misunderstandings. Anger. Depression. Death of a parent. Death of a friend. Death of a child. Our death.

But it is broader than that. A spirit of hopelessness pervades the very atmosphere in which we live.

As we approach the closing years of the twentieth century, a sense of hopelessness pervades the lives of many of us. Vast numbers are living "lives of quiet desperation". As faith has been destroyed in the lives of millions, so also has hope died, and love grown cold. Being "worldly" does not mean only conspicuous consumption and luxury; it also often means hopelessness and despair. Not only in the war-torn and famine-wracked parts of the earth has hopelessness gained sway but also in the newly "free" countries of the former Soviet Union as well as in the post-Christian cities of Europe and the Americas. The absence of genuine love, tenderness, respect, and fidelity in human relationships has led to a bitterness, cynicism, and despair that have made much of human life a struggle involving money and a futile search marked by loveless sex, filled with suspicion, the fear of betrayal, and incurable disease. This hopelessness, which has led to a cynicism and despair in human relationships, is reflected in the music we listen to; in the television shows and movies we watch; in the violence, rape, and child abuse we regularly read about in our daily newspapers.

A poem written by W. H. Auden effectively communicates this sense of hopelessness that pervades our culture:

> Faces along the bar
> Cling to their average day;
> The lights must never go out,
> The music must always play
> Lest we know where we are,
> Lost in a haunted wood,
> Children afraid of the dark
> Who have never been happy or good.[1]

Millions are asking, sometimes in groans too deep for words: Is there any hope for me? Will my life ever be a success? Will I ever find real love or ever love others truly? Is there really, after all this disappointment and sorrow and tragedy, any hope of "everything working out OK in the end"?

There are certainly enough false hopes, wishful thinking, and ill-founded optimism to go around. If we place our hopes in money, relationships, prestige, self-help techniques, or earthly security of any kind, we are ultimately bound to be disappointed, most often sooner rather than later. Is there any solidly founded hope, not dependent on personality type or worldly circumstances, that is actually accessible to the average person, you and me?

In the midst of all this, no matter what, no matter how many, no matter how long, no matter how apparently hopeless the problems are, the really good news is that there *is* hope *for you*, a hope that is born and nourished through faith in Jesus. This hope is not based on wishful thinking or restricted to certain positive personality types, nor is it the outcome of psychological techniques or theological double-talk. It is born only as we are reborn,

---

[1] "September 1939", in *The English Auden: Poems, Essays and Dramatic Writings,* ed. Edward Mendelson (New York: Random House, 1977).

through faith and baptism, in union with Jesus. And once it is born, it can grow and grow and grow until it reaches its completion as what is hoped for comes to pass: "Blessed be the God and Father of our Lord Jesus Christ! By his great mercy we have been born anew to a living hope through the resurrection of Jesus Christ from the dead, and to an inheritance which is imperishable, undefiled, and unfading, kept in heaven for you, who by God's power are guarded through faith for a salvation ready to be revealed in the last time. In this you rejoice" (1 Pet 1:3–6).

There *really is* cause for rejoicing here. The hope that is born through faith in Christ is based on the real and awesome deeds and words of Jesus, demonstrated most strikingly in his Resurrection from the dead. As we profess our faith in Jesus, we become heirs to the promise of our own glorious resurrection from the dead, and that in the end is the only thing that can make it all worthwhile.

Sometimes the circumstances of our lives can seem completely overwhelming, usually because we have never realized or have forgotten some of the most significant circumstances of our lives. These are, namely, that Jesus has offered up his life *for us,* he has risen from the dead *for us;* he is right now preparing a great heavenly inheritance *for us;* and he is interceding right now, *for us,* in the midst of all the circumstances of our lives.

The prayers of Jesus are powerful and effective. If Elijah stopped the rains in Israel for three and a half years as a result of his prayers, and if the prayers of a righteous person are powerful in their effects,[2] just think how powerful Jesus' prayers are, now, *for us!*

Jesus has not only shown us the way to happiness forever; he himself is that way. He not only reveals to us the truth; he himself is that truth. He not only has come to give us life and life in greater abundance; he himself is that life. He is not only with us but also in us and for us. He not only died on the Cross so our sin and guilt can be washed away but also rose from the dead so all our tears can be wiped away, and he sent us his Holy Spirit so our joy could be full and is with us even now no matter what we may be facing or experiencing. He not only has come to bring peace;

---

[2] James 5:16–18.

he himself is our peace. He not only founded a Church that usually meets in buildings, but he founded a Church that is his very own Body, his very own Bride, a family of brothers and sisters bound for glory.

He is so powerful, so good, so loving, and so wise that even our mistakes, sins, and failures, even all the catastrophies and tragedies, can be used by him for our great good.

The mighty sacrifice of his life is powerful in what it has opened up for us. Right now, through baptism and faith, God is pouring his love and life into our hearts through the Holy Spirit. And this is just the down payment of what he is preparing for us in heaven when we join him where he is, at our deaths or his Second Coming: "Let us hold fast the confession of our hope without wavering, for he who promised is faithful" (Heb 10:23).

There is a profound link between faith, hope, and love: "We always thank God, the Father of our Lord Jesus Christ, when we pray for you, because we have heard of your faith in Christ Jesus and of the love which you have for all the saints, because of the hope laid up for you in heaven" (Col 1:3–4).

Faith can be compared to the roots of a plant, hope to the stem, and love to the fruits: "Therefore, since we are justified by faith, we have peace with God through our Lord Jesus Christ. Through him we have obtained access [by faith] to this grace in which we stand, and we rejoice in our hope of sharing the glory of God. More than that—we rejoice in our sufferings, knowing that suffering produces endurance, and endurance produces character, and character produces hope, and hope does not disappoint us, because God's love has been poured into our hearts through the Holy Spirit which has been given to us" (Rom 5:1–3).

"For through the Spirit, by faith, we wait for the hope of righteousness. For in Christ Jesus neither circumcision nor uncircumcision is of any avail, but faith working through love" (Gal 5:5–6).

In the last analysis, the only thing that really matters in life is that we come to faith in Jesus, so hope can be born and grow and express itself in daily love.

As John Paul II has put it: "The *new Life* that has burst forth in the Resurrection is the world's only hope."[3]

Hope Is for the Future (But Brings Joy and Courage to the Present)

A classic theological definition of hope is "a supernatural virtue by which we firmly trust that God will give us everlasting life and the means to obtain it, because He is faithful to His promises".[4]

Hope is fundamentally connected to the future: "Set your hope fully upon the grace that is coming to you at the revelation of Jesus Christ" (1 Pet 1:13b).

It is the current assurance of something that is not yet fully ours but certainly will be if we continue in union with Jesus. Hope for someone who is a follower of Jesus involves, indeed, "everything working out OK in the end", despite the sorrow, disappointment, and tragedy of this life, a working out so good that it involves resurrection from the dead to eternal life and joy. The object of our hope, then, in the last analysis, is resurrection from the dead: "He saved us . . . by the washing of regeneration and renewal in the Holy Spirit, which he poured out upon us richly through Jesus Christ our Savior, so that we might be justified by his grace and become *heirs* in hope of eternal life. The saying is sure" (Titus 3:5-8).

Have you ever wished that you had a rich aunt or uncle or other friend or relative who would name you in their will? Would it not be great to receive an inheritance like that? It sure would. But whether we receive a material inheritance in this life or not, all of us who have put our faith in Jesus, been baptized and joined to him, and continue in faith and union with him have been named in God the Father's will as coheirs along with Christ and will receive an absolutely stunning inheritance.

Great explorers like Ponce de León expended much time, effort, and wealth in searching for the "fountain of youth". He did

[3] Pope John Paul II, "Jesus' New Life Is the World's Only Hope", *L'Osservatore Romano* (English ed.), August 25, 1993, p. 5.

[4] James F. McElhone, C.S.C., *Particular Examen* (Harrison, N.Y.: Roman Catholic Books, 1952), p. 149.

not find it, but it is available, free, for those who put their trust in Jesus!

Immense effort, time, and wealth are expended today trying to push back death and prolong youth, whether through cosmetics, fitness, diet, or medical research. Yet only relatively modest gains have been made. All of us remain terminally ill, destined to die. How much would men be willing to pay to live forever? A thousand dollars? A million dollars? A billion? Everything we have? What if only a limited number of people were able to obtain the secret of eternal life? What competition there would be for the secret!

The secret is now revealed; the cost is repentance and faith in Jesus, and there is no limit to how many can avail themselves of the offer! "On the last day of the feast, the great day, Jesus stood up and proclaimed, 'If any one thirst, let him come to me and drink. He who believes in me, as the scripture has it, "Out of his heart shall flow rivers of living water." ' Now this he said about the Spirit, which those who believed in him were to receive" (Jn 7:37–39).

The Scripture frequently speaks of the inheritance that those who are faithful to Christ in this life will receive: "And now I commend you to God and to the word of his grace, which is able to build you up and to give you *the inheritance* among all who are sanctified" (Acts 20:32).

"May you be strengthened with all power, according to his glorious might, for all endurance and patience with joy, giving thanks to the Father, who has qualified us to share in *the inheritance* of the saints in light" (Col 1:11–12).

"Whatever your task, work heartily, as serving the Lord and not men, knowing that from the Lord you will receive *the inheritance* as your reward; you are serving the Lord Christ" (Col 3:23–24).

"Therefore he is the mediator of a new covenant, so that those who are called may receive the promised eternal *inheritance,* since a death has occurred which redeems them from the transgressions under the first covenant" (Heb 9:15).

"Blessed be the God and Father of our Lord Jesus Christ! By his great mercy we have been born anew to a living hope through the resurrection of Jesus Christ from the dead, and to an *inheritance* which is imperishable, undefiled, and unfading, kept in heaven for you, who by God's power are guarded through faith for a salvation ready to be revealed in the last time. In this you rejoice" (1 Pet 1:3–6).

"Delivering you from the people and from the Gentiles—to whom I send you to open their eyes, that they may turn from darkness to light and from the power of Satan to God, that they may receive forgiveness of sins and a place among those who are sanctified by faith in me" (Acts 26:17–18).

The Spirit "is the guarantee of our *inheritance* until we acquire possession of it, to the praise of his glory" (Eph 1:14).

"And because you are sons, God has sent the Spirit of his Son into our hearts, crying, 'Abba! Father!' So through God you are no longer a slave but a son, and if a son then an *heir*" (Gal 4:6–7).

"For in Christ Jesus you are all sons of God, through faith.... And if you are Christ's, then you are Abraham's offspring, *heirs* according to promise" (Gal 3:26, 29).

"Having the eyes of your hearts enlightened, that you may know what is the hope to which he has called you, what are the riches of his glorious *inheritance* in the saints" (Eph 1:18).

What is this inheritance? Nothing less than eternal life. Not just unending life, although that it is, but life of an immeasurably higher order, of an immeasurably greater glory and splendor. Like unto life on this earth in this body and yet gloriously renewed and transformed. Beyond our fondest hopes and dreams. Greater than we can imagine.

The words that Scripture uses to describe the inheritance that is ours only point in the direction of indescribable glory. Unfading. Imperishable. Undefiled. Unfading. Full redemption. Riches of glory.

This kingdom, this treasure, this inheritance is truly like the treasure buried in the field or like the "pearl of great price", worth "selling everything" in order to possess it.

How can we enter into such a great inheritance?

Through repentance and faith: "Be sure of this, that no immoral or impure man, or one who is covetous (that is, an idolater), has any *inheritance* in the kingdom of Christ and of God" (Eph 5:5).

"Now the works of the flesh are plain: immorality, impurity, licentiousness, idolatry, sorcery, enmity, strife, jealousy, anger, selfishness, dissension, party spirit, envy, drunkenness, carousing, and the like. I warn you, as I warned you before, that those who do such things *shall not inherit* the kingdom of God" (Gal 5:19–21).

We need to turn from sin and to Jesus and allow him to wash us clean: "Peter said to him, 'You shall never wash my feet.' Jesus answered him, 'If I do not wash you, you have no part in me' " (Jn 13:8).

And we need simply to stay united to Jesus, through thick and thin, through good times and bad times, uniting our suffering to his, for us surely to come into this utterly magnificent inheritance: "For all who are led by the Spirit of God are sons of God. For you did not receive the spirit of slavery to fall back into fear, but you have received the spirit of sonship. When we cry, 'Abba! Father!' it is the Spirit himself bearing witness with our spirit that we are children of God, and if children, then heirs, heirs of God and fellow heirs with Christ, provided we suffer with him in order that we may also be glorified with him" (Rom 8:14–17).

Hope Gives Us Strength Now

In this now-oriented culture anything that has to do with the future can seem somewhat suspect. One critique of Christianity is that its future orientation takes away from attention to the here and now. The truth, though, is that the future hope that we have because of Christ releases an energy, joy, and confidence that make a huge difference for living life and living it abundantly here and now.

Remember the results of a recent study on the link between religious faith and mental health, which we considered in a previous chapter? "Followers of 'that old time religion', a favorite target of comics, may have the last laugh: Their faith gives them a strong mental health edge.... [They] are far more optimistic than followers of moderate or liberal religions, a new study suggests.

" 'We know optimistic people are less vulnerable to depression, and optimism correlates with high achievement', says psychologist Sheena Sethi of Stanford University."[5]

Mental health professionals and many medical doctors tell of the difference hope makes in the recovery and well-being of their patients. The thing about hope is that you cannot manufacture it or fake it. Real, well-grounded hope is born in a relationship with the one who is able to save us from death, God: "And you will have confidence, because there is hope; you will be protected and take your rest in safety" (Job 11:18).

I remember one time on an airplane trip sitting next to a fellow passenger who turned out to be a Southern Baptist minister. We started visiting, and I discovered he was the father of five children and that he and his wife and family were about ready to return to an African country where they were serving as missionaries. The country at the time was a difficult place to live and suffered from political and economic instability. I asked him if he felt that it was a safe place for him to take his family. His answer has remained with me to this day: "The safest place for my family and myself is the place where God wants us to be, doing his will. If I stayed in the most secure American city and it wasn't God's will, I'd be putting my family in grave danger. Our safety, our only place of safety is to be doing his will": "Be strong, and let your heart take courage, all you who wait for the Lord" (Ps 31:24).

"Rejoice in your hope, be patient in tribulation, be constant in prayer" (Rom 12:12).

"They who wait for the Lord shall renew their strength, they shall mount up with wings like eagles, they shall run and not be weary, they shall walk and not faint" (Is 40:31).

What an amazing promise! And it is true. As we hope in the Lord, our strength will be replenished, and we will be able not only to endure in affliction but also to triumph in Christ. Time

[5] "Strict Religious Faith Lifts Mind as Well as Spirit", *USA Today,* August 2, 1993, p. D1.

and time again I have found this to be true in my own life, and I am profoundly grateful to God for the strength he gives me through my faith and hope in him. As a husband and father of six children, in a challenging occupation, I really need to depend on Christ in a daily way for strength, courage, and wisdom to persevere on the way he has set out for me to travel. Having hope that is solidly grounded is essential for going on: "We always thank God, the Father of our Lord Jesus Christ, when we pray for you, because we have heard of your faith in Christ Jesus and of the love you have for all the saints, because of *the hope* laid up for you in heaven" (Col 1:3–5).

Hope helps us to get out of bed in the morning and try again. Hope moves us to keep on serving, keep on loving, keep on forgiving, keep on praying. What joy, what delight, to have real hope because of our relationship with God; how life-giving, energizing, freeing. Indeed, "happy is he whose help is the God of Jacob, whose hope is in the Lord his God" (Ps 146:5).

When we live reconciled to God through Jesus Christ, in the power of the Holy Spirit, nothing can ultimately destroy us; whether in death or life we share in the ultimate and glorious victory of the risen Christ. This was the "secret" of the freedom from fear that Paul had in his challenging life: "It is my eager expectation and hope that I shall not be at all ashamed, but that with full courage now as always Christ will be honored in my body, whether by life or by death" (Phil 1:20).

The hope we have because of Christ and our relationship to him gives us the courage and freedom to speak and act as we are moved by his Spirit: "Since we have such a hope, we are very bold" (2 Cor 3:12).

As Catholics we are sometimes characterized by our lack of boldness and confidence when it comes to our own relationship with God or sharing the good news with others. While certain cultural factors are relevant, I believe the main factor is a fundamental lack of clarity and understanding about the basis of our standing with God, about the basics of salvation.

As Father Avery Dulles, a prominent Catholic theologian, has pointed out, "Too many Catholics of our day seem never to have encountered Christ. They know a certain amount about him from the teaching of the Church, but they lack direct personal familiarity. ... The first and highest priority is for the Church to proclaim the good news concerning Jesus Christ as a joyful message to all the world."[6]

Catholics quite simply need to know Christ more. We need to know how great his love is, how great his sacrifice for us is, how steadfast his love for us is, so we can repent and believe and let the hope that brings freedom and boldness be born and grow in our hearts.

Even if, as we Catholics believe, when we die there may still be a need for a final purification before we are able to see God face to face, there is already cause for great rejoicing. John Paul II has emphasized this important but often underemphasized extraordinarily positive aspect of the reality of Purgatory.

"One further point should be made: life's earthly journey has an end that, if a person reaches it in friendship with God, coincides with the first moment of eternal bliss. Even if in that passage to heaven the soul must undergo the purification of the last impurities through Purgatory, it is already filled with light, certitude, and joy, because the person knows that he belongs forever to God."[7]

While there are many in the world today who are hopeless, and it seems their numbers are growing if the startling increase in youth suicides is any indicator, there are also many who are clinging desperately to false hopes. It is possible to "hope" in a completely groundless manner.

Groundless Hope

The only solid basis of hope that any man can have is if he has cast himself on the mercy of Jesus Christ and become heir to the

[6] Fr. Avery Dulles, S.J., *John Paul II and the New Evangelization* (New York: Fordham University, 1992), pp. 16–17.

[7] John Paul II, "Spirit: Pledge of Eschatological Hope", *L'Osservatore Romano* (English ed.), July 8, 1991, p. 11.

glorious future of Jesus and those who are united to him. To hope in anyone or anything else is to assure oneself a future of bitter disappointment: "The hope of the righteous ends in gladness, but the expectation of the wicked comes to nought" (Prov 10:28).

"When the wicked dies, his hope perishes, and the expectation of the godless comes to nought" (Prov 11:7).

"Such are the paths of all who forget God; the hope of the godless man shall perish" (Job 8:13).

"They shall be dismayed and confounded because of Ethiopia their hope and of Egypt their boast" (Is 20:5).

"Put no confidence in extortion, set no vain hopes on robbery; if riches increase, set not your heart on them" (Ps 62:10).

The story of Israel is the story of a people who time and time again put their hope or trust in someone or something other than God himself and eventually experienced the bitter consequences. Whether it was a seemingly shrewd alliance with neighboring countries or a trust in their own strength or wealth, they discovered repeatedly that all their blessings came from God and only God and that their only hope rested in trusting in and obeying God. Jesus himself warned of the same danger to those who were his disciples: "And do not seek what you are to eat and what you are to drink, nor be of anxious mind. For all the nations of the world seek these things; and your Father knows that you need them. Instead, seek his kingdom, and these things shall be yours as well" (Lk 12:29–31).

Solidly Grounded Hope Is in the Lord and His Word

"Then you will know that I am the Lord; those who wait for me shall not be put to shame" (Is 49:23).

"Blessed is the man who trusts in the Lord, whose trust is the Lord" (Jer 17:7).

"And now, Lord, for what do I wait? My hope is in thee" (Ps 39:7).

"For thou, O Lord, art my hope, my trust, O Lord, from my youth" (Ps 71:5).

"Remember thy word to thy servant, in which thou hast made me hope" (Ps 119:49).

"Your faith and hope are in God" (1 Pet 1:21b).

Ultimately, Christ himself is our hope, and most strikingly of all Christ in us, our hope for glory: "Paul, an apostle of Christ Jesus by command of God our Savior and of *Christ Jesus our hope*" (1 Tim 1:1).

"To them God chose to make known how great among the Gentiles are the riches of the glory of this mystery, which is *Christ in you, the hope of glory*" (Col 1:27).

Or as Julian of Norwich puts it, true hope is in God's "endless love".[8]

How Can Hope Be Born and Grow?

The same way that faith is born and grows: "For, 'every one who calls upon the name of the Lord will be saved.' But how are men to call upon him in whom they have not believed? And how are they to believe in him of whom they have never heard? And how are they to hear without a preacher? And how can men preach unless they are sent? As it is written, 'How beautiful are the feet of those who preach good news!' . . . *Faith comes from what is heard,* and what is heard comes by the preaching of Christ" (Rom 10:13–17).

"Whatever was written in former days was written for our instruction, that by steadfastness and by the encouragement of the scriptures we might have hope" (Rom 15:4).

Faith comes through hearing, and so does hope. Hearing the word of God and the wonderful promises and deeds of Christ increases our faith and our hope. Knowing Jesus and his word more helps us to believe more and hope more. Prayer. Scripture reading. Regular contact with others who believe and hope in him. The Eucharist. Spiritual reading. Faith- and hope-filled music. Contact with Christ in his word, his Spirit, his Body, his people,

---

[8] Julian of Norwich, *Showings,* chap. 47.

his gifts helps us grow in faith and hope. Hope comes from God. Seeking God, hungering for him, going where we can have contact with him, doing what will bring us closer. Seeking him and his kingdom, first: "For God alone my soul waits in silence, for my hope is from him" (Ps 62:5).

"You have heard [of this hope] before in the word of the truth, the gospel which has come to you, as indeed in the whole world it is bearing fruit and growing—so among yourselves" (Col 1:5–6).

"But whatever gain I had, I counted as loss for the sake of Christ. Indeed I count everything as loss because of the surpassing worth of knowing Christ Jesus my Lord. For his sake I have suffered the loss of all things, and count them as refuse, in order that I may gain Christ and be found in him, not having a righteousness of my own, based on law, but that which is through faith in Christ, the righteousness from God that depends on faith; that I may know him and the power of his resurrection, and may share his sufferings, becoming like him in his death, that if possible I may attain the resurrection from the dead.

"Not that I have already obtained this or am already perfect; but I press on to make it my own, because Christ Jesus has made me his own. Brethren, I do not consider that I have made it my own; but one thing I do, forgetting what lies behind and straining forward to what lies ahead, I press on toward the goal for the prize of the upward call of God in Christ Jesus. Let those of us who are mature be thus minded; and if in anything you are otherwise minded, God will reveal that also to you. Only let us hold true to what we have attained" (Phil 3:7–16).

The more we give ourselves to him, the more we realize he is our treasure, the more we seek him, night and day, the more he is able to give himself to us. And the more that faith, hope, and love will grow in us and give birth to security, confidence, joy, peace, and freedom.

My prayer for you, indeed, for all of us, is the same as Paul's: "We always thank God, the Father of our Lord Jesus Christ, when we pray for you, because we have heard of your faith in Christ Jesus and of the love which you have for all the saints, because of the hope laid up for you in heaven" (Col 1:3–4).

"May the God of hope fill you with all joy and peace in believing, so that by the power of the Holy Spirit you may abound in hope" (Rom 15:13).

"That the God of our Lord Jesus Christ, the Father of glory, may give you a spirit of wisdom and of revelation in the knowledge of him, having the eyes of your hearts enlightened, that you may know what is the hope to which he has called you, what are the riches of his glorious inheritance in the saints, and what is the immeasurable greatness of his power in us who believe" (Eph 1:17–19).

May it indeed be so!

Chapter Five

The Greatest of These

One of the great philosophical questions is: Why is there being rather than nothingness? Why does anything exist at all?

A well-known philosophical principle is: Good is diffusive of itself. We are so used to the daily routine of life that we seldom step back and notice the obvious. We exist, and we do not have to.

God in his great goodness and love brought into existence us and the whole universe as a way of sharing his immense glory. The initiative has been with him since the beginning. Out of love he created us. He created us with a dignity and freedom that partook of something of his own nature. In his own image we were created, in the image of God; male and female were we created. He did not make us as robots or automatons; he bestowed on us the dignity of freedom.

When we used that freedom to turn away from him in a foolish quest for eternal life apart from him, he did not destroy us or abandon us to our nothingness but instead determined to offer us a chance at restoration and reconciliation in a display of love even more breathtaking than the creation.

While we were still locked in our sin—and sin is nothing if it is not ugly—in our hostility, selfishness, lust, greed, and blasphemous arrogance, he loved us and came to us in an overwhelmingly generous act of love: "But God shows his love for us in that while we were yet sinners Christ died for us" (Rom 5:8).

"And you, who once were estranged and hostile in mind, doing evil deeds, he has now reconciled in his body of flesh by his death, in order to present you holy and blameless and irreproachable before him, provided that you continue in the faith, stable and steadfast, not shifting from the hope of the gospel which you heard" (Col 1:21–23).

"In this the love of God was made manifest among us, that God sent his only Son into the world, so that we might live through him. In this is love, not that we have loved God but that he loved us and sent his Son to be the expiation for our sins" (1 Jn 4:9–10).

Father Raniero Cantalamessa makes the interesting point that perhaps because of the natural tendency of human reason or perhaps because of the influence of Aristotelian philosophy on the life of the Church, we have a tendency to put first the duty of us loving God rather than the primary fact of God loving us first: "But revelation gives more importance to the second meaning; to God's love for us rather than to our love for God. Aristotle said that God moves the world in so far as he is loved, that is, in so far as he is the object of love and the final cause of all its creatures (Metaf. XII, 7, 1072b); but the Bible says the exact opposite, that God creates and moves the world in so far as he loves the world. Concerning God's love, therefore, the most important thing is not that man should love God but that God loves man and that he loved him first. . . . Everything else depends on this including our own chance of loving God."[1]

"For we ourselves were once foolish, disobedient, led astray, slaves to various passions and pleasures, passing our days in malice and envy, hated by men and hating one another; but when the goodness and loving kindness of God our Savior appeared, he saved us, not because of deeds done by us in righteousness, but in virtue of his own mercy, by the washing of regeneration and renewal in the Holy Spirit, which he poured out upon us richly through Jesus Christ our Savior, so that we might be justified by his grace and become heirs in hope of eternal life. The saying is sure" (Titus 3:3–8).

"See what love the Father has given us, that we should be called children of God; and so we are" (1 Jn 3:1).

---

[1] Fr. Raniero Cantalamessa, *Life in the Lordship of Christ* (Kansas City, Mo.: Sheed and Ward, 1990), p. 3.

"In him we have redemption through his blood, the forgiveness of our trespasses, according to the riches of his grace which he lavished upon us" (Eph 1:7–8).

"For God so loved the world that he gave his only Son, that whoever believes in him should not perish but have eternal life" (Jn 3:16).

Again, as Father Cantalamessa points out, drawing from the tradition of the Church:

> The whole Bible, St. Augustine observes, does nothing but tell of God's love (*Cat.rud.* I, 8, 4; PL 40, 319); it is, so to say, full of it. This is the message that supports and explains all the other messages. The love of God is the answer to all the "why's" in the Bible; the why of Creation, the why of the Incarnation, the why of Redemption. . . . If the written word of the Bible could be changed into a spoken word and become one single voice, this voice, more powerful than the roaring of the sea would cry out: *The Father loves you!* (Jn 16:27). Everything that God does and says in the Bible is love, even God's anger is nothing but love. God "is" love! It has been said that it is not so important to know whether God exists or not; what is important is to know whether he is love (Kierkegaard, *The Gospel of Suffering,* IV). And the Bible assures us that he is love![2]

> And you he made alive, when you were dead through the trespasses and sins in which you once walked, following the course of this world, following the prince of the power of the air, the spirit that is now at work in the sons of disobedience. Among these we all once lived in the passions of our flesh, following the desires of body and mind, and so we were by nature children of wrath, like the rest of mankind. But God, who is rich in mercy, out of the great love with which he loved us, even when we were dead through our trespasses, made us alive together with Christ (by grace you have been saved), and raised us up with him, and made us sit with him in the heavenly places in Christ Jesus, that in the coming ages he might show the immeasurable riches of his grace in kindness toward us in Christ Jesus. For by grace you have been saved through faith; and this is not your own doing, it is the gift of

[2] Ibid., pp. 3–4.

God — not because of works, lest any man should boast. For we are
his workmanship, created in Christ Jesus for good works, which
God prepared beforehand" (Eph 2:1–10).

How extraordinary is the love of God! How undeserved, how
unmerited, how generous, how far beyond what we could have
asked or imagined. And we are getting just glimpses of it, although
what inspired glimpses! Scripture hints about even more wonderful
things unfolding in the "ages to come", even greater manifestations and celebrations of the unfathomable love of God way
beyond our present experience or ability to comprehend: he
"raised us up with him, and made us sit with him in the heavenly
place in Christ Jesus, that in the coming ages he might show the
immeasurable riches of his grace in kindness toward us in Christ
Jesus" (Eph 2:6–7).

"Beloved, we are God's children now; it does not yet appear
what we shall be, but we know that when he appears we shall be
like him, for we shall see him as he is. And every one who thus
hopes in him purifies himself as he is pure" (1 Jn 3:2–3).

"I consider that the sufferings of this present time are not worth
comparing with the glory that is to be revealed to us. For the
creation waits with eager longing for the revealing of the sons of
God. . . . We know that the whole creation has been groaning in
travail together until now; and not only the creation, but we
ourselves, who have the first fruits of the Spirit, groan inwardly as
we wait for adoption as sons, the redemption of our bodies. For in
this hope we were saved. Now hope that is seen is not hope. For
who hopes for what he sees? But if we hope for what we do not
see, we wait for it with patience" (Rom 8:18–19, 22–25).

Something truly extraordinary has happened in the creation
and redemption of the world; something truly extraordinary
awaits us in the future as God prepares to manifest his gracious,
saving love in amazing ways. O the depth and the riches and the
greatness of the mercy and love of God!

One of the greatest depths of God's love involves his breathtaking humility.

The Humility of God

God does not force us to love him. If he did, it would not really be love. He shows an immense respect for our freedom and invites but does not force. I would go so far as to say that the respect he shows us, his humility, is scandalous.

I remember as a young boy, perhaps as a preteen, praying that God would take away my freedom to reject him. Thanks to the grace of God working through my parents and Church, I was growing up with a genuine love and appreciation for God and never wanted to do anything to offend him or reject him. I was afraid, and rightly so, of offending him or even rejecting him as I grew older. God did not grant my request, and I did go through some painful times as I "grew up", but I know now that unless love is freely given, it really is not love. God in his great wisdom has decided that the preciousness of love freely given outweighs the awful cost of the probable rejection of many. Freely given love must really be special for it to be worth such a risk of rejection. That is exactly what his love is like. May we recognize the holy depth of humble love revealed in the coming of Jesus!

> In the beginning was the Word, and the Word was with God, and the Word was God. He was in the beginning with God; all things were made through him, and without him was not anything made that was made. In him was life, and the life was the light of men. The light shines in the darkness, and the darkness has not overcome it. . . . He was in the world, and the world was made through him, yet the world knew him not. He came to his own home, and his own people received him not. But to all who received him, who believed in his name, he gave power to become children of God; who were born, not of blood nor of the will of the flesh nor of the will of man, but of God. And the Word became flesh and dwelt among us, full of grace and truth; we have beheld his glory, glory as of the only Son from the Father (Jn 1:1–5, 10–14).

May we be given the grace to weep at these words: "He was in the world, and the world was made through him, yet the world knew him not. He came to his own home, and his own people received him not."

He wept, in love and sorrow, as he was rejected by his own. May the Spirit of God join us to him in his love and sorrow, for if we do not share his sorrow, we will not share his glory. Love unites us with the Beloved in sorrow as well as in joy. It reminds me of the words of Jesus to St. Margaret Mary: "Behold this heart which has so loved men, and is so little loved in return": "And when he drew near and saw the city he wept over it, saying, 'Would that even today you knew the things that make for peace! But now they are hid from your eyes. . . . you did not know the time of your visitation' " (Lk 19:41–42, 44).

The humility of God to come to his own and not overwhelm them with his divinity; the humility of God to come, showing a depth of love the world has never seen. A pure love, an unselfish love, a love that had the good of the loved at heart, a love that had treasures to share and longed to share them, a love that had eternal life to give and wanted to give it. A love that was hidden and humble, lowly and meek; a love that could be rejected, and was, and is: Jesus, "though he was in the form of God, did not count equality with God a thing to be grasped, but emptied himself, taking the form of a servant, being born in the likeness of men. And being found in human form he humbled himself and became obedient unto death, even death on a cross. Therefore God has highly exalted him and bestowed on him the name which is above every name, that at the name of Jesus every knee should bow, in heaven and on earth and under the earth, and every tongue confess that Jesus Christ is Lord, to the glory of God the Father" (Phil 2:6–11).

The Father is giving a great and precious gift to men in the Person of his Son, Jesus. A gift can be received; a gift can also be rejected. The gift is the gift of pure and holy love, of eternal love, a love stronger than death that will save all those who trust themselves to it. But Jesus can save only those who trust him, those who surrender to his love, those who accept being loved by him. Pride often gets in the way: "Jesus, knowing that the Father had given all things into his hands, and that he had come from God and was going to God, rose from supper, laid aside his garments, and girded himself with a towel. Then he poured water into a basin, and began to wash the disciples' feet, and to wipe them with the towel with which he was girded. He came to Simon Peter; and Peter said to him, 'Lord, do you wash my feet?' Jesus answered him, 'What I am doing you do not know now, but afterward you will understand.' Peter said to him, 'You shall never wash my feet.' Jesus answered him, 'If I do not wash you, you have no part in me.' Simon Peter said to him, 'Lord, not my feet only but also my hands and my head' " (Jn 13:3–9).

It is sometimes more difficult to be loved than to love, to accept love than to give love, particularly for people who pride themselves on being "strong" or "together". It is humbling in a way to receive and accept love. It makes us vulnerable, revealing a need, a humanness, a lack of completeness. It also draws forth a reciprocal response that further makes us vulnerable. When Jesus approaches to love us, we can feel threatened, vulnerable, and draw back or close ourselves off. We can feel fear or anxiety, dimly wondering if we can survive the surrender and the upheaval in the carefully constructed approach to life that has shaped our personality and relationships. To let go and accept being loved with the immense love of Jesus, and to love in return, is the only way of reaching heaven. In fact, it is the definition of heaven, and it needs to begin now.

Peter was humbled by Jesus' humility. Peter was not prepared to be loved in such a humble and profound way. Yet when Jesus indicated to Peter it was the only way Peter could really be connected to Jesus, Peter responded in total surrender. It was not a surrender that made him perfect, but it was a surrender that enabled him to experience being loved perfectly. Perhaps it was the memory of that love that enabled him to repent and return after his terrible fall rather than kill himself in despair as Judas did.

It is the humble pouring out of the life of Jesus that saves the world; it is our receiving that humble love that saves us. Jesus, out of the depths of his humble love, calls out to us: "Come to me, all who labor and are heavy laden, and I will give you rest. Take my yoke upon you, and learn from me; for I am gentle and lowly in heart, and you will find rest for your selves. For my yoke is easy, and my burden is light" (Mt 11:28–30).

In the face of such love, of such mystery, of such depth, words fail us. Only love calling to love, humility to humility suffices. In fact, that is how it all began:

> In the sixth month the angel Gabriel was sent from God to a city of Galilee named Nazareth, to a virgin betrothed to a man whose name was Joseph, of the house of David; and the virgin's name was Mary. And he came to her and said, "Hail, O favored one, the Lord is with you!" But she was greatly troubled at the saying, and considered in her mind what sort of greeting this might be. And the angel said to her, "Do not be afraid, Mary, for you have found favor with God. And behold, you will conceive in your womb and bear a son, and you shall call his name Jesus. He will be great, and will be called Son of the Most High; and the Lord God will give to him the throne of his father David, and he will reign over the house of Jacob for ever; and of his kingdom there will be no end." And Mary said to the angel, "How shall this be, since I have no husband?" And the angel said to her, "The Holy Spirit will come upon you, and the power of the Most High will overshadow you; therefore the child to be born will be called holy, the Son of God. And behold your kinswoman Elizabeth in her old age has also conceived a son; and this is the sixth month with her who was called barren. For with God nothing will be impossible." And Mary said, "Behold, I am the handmaid of the Lord; let it be to me according to your word." And the angel departed from her (Lk 1:26–38).

Mary was afraid at the approach of Divine Love but responded to the grace God was giving her to surrender. Her whole life changed with that humble Yes. And so did ours. Her heart was so full of joy and wonder at the greatness of God and the wonders of his love that she sang out in response to Elizabeth's greeting:

> "Blessed is she who believed that there would be a fulfilment of what was spoken to her from the Lord." And Mary said, "My soul magnifies the Lord, and my spirit rejoices in God my Savior, for he has regarded the low estate of his handmaiden.

For behold, henceforth all generations will call me blessed; for he who is mighty has done great things for me, and holy is his name. And his mercy is on those who fear him from generation to generation. He has shown strength with his arm, he has scattered the proud in the imagination of their hearts, he has put down the mighty from their thrones, and exalted those of low degree; he has filled the hungry with good things, and the rich he has sent empty away. He has helped his servant Israel, in remembrance of his mercy, as he spoke to our fathers, to Abraham and to his posterity for ever" (Lk 1:45–55).

The humility of God approached the God-given humility of Mary, a daughter of men, and her response gave hope to us all.

The Example of Humble Love

The pattern of humility we see in the Divine Love is a pattern explicitly offered as a pattern that the Spirit of God in his mercy and wisdom will draw us into. What Jesus did and how he did it are intended to be examples of what the life of heaven is like and the life of the redeemed is also to become, starting already in this life.

In some of the very passages we have examined to understand better the humility of God's love we see, along with the striking descriptions, exhortations to follow the pattern ourselves now that the grace of God is at work in our life to make such humble love possible.

The striking hymn of the servanthood of Christ in Philippians begins with this exhortation: "Have this mind among yourselves, which was in Christ Jesus" (Phil 2:5).

Also, when we learn from him, who is meek and lowly of heart, what we learn are humility and meekness. Scripture also indicates that because God is giving us the grace to humble ourselves, we can "lean into" humility, as it were: "But he gives more grace; therefore it says, 'God opposes the proud, but gives grace to the humble' " (James 4:6).

"Humble yourselves therefore under the mighty hand of God, that in due time he may exalt you" (1 Pet 5:6).

"Whoever exalts himself will be humbled, and whoever humbles himself will be exalted" (Mt 23:12).

The pattern of humble love is to be characteristic not just of our relationship with God but also of our relationships with one another. The love with which we are loved by God frees us, calls us, and empowers us to love one another.

Love One Another

The greatness of Christ's sacrifice releases a power into the lives of those in union with him that as it purifies us and frees us progressively enables us to grow into the pattern of his love in our relationships with others. So great are the sacrifice and the Covenant made with us in his blood, so great is the power released into our lives, that Jesus speaks of a "new" Commandment that summarizes what his will is for our relationships with one another: "A new commandment I give to you, that you love one another; even as I have loved you, that you also should love one another. By this all men will know that you are my disciples, if you have love for one another" (Jn 13:34–35).

"As the Father has loved me, so have I loved you; abide in my love. If you keep my commandments, you will abide in my love, just as I have kept my Father's commandments and abide in his love. These things I have spoken to you, that my joy may be in you, and that your joy may be full. This is my commandment, that you love one another as I have loved you. Greater love has no man than this, that a man lay down his life for his friends" (Jn 15:9–13).

Jesus has taken the disciples up to the top of a high diving board and is now telling them to jump. He is telling them that they are expected now to enter into the realm of humble, steadfast love that is characteristic of the relationships between Father, Son, and Holy Spirit. He is inviting them to step into divine life and love and to allow the Father, Son, and Holy Spirit to impart their own life and the pattern of their love to "mere mortals". The implication is that the life of discipleship, of renouncing self to take up the cross of humble, steadfast love, is the life of God himself, is the life of heaven itself. As we progressively surrender to God's love and enter into the pattern of his love in relationship with others, we are promised that our joy will be complete.

This love is neither impersonal nor inhuman. It is, when lived authentically, intensely human and intensely personal. "Agape" love is not love freed of emotion; it is love freed of impurity.

Sometimes we can have a distorted notion of what the love of God is and therefore of what our love for one another should be, a notion that is affected by the influence of Greek philosophy on certain approaches to spirituality. Properly understood, God's love is passionate and compassionate, and our love for one another is to be as truly human and fervent as it is pure:

> The theme of the compassion of the Father disappeared from the language and conscience of the Church; it was completely disregarded. ... The general and inexorable process of adaptation to the culture of the time caused the Biblical idea of God's suffering to be sacrificed to the Greek idea of God's impassibility. It was also influenced by the fact that the impassibility (*apatheia*) became, in certain monasteries, the highest ascetic ideal, the very peak of sanctity, causing it to be supremely attributed to God. "Thus ontological metaphysics was able to penetrate theology gradually and definitely supplanting the biblical way of thinking. ... The immediate consequence was that the image of God as defined by tradition took on, against the intentions of the Councils of Nicaea and Constantinople, the typically Greek features of an immobile and indifferent God" (W. Kasper, *Jesus der Christus,* III, 1, 2, Mainz, 1974).[3]

St. Augustine, for all his sensitivity of conscience and ideal of high holiness, very early on reacted against a certain interpretation of the Greek ideal of *apatheia* — freedom from passion. He saw the progress of the Christian life as rightly ordering our passions, not destroying them. "If that is to be called apathy (apathia), where the mind is the subject of no emotion, then who would not consider this insensibility to be worse than all vices?"[4]

[3] Ibid., pp. 107–8.
[4] Augustine, *City of God,* xiv, 9.

Augustine pointed out that Christ experienced all human emotions—sorrow, fear, compassion, love, delight—fully and really and declared of those who think they have put emotion behind them that "such persons rather lose all humanity rather than obtain true tranquillity. For a thing is not necessarily right because it is inflexible, nor healthy because it is insensible."[5]

"Let love be genuine; hate what is evil, hold fast to what is good; love one another with brotherly affection; outdo one another in showing honor" (Rom 12:9–10).

"Let all that you do be done in love" (1 Cor 16:14).

"I therefore, a prisoner for the Lord, beg you to live a life worthy of the calling to which you have been called, with all lowliness and meekness, with patience, forbearing one another in love" (Eph 4:1–2).

" . . . The aim of our charge is love that issues from a pure heart, and a good conscience and sincere faith" (1 Tim 1:5).

"Having purified your souls by your obedience to the truth for a sincere love of the brethren, love one another earnestly from the heart" (1 Pet 1:22).

Even the Spanish mystics, John of the Cross and Teresa of Avila, well known for their intensive treatment of the purification needed in order to be fully united with God, also speak of the intensity of human love that should flow from a pure heart. As Father Dubay puts it in his commentary on their work: "A burning love for God does imply and bring about a disappearance of self-centered clingings and egoisms, but it does not destroy the reciprocity of interpersonal human love. On the contrary, divine love intensifies human love. Reality, another name for sanctity, is an integrated whole: everything fits with and reinforces everything else. Truth is indeed symphonic."[6]

C. S. Lewis makes the same point in his typically breathtakingly insightful way: "When I have learnt to love God better than my earthly dearest, I shall love my earthly dearest better

---

[5] Ibid.

[6] Fr. Thomas Dubay, S.M., *Fire Within* (San Francisco: Ignatius Press, 1989), p. 277.

than I do now. In so far as I learn to love my earthly dearest at the expense of God and instead of God, I shall be moving toward the state in which I shall not love my earthly dearest at all. When first things are put first, second things are not suppressed but increased."[7]

In Deeds, Not Just Words

Christ's love was expressed not just in words but also in deeds: daily deeds of patient, humble, loving service; extraordinary deeds of healing, deliverance, preaching, teaching, and miracles; and the most extraordinary deed of all, becoming man, in obedience to the Father, an obedience that led to total surrender in death on the Cross.

Faith, hope, and love, if they are genuine, will lead to walking in the deeds that God has prepared in advance for us. Faith releases power to act; hope gives us motivation to do; love impels us to love, in deed as well as word.

In fact, love that expresses itself in deeds is the measure of true spirituality, the measure of authentic relationship with God: "By this we know love, that he laid down his life for us; and we ought to lay down our lives for the brethren. But if any one has the world's goods and sees his brother in need, yet closes his heart against him, how does God's love abide in him? Little children, let us not love in word or speech but in deed and in truth" (1 Jn 3:16–18).

"Beloved, let us love one another; for love is of God, and he who loves is born of God and knows God. He who does not love does not know God; for God is love" (1 Jn 4:7–8).

"We know that we have passed out of death into life, because we love the brethren. He who does not love remains in death" (1 Jn 3:14).

"By this it may be seen who are the children of God, and who

[7] C. S. Lewis, "Letter to a Lady", November 8, 1952, in W. H. Lewis, ed., *Letters of C. S. Lewis,* p. 248; cited in: Dubay, *Fire Within,* p. 286.

are the children of the devil: whoever does not do right is not of God, nor he who does not love his brother. For this is the message which you have heard from the beginning, that we should love one another" (1 Jn 3:10–11).

"If any one says, 'I love God,' and hates his brother, he is a liar; for he who does not love his brother whom he has seen, cannot love God whom he has not seen. And this commandment we have from him, that he who loves God should love his brother also" (1 Jn 4:20–21).

It is strong, clear, and challenging. It reminds me of what someone once said: "It's not the parts of the Bible that I don't understand that bother me, but the parts that I do understand."

But Jesus does not just invite us to jump off the diving board (or step out of the boat) and leave us to our own resources. He jumps off with us, walks on the water with us, and does all he can not just by his example but also by his personal presence with us, his steadfastly loving us and teaching us, to help us to "grow into" the sacrificial love of the Trinity.

Of course none of this is possible except for the gift of the Spirit, with which the law of God is now written on our hearts, which we will consider shortly.

It is a lifelong process. But it is sure good to get started: repenting, forgiving, asking for his help. If we run into blocks and obstacles, there are all kinds of books today and small groups of Christians who can help us remove the obstacles and open our hearts wider to forgiveness and love, in deed as well as in word.

Jesus also knows that sometimes we just cannot learn through "teachings" or words but that a certain amount of suffering is necessary to break our pride, humble our hearts, and widen them to mercy and compassion. He is the divine physician and will do whatever soul surgery is necessary so we can walk in love as his beloved children. We can trust his skillful hand on our lives, ordering the events and circumstances of our lives for our good and his glory.

Jesus especially calls us to "love one another", referring to our fellow Christians, as a sign of his presence among his people, who have responded to the offer of salvation. But he also makes clear that his love, and our love, is to be inclusive and is to reach out to all of humanity.

The Inclusiveness of God's Love

Sometimes "religion" can become closed in on itself, self-righteous, and judgmental and condemnatory of those "outside" it: a sad but common perversion of what God intended the gathering of his people to be. Rather than loving those "outside", our fallen human natures tend to use "our religion" as a bolster for our own egos, as a way of feeling superior to others. We make a system or ideology out of the living union with Jesus, or as a substitute for that union, and use it to judge and condemn others. How different from what Jesus intended and intends!

> "But I say to you that hear, Love your enemies, do good to those who hate you, bless those who curse you, pray for those who abuse you. To him who strikes you on the cheek, offer the other also; and from him who takes away your coat do not withhold even your shirt. Give to every one who begs from you; and of him who takes away your goods do not ask them again. And as you wish that men would do to you, do so to them.
>
> "If you love those who love you, what credit is that to you? For even sinners love those who love them. And if you do good to those who do good to you, what credit is that to you? For even sinners do the same. And if you lend to those from whom you hope to receive, what credit is that to you? Even sinners lend to sinners, to receive as much again. But love your enemies, and do good, and lend, expecting nothing in return; and your reward will be great, and you will be sons of the Most High; for he is kind to the ungrateful and the selfish. Be merciful, even as your Father is merciful.
>
> "Judge not, and you will not be judged; condemn not, and you will not be condemned; forgive, and you will be forgiven; give, and it will be given to you; good measure, pressed down, shaken together, running over, will be put into your lap. For the measure you give will be the measure you get back" (Lk 6:27–38).

When Jesus warns against judging and condemning, he is not ruling out discerning the difference between good and evil. He is not ruling out what is counseled elsewhere in Scripture: admonishing , exhorting, speaking the truth in love. He is not ruling out appealing to those locked in sin to repent or turn to the Lord or abandon their sin. He is not ruling out making a judgment in situations where we have a responsibility to do so. He is not ruling out appealing to legitimately established Church "courts" to settle serious matters. He is ruling out the smug, self-righteous definitive ruling on another's worth or value or standing in the sight of God, which is only God's place to do. That judgment, and subsequent acquittal or condemnation, belongs only to God. Once again he is looking for all things to be done in humble, steadfast, merciful love, and he does not want that love to be restricted to just our own: our own type, our own class, our own denomination or church, our own movement or group, our own race or sex, our own "religion".

The so-called wars of religion that have occurred throughout history and are occurring today are an abomination to the Lord. Whether as a rallying point against communism or a marker of identity in ethnic conflicts or a "key" to health and prosperity, religion is not to be used for our own ends. True religion is not the evil projection of our ego onto our ethnic group, religious affiliation, denominational or church identity, or national identity, but rather: "Religion that is pure and undefiled before God and the Father is this: to visit orphans and widows in their affliction, and to keep oneself unstained from the world" (James 1:27).

> Is such the fast that I choose, a day for a man to humble himself? Is it to bow down his head like a rush, and to spread sackcloth and ashes under him? Will you call this a fast, and a day acceptable to the Lord? Is not this the fast that I choose: to loose the bonds of wickedness, to undo the thongs of the yoke, to let the oppressed go free, and to break every yoke? Is it not to share your bread with the hungry, and bring the homeless poor into your house; when you see the naked, to cover him, and not to hide yourself from your own flesh? Then shall your light break forth like the dawn, and your healing shall spring up speedily;

your righteousness shall go before you, the glory of the Lord shall be your rear guard. Then you shall call, and the Lord will answer; you shall cry, and he will say, Here I am. If you take away from the midst of you the yoke, the pointing of the finger, and speaking wickedness, if you pour yourself out for the hungry and satisfy the desire of the afflicted, then shall your light rise in the darkness and your gloom be as the noonday. And the Lord will guide you continually, and satisfy your desire with good things, and make your bones strong; and you shall be like a watered garden, like a spring of water, whose waters fail not. And your ancient ruins shall be rebuilt; you shall raise up the foundations of many generations; you shall be called the repairer of the breach, the restorer of streets to dwell in (Is 58:5–12).

Deep within our hearts is a selfish tendency to narrow the circle of love, to exclude others from our love and from the love of God. Even those who were closest to Jesus, even after Pentecost, had to struggle with this tendency. It took extraordinary visions and "divine appointments" for Peter to widen his heart to love and accept Gentiles as brothers in Christ (see Acts 10): "You yourselves know how unlawful it is for a Jew to associate with or to visit any one of another nation; but God has shown me that I should not call any man common or unclean" (Acts 10:28).

Jesus illustrated the message of universal love and mercy in many of his parables. Whether in the parable of the good Samaritan, the wedding feast, or the vineyard and the laborers, Jesus made it clear that whoever is in need is our neighbor, and just because we are already his disciples does not give us warrant to look down on others or narrow the circle of love: "John said to him, 'Teacher, we saw a man casting out demons in your name, and we forbade him, because he was not following us.' But Jesus said, 'Do not forbid him; for no one who does a mighty work in my name will be able soon after to speak evil of me. For he that is not against us is for us' " (Mk 9:38–40).

"And men will come from east and west, and from north and south, and sit at table in the kingdom of God" (Lk 13:29).

"I have other sheep, that are not of this fold; I must bring them also, and they will heed my voice. So there shall be one flock, one shepherd" (Jn 10:16).

It is not uncommon to read of various Catholic saints extending compassion to a poor beggar or to a leper only to find that it was Christ himself.

The words of St. Augustine are a help in keeping our hearts open to those "outside": "How many wolves there are inside the fold and how many sheep outside it!"[8]

As Vatican Council II put it: "Even though incorporated into the Church, one who does not however persevere in charity is not saved. . . . All children of the Church should nevertheless remember that their exalted condition results, not from their own merits, but from the grace of Christ. If they fail to respond in thought, word and deed to that grace, not only shall they not be saved, but they shall be the more severely judged."[9]

How does all this apply to us? In so many ways!

How important it is to open our hearts to the weak, the poor, the unimportant in the eyes of the world, the uninfluential, the unpowerful (see James 2:1–9).

How important it is to love not just those of our own group or community or movement but also the whole Church.

How important it is to love not just members of our own Church, local, national, or international, but all the members of Christ's Body, in whatever denomination or Church they find themselves.

How important it is to love the Jews.

How important it is to love Buddhists and Moslems and Hindus, animists, secular humanists, liberals and conservatives, atheists, the lukewarm, black and white and brown and yellow and red, sinners and saints, male and female, sick and healthy, well balanced and dysfunctional—everyone, all whom God created and Christ died for, and the Spirit has been poured into our hearts to enable us to love.

Without at all compromising what we believe and the great

---

[8] Cited in Cantalamessa, *Life in the Lordship of Christ,* p. 152.
[9] Constitution on the Church *Lumen Gentium,* 14.

treasure with which we have been entrusted, an attitude of respect to members of the various world religions as well as to unbelievers is an essential way of showing Christ's love.

Pope John Paul II has pointed out on more than one occasion that as we proclaim Christ we need to do so "in the Gospel spirit of understanding and peace". He further points out that in his own writings on the mission of the Church there is "a message of love and respect for our brothers and sisters of other traditions".[10]

Cardinal Danneels has pointed out that the approach of Francis of Assisi to the Moslems, which was one of great respect for them and their beliefs, is still remembered to this day: "When Francis of Assisi went to talk to the Muslims and their sheik, he proclaimed Jesus with such great respect for the belief of the sheik and the Muslims that even after six centuries he is still remembered. I think that we too should aim at developing this attitude."[11]

Father Marie-Dominique Philippe puts it well: "A Catholic is someone who has a heart as big as Christ's. Therefore being 'Catholic' is the same as being 'universal'. That means to have an eye for everything just as Christ has an eye for everything. A Catholic is someone who—according to the powerful expression of a disciple of Origen—considers himself to be responsible for all of humanity through the Heart of Christ. . . . And we aren't asked to give our opinion and to say, 'Oh, what a bunch of imbeciles: where do they think they are going . . . ?' No, we are asked to *carry* them. For that matter, when we are carrying them, we are not in the least concerned about judging them since all of our energy is required to carry them and to bring them to God."[12]

An impossible task? Yes, impossible, without the help of Christ. But with him, all things are possible.

[10] John Paul II, "Dialogue Leads to Genuine Conversion", *L'Osservatore Romano* (English ed.), November 18, 1992, p. 9.

[11] Cardinal Godfried Danneels, "Do We Still Have the Courage to Proclaim Christ?" *FIAT Newsletter,* no. 3 (April 1992): 3.

[12] Fr. Marie-Dominique Philippe, O.P., *Follow the Lamb . . .* (Laredo, Tex.: Congregation of St. John, 1991), p. 35.

Love, Poured into Our Hearts

On our own, we cannot love like this. We would have a nervous breakdown if we tried. But the love of God himself, infinite love, abundant love, is poured out into our hearts by the Holy Spirit: "Therefore, since we are justified by faith, we have peace with God through our Lord Jesus Christ. Through him we have obtained access to this grace in which we stand, and we rejoice in our hope of sharing the glory of God. More than that, we rejoice in our sufferings, knowing that suffering produces endurance, and endurance produces character, and character produces hope, and hope does not disappoint us, because God's love has been poured into our hearts through the Holy Spirit which has been given to us" (Rom 5:1–5).

"I made known to them thy name, and I will make it known, that the love with which thou hast loved me may be in them, and I in them" (Jn 17:26).

"For this reason I bow my knees before the Father, from whom every family in heaven and on earth is named, that according to the riches of his glory he may grant you to be strengthened with might through his Spirit in the inner man, and that Christ may dwell in your hearts through faith; that you, being rooted and grounded in love, may have power to comprehend with all the saints what is the breadth and length and height and depth, and to know the love of Christ which surpasses knowledge, that you may be filled with all the fulness of God" (Eph 3:14–19).

The love with which we are loved, the love that has come to dwell and abide in us and with us, Christ himself, who is love and the source of all love, gives us the strength to love, to forgive, to be forgiven, and to keep on loving. We need to know with what love we are loved in order to be able to love as Christ commands us. Once we know that love and keep knowing that love, abiding in that love in union with Christ, we can then be guided, motivated, strengthened, encouraged, consoled, and empowered by it: "But, as it is written, 'What no eye has seen, nor ear heard, nor the heart of man conceived, what God has prepared for those who love him,' God has revealed to us through the Spirit" (1 Cor 2:9–10).

"Put on then, as God's chosen ones, holy and beloved, compassion, kindness, lowliness, meekness, and patience, forbearing one another and, if one has a complaint against another, forgiving each other; as the Lord has forgiven you, so you also must forgive. And above all these put on love, which binds everything together in perfect harmony" (Col 3:12–14).

"For thy steadfast love is before my eyes, and I walk in faithfulness to thee" (Ps 26:3).

"I will rejoice and be glad for thy steadfast love" (Ps 31:7).

"Many are the pangs of the wicked, but steadfast love surrounds him who trusts in the Lord" (Ps 32:10).

"How precious is thy steadfast love, O God! The children of men take refuge in the shadow of thy wings" (Ps 36:7).

Once we know the riches and treasures, the steadfastness, purity, and power of God's love for us, we can then love what that love loves, genuinely, from the heart.

Rather than love money, wickedness, places of honor, the appearance of being good, the praises of men, once we know with what love we are being loved, we can love goodness, the praise that comes from God, his kingdom, his name, his will, his people, his word, his truth, his judgments, his commands, his ways (see Ps 119:97, 119, 127, 167).

Only when we know how we are loved can we definitively turn from the "sin that clings so closely" in the deepest recesses of our mind, heart, emotions, and will and love goodness and hate wickedness. The secret tolerance of wickedness, affection for wickedness, indulged attraction to wickedness can be broken only by the love that sets us free. Only when we have confidence that the eternal love calling us to surrender far surpasses the secret attraction of sin and its false but powerful allure will we have the freedom and courage really to break with it, burn our bridges, and put it to death.

Only when we know something of the depth of the love with which we are loved can we trust that in all the circumstances of life, even the most difficult, and seemingly most tragic, love will find a way to bring victory out of apparent defeat: "Do not be afraid of sudden panic, or of the ruin of the wicked, when it comes; for the Lord will be your confidence and will keep your foot from being caught" (Prov 3:25–26).

I was very touched a few years ago when Cardinal Suenens sent me a copy of a short spiritual autobiography he had written as he prepared for death. It sums up the spiritual lessons he learned over a long lifetime of following the Lord:

> At 86 years, the Eternal tomorrow is near. . . . I am experiencing again today my childhood intuition, which understood, from life's very start, how transient it is, and that only eternal life is really life.
>
> This life of tomorrow will be the definite entry into the Kingdom of God where all is light, love and tenderness. . . . As death approaches, I see on every page of my life a watermark, so to say, that shows how the attentive Love of God has watched over my daily goings and comings, so much is it true that what we called chance or coincidental circumstances were but Providence at work with infinite delicacy. . . . As a farewell to those who read this booklet, I should like to say to them:
>
> The secret of Christian life and of its serenity is nothing else but total and trusting abandonment to the indefectible Love of God, in *all* circumstances.
>
> and ALL means ALL
> THANK YOU, LORD
> For YESTERDAY, for TODAY, for TOMORROW.[13]

Love and Power

There is a surprising link between Christian love and spiritual power that we need to look at. The love of God that is poured out into our hearts is just that, the love of God. That love is profoundly humble, but it is also profoundly free and powerful. It does not often look like the freedom and power that the world recognizes, but it is a freedom and power that make what the world calls freedom and power pale in comparison. Immediately

[13] Cardinal Suenens, *Spiritual Journey* (Gravenplein, Belgium: F.I.A.T. Publications, 1990), pp. 63–71.

after the great hymn to love in 1 Corinthians 13, Paul goes on to say: "Make love your aim, and earnestly desire the spiritual gifts, especially that you may prophesy" (1 Cor 14:1).

This is a very strong exhortation to seek after love *and* the gifts of the Spirit. Sometimes the two are put in opposition. Some give the impression that since "the greatest of these is love", that the gifts of the Spirit for action, often "external", are unimportant or somehow beneath a truly spiritual or "interior" person. Others may give the impression that what really matter are the gifts of the Spirit for action and that love is nice but not really "where it's at". The teaching of Scripture is to make love our aim *and* earnestly desire spiritual gifts. "Make love your aim" and "earnestly desire" are very strong exhortations indeed. The love of God seeks to manifest itself in actions inspired by and gifts given by the Holy Spirit. Goodness and love are diffusive of themselves.

John Paul II has recently made some very strong statements on the importance of the charisms for the life of the Church. He begins by quoting the Second Vatican Council: "It is not only through the sacraments and the ministrations of the Church that the Holy Spirit makes holy the People of God, leads them and enriches them with his virtues. Allotting his gifts as he wills (cf. 1 Cor 12:11), he also distributes special graces among the faithful of every rank. By these gifts he makes them fit and ready to undertake various tasks and offices for the renewal and building up of the Church" (Constitution on the Church *Lumen Gentium,* 12). He goes on to say:

> Therefore the People of God's sharing in the messianic mission is not obtained only through the Church's ministerial structure and sacramental life. It also occurs in another way, that of the spiritual gifts or charisms.
>
> This doctrine, recalled by the Council, is based on the New Testament and helps to show that the development of the ecclesial community does not depend only on the institution of ministries and sacraments, but is also furthered by the free and unforeseeable gifts of the Spirit, who works outside established channels, too. Because of this bestowal of special graces it is apparent that the universal priesthood of the ecclesial

community is led by the Spirit with a sovereign freedom ("as he wishes", St. Paul says [1 Cor 12:11]) that is often amazing.... Each of us receives from God many gifts which are appropriate for us personally and for our mission. Because of this diversity, no individual way of holiness or mission is ever identical to the others. The Holy Spirit shows respect for each person and wants to foster in each one an original development of the spiritual life and the giving of witness.

After singling out the importance of the prophetic function in the Church and the importance of responsible freedom of speech, the Pope concludes: "If this is the profile of freedom of speech, we can say that there is no opposition between charism and institution, because it is the one Spirit who enlivens the Church with the various charisms. The spiritual gifts also help in exercising the ministries. They are bestowed by the Spirit to help advance the kingdom of God. In this sense we can say that the Church is a community of charisms."[14]

And Vatican II, in its Decree on the Ministry and Life of Priests, specifically urges the official pastors of the Church to foster and encourage the charismatic gifts of the Spirit: "While trying the spirits if they be of God, they must discover with faith, recognize with joy, and foster with diligence the many and varied charismatic gifts of the laity, whether these be of a humble or more exalted kind."[15]

Of course, in practice it is often not easy for new things the Spirit is doing to find their proper place in the life of the Church; love and patience are much needed.

As Bishop Cordes has pointed out in a recent book, we have much to learn from our history in this regard:

Yet the duty of fostering these charisms urged by the Council does not seem to be easy to fulfil. Already at the biblical level the Apostle of the Gentiles felt obliged to admonish his community: "Quench not the Spirit. Despise not the gift of prophecy!" (1 Thess 5:20) ... The Apostle of the Gentiles himself

---

[14] John Paul II, "Charisms Have Role in Church's Life", *L'Osservatore Romano* (English ed.), July 1, 1992, p. 11.

[15] Decree on the Ministry and Life of Priests *Presbyterorum Ordinis, 9.*

had to struggle for the essential nucleus of the Gospel of salvation, which he saw jeopardized among the Galatians (cf. Gal 3:1). . . . Evidently the ecclesial community has difficulty in allowing new expressions or movements of the spirit, however well-tested and approved, to operate freely. . . . Spiritual movements are not appreciated in the way that the statistical recurrence of the expression would suggest. On the contrary, their impulses are greeted with scepticism; they come into friction with the traditional structures; they frequently fail to clear the hurdles of the postconciliar consultative bodies; they are often passed over in silence by the Church's media; they are regarded as playgrounds for outsiders . . . even more striking is the lesson of history which shows how God's salvific initiative is often hindered by human blindness. This is borne out by the life and work of some great renewers: Anthony, the father of the desert; Athanasius, the theologian; Benedict, the founder of the Benedictine order; Francis and Ignatius. All these and many others have a warning for us: it was only after their death that they were accorded the "honours of the altar"; during their lifetime they ran up against the most obstinate resistance at every level of the ecclesiastical hierarchy.[16]

It is not enough to sit back and let love come to us. We are told to seek eagerly after love, to seek God himself, to seek eagerly to walk the way of love.

It is not enough to be "open" to the spiritual gifts; instead we must set our hearts on them, positively to desire them, pray for them, and desire to yield to them. Love impels us to avail ourselves of all that God is willing to make available as a way of helping and serving others, of setting others free, of encouraging and strengthening them. Not to set our hearts on spiritual gifts is to fall back into that cowardice, timidity, or fear that Scripture explicitly warns us against: "Hence I remind you to rekindle the gift of God that is within you through the laying on of my hands; for God did not give us a spirit of timidity but a spirit of power and love and self-control" (2 Tim 1:6–7).

A contemporary prophetic preacher puts it well: "We must recover holiness without legalism, boldness without presumption

---

[16] Bishop Paul Cordes, *Charisms and New Evangelization* (Middlegreen, Slough, U.K.: St. Paul Publications, 1992), pp. 10–14.

and power without pride. When the church does this she will gain the attention of both the heavens and the earth, because her God will be with her in His manifest presence."[17]

There is an energy, a power, a strength imparted by God through the Holy Spirit, love poured out into our hearts that energizes us to act: "Him we proclaim, warning every man and teaching every man in all wisdom, that we may present every man mature in Christ. For this I toil, striving with all the energy which he mightily inspires within me" (Col 1:28–29).

Love and spiritual power are intended to be profoundly linked; when they are not, something less than the fullness of the gospel is present.

Strengthened now, in faith, hope, love, and spiritual power, let us look again at the situation in which we and the whole Church are living.

[17] Paul Cain, "The Jealousy of God", *Morning Star Journal,* vol. 2, no. 3, p. 49.

Chapter Six

Jesus, Us, and the End of an Age

There certainly have been terrible times in the history of the world and the history of the Church.

Listen to the words of St. Jerome, who died in the early fifth century (419), about the state of the clergy in his time, a time still referred to as the "early Church":

> There are others—and here I am speaking of men of my own class—who aspire to the office of presbyter or deacon just for the purpose of seeing women with greater freedom. As a consequence their one concern is about their dress, that it may be finely perfumed, and that their foot may not puff out because of a loose shoe. They roll their hair into ringlets with the aid of curling tongs, their fingers sparkle with rings. If they go into the street when it's wet, they walk mincingly, scarcely touching the ground, so as not to spatter their feet with mud. When one sees them, one would take them for suitors rather than priests. For some of these men the whole business of their life consists in discovering the names of married women and finding out about their homes and characters.[1]

And the Roman Empire in which the early Church found herself was in its later stages certainly corrupt in ways very similar to our own society today.

Yet in our time there is a quality to the evil that is unfolding and a worldwide scope that is perhaps unique. Never before have

[1] Cited in Bishop Paul Cordes, *Charisms and New Evangelization* (Middlegreen, Slough, U.K.: St. Paul Publications, 1992), p. 25.

the means been available for the entire planet to be turned into a global village through the advances in telecommunications. Even as I write new worldwide satellite systems are being prepared, and telecommunications and computer technologies are converging in the service of international business, entertainment, and education.

The accompanying breakdown of traditional cultures and societies where religious, moral, and family ties were strong and the mass migration from rural areas to urban centers happening all over the world are unfortunately leaving the individual more and more isolated, alone, and vulnerable to the destruction of traditional values being promoted by the international pagan culture. Mesmerized, almost lulled or drugged, by increasingly spectacular advances in color, sound, and sensation, "virtual reality", men are in danger of being turned into zombies, consuming pawns of an international culture driven by greed, lust, and perhaps a hatred of God.

We have seen the statistics. Has there ever been such a mass turning away from Christ and the Church in all the "Christian" lands such as we have seen in our lifetime?

I think the answer is clearly not. Seventeen hundred years of Christendom are falling into ruins around us. An age is coming to an end, not just the end of a remarkable century but the end of seventeen hundred years of Christendom. The greatest apostasy since the birth of the Church is clearly far advanced all around us. Whether it is *the* great apostasy spoken of by the Scriptures that must take place before the Lord's return time will certainly tell: "Now concerning the coming of our Lord Jesus Christ and our assembling to meet him, we beg you, brethren, not to be quickly shaken in mind or excited . . . unless the apostasy comes first, and the man of lawlessness is revealed. . . . And you know what is restraining him now so that he may be revealed in his time. For the mystery of lawlessness is already at work; only he who now restrains it will do so until he is out of the way. And then the lawless one will be revealed, and the Lord Jesus will slay him with the breath of his mouth and destroy him by his appearing and his coming. The coming of the lawless one by the activity of Satan will be with all power and with pretended signs and wonders" (2 Th 2:1–9).

But while the smoke of Satan, as Paul VI described it, may indeed have entered the Church, the source of the fire of Satan is "in the world", where it also devours souls.

The apostasy that is spoken of in Scripture not only describes a great falling away from God in the Church but also has overtones of a generalized rebellion against God that permeates society as a whole and the political and legal and educational powers of the age. Here we clearly see the hand of the "lawless one" and the progressive removal of any restrainer on the disordered desires of fallen humanity.

The sexual revolution, which is perhaps the special characteristic of our generation, is at heart a massive rebellion against God: against his ways, his laws, his nature, the structure of creation itself. As such it is profoundly unrealistic and suicidal. Yet even when the unrealistic, self-destructive, suicidal aspects of this rebellion are clear to see, those who are committed to it would prefer to proceed with it, no matter what the cost, even if it be the destruction of vast numbers of their fellows and themselves as well. The words of Scripture come to mind: "And then the lawless one will be revealed ... with all wicked deception for those who are to perish, because they refused to love the truth and so be saved. Therefore, God sends upon them a strong delusion, to make them believe what is false, so that all may be condemned who did not believe the truth but had pleasure in unrighteousness" (2 Th 2:8, 10–11).

It is becoming clearer that in the ranks of the radical feminists, in their quest for what they euphemistically call "reproductive freedom", and in the ranks of the gay movement, in their futile effort to call sin virtue, and virtue sin, there is a "spiritual" commitment that will not be dissuaded by the facts but sometimes contains an element of profound hatred of God and of the one whom he has sent, Jesus, and the Church, which is his Body. When such is the case, we see the spirit of the anti-Christ here.

It is particularly disturbing when we see signs of this within the heart of the Church.

About 2,000 women from major Protestant denominations gathered in Minneapolis where they gave praise to a female personification of God, laughed at the patriarchal tradition of the church and shared honeyed milk in a ritual that affirmed the sensuality of women.... "Our maker Sophia, we are women in your image; with the hot blood of our wombs we give form to new life.... With nectar between our thighs we invite a lover.... With our warm body fluids we remind the world of its pleasures and sensations...." The critics are also protesting a speaker's call for "lesbian, bisexual and transsexual women" to join her onstage. The audience applauded as about 100 women answered.... "We did not last night name the name of Jesus," said the Rev. Barbara K. Lundblad, the pastor of Our Savior's Atonement Lutheran Church in New York City. "Nor have we done anything in the name of the Father and of the Son and of the Holy Spirit," she continued, stirring laughter and cheers.... "I don't think we need a theory of atonement at all," said the Rev. Delores S. Williams, who teaches at Union Theological Seminary in New York. "I don't think we need folks hanging on crosses and blood dripping and weird stuff...." "We will all shed the excess baggage of patriarchy and assume the interwoven stance of a people doing justice or we will die trying," said Mary Hunt, co-director of the Women's Alliance for Theology, Ethics and Ritual. "Whether it is Christian or not is frankly, darling, something about which I no longer give a pope."[2]

A "brave, new world" without the traditional family is being heralded, made possible by the artificial insemination of lesbians, patriarchy banished, children raised by paid workers from birth onward. The terror of Aldous Huxley's *Brave New World*, of George Orwell's *1984* is already here, just a few years later than expected. *That Hideous Strength* of C. S. Lewis can be seen from time to time exposed in the pictures of hatred, rage, and lawlessness that occasionally make it into print. Whether it be the desecration of the Eucharist at St. Patrick's Cathedral in the name of "gay

---

[2] Peter Steinfels, "Female Concept of God Is Shaking Protestants", *New York Times*, May 14, 1994, p. 7.

rights" or the arrogance of television executives who boast of the revolution in values they have pulled off, we see again what Psalm 2 speaks of as "the nation's rage".

With the collapse of communism came hopes for peace and prosperity and a "new world order". With the signing of an agreement between Israel and the Palestine Liberation Organization, hope surged again. Yet increasingly there is a rumbling under the surface of the nations. Age-old hatreds and manifestations of evil are erupting, economic problems are mounting, nuclear weapons do not seem to be disappearing but may be proliferating, and increasingly the situation looks like it is out of the control of mere politicians.

As Cardinal Ratzinger has recently put it: "It is evident today that all the great civilizations are suffering in varying ways from the crises of values and ideas which in some parts of the world assume dangerous forms. . . . In many places, we are on the brink of ungovernability."[3]

An article recently appeared in the *Atlantic Monthly* entitled "The Coming Anarchy", which painted a frightening picture of the growing chaos in the world and descent into lawlessness.[4]

Prophetic voices are being raised warning us not to be lulled into complacency or false hopes: "We must realize the seriousness of these times. There is no greater judgment than war. There is no greater devastation than when modern armies sweep over a land unleashing their powers of destruction and death. With the collapse of communism the whole world seemed to breathe a sigh of relief, but as the apostle Paul warned, 'When people say "There is peace and security," then sudden destruction will come upon them as travail comes upon a woman with child; and there will be no escape' (1 Th 5:3). At the very time when men begin to think that peace and safety are really possible, the most devastating wars of all are looming in our future—wars

[3] Cardinal Joseph Ratzinger, "Ratzinger Speaks", *Catholic World Report*, January 1994, p. 24.

[4] Robert D. Kaplan, "The Coming Anarchy", *Atlantic Monthly*, February 1994, pp. 44–76.

that will arise between peoples within every nation, even every city."[5]

Zbigniew Brzezinski, who played a key role in the administration of President Jimmy Carter as national security advisor, has recently written a book, *Out of Control,* where he makes precisely that point.[6] He points out that while the collapse of communism has given way to an out-of-control situation in the former Soviet empire, the Western liberal democracies as they lose their grounding in absolute moral values have virtually nothing of substance to offer, and this vacuity is increasingly being perceived.

> But the rich West today increasingly projects to the rest of the world an image of hedonistic, morally relativistic, value-neutral social order which I fear will not be adequately responsive to the socio-economic and emotional dilemmas that the vast majority of the global population living in poor countries faces. . . . If liberal democracy is not able to infuse its culture and philosophical character with a somewhat more morally driven set of imperatives, then I fear that what the West stands for today will be seen increasingly as an empty shell, as reflecting progressive demoralization, as foreshadowing a way of life that is ultimately aimless. . . . When I talk of our global situation being out of control, I have very much in mind also the fact we are now at a time in which we are gaining all sorts of powers which we have never had before, but we have no standard or criteria with which to determine how we should use these powers.
>
> I think genetic self-alteration is very much an example of this, and we're going to be able to do things to ourselves which are literally unimaginable. We are going to have transplants, genetic manipulations; we are going to have alterations of personalities, bodies, brains, memories. Unless we have some criteria for judgment, . . . it will be a mechanical, amoral, de-humanized process and it will probably be pursued in a setting of mass global inequality . . . the human being may alter himself to the degree he ceases to be "human". . . . If we do not know

[5] Rick Joyner, "The Coming Catastrophe", *Morning Star,* September 1993, p. 2.

[6] Zbigniew Brzezinski, *Out of Control: Global Turmoil on the Eve of the Twenty-first Century* (New York: Macmillan, 1993).

what is right and what is wrong, if we do not have some notion of the superiority of the spirit over the material we are going to lose over time the essence of our humanness. I think that is ultimately what is at stake in the contemporary global crisis of the spirit.[7]

But the very evil that men do and God permits contains within it the seeds of redemption. It is very true that where sin abounds, grace abounds still more.

As Chiara Lubich, foundress of the Focolari Movement, has said, "With His Divine pedagogy, through the collapse of all things, He is showing us today . . . that He is All."[8]

These words of Chiara Lubich remind me of a prophecy that was given at St. Peter's Basilica in Rome in 1975 when the Catholic charismatic renewal movement was received for the first time in a public way by the Pope. It seems relevant here.

> Because I love you I want to show you what I am doing in the world today. I want to prepare you for what is to come. Days of darkness are coming on the world, days of tribulation. . . . Buildings that are now standing will not be standing. Supports that are there for my people now will not be there. I want you to be prepared, my people, to know only me and to cleave to me and to have me in a way deeper than ever before. I will lead you into the desert. . . . I will strip you of everything that you are depending on now, so you depend just on me. A time of darkness is coming on the world, but a time of glory is coming for my church, a time of glory is coming for my people. I will pour out on you all the gifts of my Spirit. I will prepare you for spiritual combat; I will prepare you for a time of evangelism that the world has never seen. And when you have nothing but me, you will have everything: land, fields, homes, and brothers and sisters and love and joy and peace more than ever before. Be ready, my people, I want to prepare you. . . . [9]

[7] Peter Mullen, "Deeply Ingrained, Almost Instinctive, Imperatives: An Interview with Zbigniew Brzezinski", *Catholic World Report,* August–September 1993, pp. 50–53.

[8] Chiara Lubich, "A Number of Theological-Spiritual Aspects for Deepening the Faith Today", published in the 1991–1992 bulletin of the Pontifical Council for the Laity, *Spectacle of Holiness for the World,* p. 84.

[9] *New Covenant,* July 1975, p. 26.

And the witness of those who have already lived through this stripping is also relevant. For the African, faced with the growing chaos in Africa, Cardinal Vlk, of the Czech Republic, shared his own testimony as an encouragement.

> Hearing them speak of the enormous problems of evangelization in Africa, I thought of that collapse of all the structures and all those means which we experienced in Eastern and Central Europe under the communist persecution. In that situation only Jesus remained; only his gospel, the sacraments and communion among us in small underground groups where reciprocal love reigned. Thus the Church and her evangelizing mission developed. Stripped of everything, we have discovered "the nearness of God", the presence of the risen Christ there "where two or three are gathered in his name" (cf. Mt 18:28).[10]

No matter how great the power of evil at work in the world, the power at work in the sons and daughters of God, in the Church, is greater by far. God will always preserve a remnant, bigger than we might expect, who will be his own in a special way. The evil and suffering God permits men to do have as one of their purposes the purification and preparation of a remnant that belongs to him:

> For I will leave in the midst of you
> a people humble and lowly.
> They shall seek refuge in the name of the Lord,
> those who are left in Israel;
> they shall do no wrong
> and utter no lies,
> nor shall there be found in their mouth
> a deceitful tongue (Zeph 3:12–13).

God is looking for a meek and humble people who will simply trust in him:

> In the whole land, says the Lord,
> two thirds shall be cut off and perish,

---

[10] Archbishop Miloslav Vlk, "The Exchange of Gifts", *L'Osservatore Romano* (English ed.), April 27, 1994, p. 10.

and one third shall be left alive.
And I will bring this third into the fire,
and refine them as one refines silver,
and test them as gold is tested.
They will call on my name,
and I will hear them.
I will say, "They are my people";
and they will say, "The Lord is my God" (Zech 13:8–9).

And even when things look extremely bad, there are always more who are faithful to him than zealous prophets or renewal movements might expect. When Elijah reached a point of great discouragement, God pointed out to him that he was not alone, that there were seven thousand who had remained faithful to God (see 1 Kings 19:14–18).

God has made all mankind with an instinct for truth, a sense of right and wrong, and most of all a hunger for himself. Quite simply, we are constructed in such a way as never to be able to reach happiness apart from God. As we try one thing and another apart from God, we doom ourselves to frustration and eventual failure.

Eventually, truth will out. Perhaps after great suffering and great waiting, but truth will eventually out.

Even in the concentration camps of World War II, where evil was so concentrated and so apparently triumphant, story after story of the powerful working of God's grace continues to be revealed. The life of St. Maximillian Kolbe is increasingly well known. One story that is not is that of a secularized Jewish agnostic, Etty Hillesum, a young Dutch woman whose diaries have only recently been discovered, who by the grace of God was being led to a life of faith and prayer and love all the way to Auschwitz and who was able to interpret something of the "signs of the times". These words were written during a short respite from a transit camp in Holland shortly before she was sent to Auschwitz, where she and her whole family died: "How is it that this stretch of heathland surrounded by barbed wire, through which so much human misery has flooded, nevertheless remains inscribed in my memory as something almost lovely? How is it that my spirit, far from being oppressed, seemed to grow lighter and brighter there? It is because I read the signs of the times and they did not seem meaningless to me . . . there among the barracks, full of hunted and persecuted people, I found confirmation of my love of life. . . . After this war two torrents will be unleashed on the world: a torrent of loving-kindness and a torrent of hatred. And then I knew: I should take the field against hatred."[11]

In the very darkest days and hours, in the midst of what is certainly a great apostasy, the seeds of a new Pentecost and a new evangelization are being sown.

The first signs of this new springtime can already be seen. We have done our best in this book to present some of them to you. A century that has been marked by the sign of the greatest global evil that has yet been seen may eventually be seen as a century in which God poured out his Holy Spirit and the gospel was preached with more effect than at any time since the early days of the Church.

As we approach the end of the century, it appears that the darkness is growing darker and yet the light is shining more brightly.

Hans Urs von Balthasar points out why this is so:

As far as the person of Jesus is concerned, the Incarnation of the Word is complete when he returns, glorified, to the Father; but it still remains to be carried out with regard to mankind as a whole. The intention is that mankind will be incorporated in the new and ultimate principle through the sacramental mediation of the "body" of Christ, the Church. The individual can freely allow this to happen, but he can also freely refuse; *and since, as a result of Christ's victory, the anti-Christian powers have become really alert and ready for combat, his victory ushers in the most decidedly dramatic period of world history.* As the history of man's theological liberation marches forward, the pendulum swings more and more freely, both for each individual and for mankind as a whole, between Yes and No. The Apocalypse that concludes the word of God shows in the clearest manner that

---

[11] Etty Hillesum, *An Interrupted Life* (New York: Washington Square Press, Pocket Books, 1985), p. 219.

there can be no question of one-dimensional progress in history: *the nearer the end approaches, the more fierce becomes the battle. . . . The more the Holy Spirit becomes present in history, the more prevalent is what Jesus calls the sin against the Holy Spirit.* [12]

At one time in Israel's history these woeful words were spoken: "And there was no prophet in those days; the voice of the Lord was not heard in the Land." That cannot be said today. Many voices are being raised in warning, pointing out, in a remarkable unity, the way the Spirit is leading us to go. I have tried to acquaint you with some of these voices in this book.

There seems to be an intensification in the work of the evil one; perhaps he knows his days are short. But rather than fear what is unfolding, we need to see it as an opportunity for God to show his power. Truth will out, and we need to remember that the truth is Jesus. Jesus reigns, in the midst of his enemies; in the midst of conflict and setbacks and temporary satanic victories, Jesus reigns. But the day is coming when he will arise, and his enemies will be scattered, and the kingdoms of this world will become the kingdom of God and of his Son.

Are there not signs already that "the wrath of God is revealed from heaven against all ungodliness and wickedness of men who by their wickedness suppress the truth" (Rom 1:18)?

The little-told story of the early 1994 Southern California earthquakes is amazing:

The overwhelming media coverage of last week's California earthquake failed to mention that the quake's epicenter is the hub of America's $3 billion X-rated video industry.

The triangle formed by the San Fernando Valley communities of Chatsworth, Northridge and Canoga Park—tightly encircling the epicenter of the powerful quake—contains nearly 70 companies that crank out more than 95 percent of the roughly 1,400 pornographic videos made every year in the United States. . . .

God's will or not, there is no doubt that the devastation in

---

[12] Hans Urs von Balthasar, *Theo-Drama*, vol. 3, *The Dramatis Personae: The Person in Christ* (San Francisco: Ignatius Press, 1992), pp. 37–38. Emphasis mine.

California's video-Sodom has been close to apocalyptic. A telephone survey of various Northridge and other Valley-area studios discloses that—with no exceptions—every company has suffered some major damage, much of it immobilizing.

Probably the most devastated has been the giant of the industry.... "It's all over for them.... Their whole operation is gone—all their equipment and masters."[13]

We are privileged now to live in a time that while exceedingly difficult is also a time where we have seen and will see yet more of the great interventions of God.

How long will it be? How long can we last, can our children last, in such a powerful pagan culture and such a weakened Church? No matter how long: he will be with us every step along the way, every moment of every day, in the midst of every difficulty.

I suspect that the length of the tribulations is somehow bound up with our response. It remains true for us today, as it was for God's people of old: "When I shut up the heavens so that there is no rain, or command the locust to devour the land, or send pestilence among my people, if my people who are called by my name humble themselves, and pray and seek my face, and turn from their wicked ways, then I will hear from heaven, and will forgive their sin and heal their land" (2 Chron 7:13–14).

I suspect that whether the days of our exile are shortened or not depends on the honesty and depth of our repentance, humility, and prayer as well as on the mercy of God.

But one thing is sure. God is not worried about the situation. He is not anxious. He is not afraid. He is in control and will see that all things work out to the good of those who love him. The nations may rage in their folly; God "laughs":

> Why do the nations conspire
> and the peoples plot in vain?
> The kings of the earth set themselves,

[13] William Arnold, "Pornography Industry Disrupted by Quake", New York Times News Service, published in the *Ann Arbor News,* January 25, 1994, p. A3.

and the rulers take counsel together,
against the Lord and his anointed, saying,
"Let us burst their bonds asunder,
and cast their cords from us."
He who sits in the heavens laughs;
the Lord has them in derision.
Then he will speak to them in his wrath,
and terrify them in his fury, saying,
"I have set my king
on Zion, my holy hill" (Ps 2:1–6).

As one contemporary Christian writer has put it:

The Lord laughs at the foolishness of those in the rebellion, that
they imagine God's judgements cannot reach them. In truth,
our cities' decline, our insurmountable national debt, the AIDS
crisis, the breakdown of our families are all consequences of our
sins, the result of God's disapproval with our nation. Consider
the Soviet communists. Even as they were shaking their fists
toward God, He was undermining their rebellion against Him.
And, even as they are now experiencing a national spiritual
awakening, so the hour of God shall once again come to our
nation.... Yet more than waiting for evil to ripen, the Lord
waits for us, His church. For while the world shall demand, and
receive, the reign of hell, the goal of the praying church shall be
for the reign of heaven. You see, *all* of God's prophecies shall
be fulfilled: those concerning evil and those concerning good....
As Christ's church, we do not deserve a national revival, but
Jesus does!... Therefore, while the perverse strive toward complete rejection of God, even as their mocking words fill the air
with curses, God's unchangeable promise to us is "ASK OF ME,
and I will surely give the nations!"
   While you sit in jail for your protest against abortion, even as
witchcraft flourishes in our schools, while our government
leaders counsel against the Lord—ASK![14]

As the prayer at the sign of peace in the eucharistic liturgy says:
"Look not upon our sins, but on the faith of your Church."

[14] Francis Frangipane, "Ask of Me!", *River of Life Newsletter,* January 1993,
p. 3.

The faith of the Church is ultimately the faith of Jesus dwelling in her, praying for her and with her, worshipping the Father in spirit and in truth.

Our task in the difficult times ahead is simply to abide in him, believe in him, and do whatever he tells us.

But already a great light is shining in the darkness, and the darkness will never be able to put it out. The Son of God is rising, eyes are turning toward him, and the Spirit is being poured out, disciples made, the gospel preached, and works of mercy done. You can see it all around you if you have eyes to see and ears to hear.

He is coming to destroy "the covering that is cast over all peoples, the veil that is spread over all nations" (Is 25:7).

You can find it in small parish communities across the world where those who believe and pray are finding each other at daily Mass and elsewhere, are loving each other and caring for one another and praying for and sharing the good news with others. You can see it in the many movements that are helping so many live a life for and with Christ. You can see it in the new religious orders that are arising where men and women are once again willing to "sell everything" to follow Christ. You can find it at nighttime when holy bishops and priests weighed down by the impossibility of the situation stop in the chapel or in the quiet of their room to cry out to God for help and mercy, for the gift of his Spirit for themselves and their people. You can see it when John Paul II prays by himself in his chapel in his residence early in the morning and keeps praying when others join him for the remembrance and making present of the sacrifice of Jesus on the Cross. You can see it in the persevering faith of so many parents who struggle with the devil for the souls of their children in prayer and sacrifice. You can see it in the faces of thousands of young people around the world who have heard the good news and are responding wholeheartedly. You can see it in the great Pentecostal healing services where true signs and wonders of the kingdom are done by a merciful and powerful God.

As Cardinal Groër of Austria has said: "Everywhere I see proof of the primordial force of grace, above all in young people, but also in adults. Fortunately here in the Vienna diocese we have a very good, healthy core in every parish. And it is astonishing in how many young people something miraculous happens—not in the traditional organizations set up 40 years ago, no, not there, but where the Holy Spirit works in silence."[15]

And as Pope John Paul II has said:

> The number of those who do not know Christ and do not belong to the Church is constantly on the increase. Indeed, since the end of the Council it has almost doubled. When we consider this immense portion of humanity which is loved by the Father and for whom he sent his Son, the urgency of the Church's mission is obvious.... God is opening before the Church the horizons of a humanity more fully prepared for the sowing of the Gospel. I sense that the moment has come to commit all of the Church's energies to a new evangelization and to the mission *ad gentes.* No believer in Christ, no institution of the Church can avoid this supreme duty: to proclaim Christ to all peoples.... If we look at today's world, we are struck by many negative factors that can lead to pessimism. But this feeling is unjustified: we have faith in God our Father and Lord, in his goodness and mercy. As the third millennium of the redemption draws near, God is preparing a great springtime for Christianity, and we can already see its first signs.[16]

As this springtime unfolds, we must not forget the lessons we learned in affliction, poverty, and humiliation. We must beg God to help us remember always our utter poverty and dependence on him, even as the new Pentecost and the new evangelization unfold in ever-widening circles.

Father Marie-Dominique Philippe puts it well:

> You see, the great drama of Vatican II is a little bit like this. We have to say, "All right! Accept the fact that the great tradition must be taken back to its source in poverty", the "Church of the Poor", this is what we are living.... And we must go through

[15] Guido Horst, "The Primordial Force of Grace: An Interview with Cardinal Hans Hermann Groër", 30 *Days,* no. 6 (1993): 64.

[16] John Paul II, Encyclical *Redemptoris Missio (Mission of the Redeemer),* 3, 86.

this in the midst of a springtime blossoming . . . the Church of the poor and the mystery of spring—must be experienced simultaneously. . . . Isn't this basically the major demand of the Holy Spirit? Especially if the Church must live the last era before Christ's Second Coming, if we are coming to the end of the great anticipation of Christ's Second Coming! . . . I believe that the Church is going through a final stage. . . . It can last a while, but it's a final stage. . . . The Church must simultaneously become poorer, live the mystery of John the Baptist (since John the Baptist must return at the end of time, clothed with the spirit of Elijah, to announce Christ's Second Coming) and it must live a springtime blossoming at the same time. . . . Otherwise it would never be able to accept Christ's Second Coming. How many Christians today cannot accept the fact that Christ will return?[17]

It is not a time for giving up but a time for going on. With joy, with confidence, in humility, poverty of spirit, and total dependence on God, in the glorious freedom of being sons and daughters of God.

As Cardinal Suquia of Spain has pointed out, as difficult as things are today, we must not forget how difficult they were when the Christians were a small, persecuted minority in the midst of an idolatrous, immoral, pagan empire and the secret of their success.

Looking at the first evangelization, one sees at a glance that the Church in the first centuries lacked many institutions, pastoral projects, and intellectual traditions that we have today. The difficulties for the spread of Christianity in the ancient world were not fewer than those of today, nor was the Christian faith less strange to the culture that dominated the world, a culture with a strong consciousness of its superiority and proud of itself. And, nevertheless, it is impossible not to marvel at the imposing missionary capacity of the young Church. That capacity rested only on its belonging to the resurrected Christ, on the certainty of participating in his heritage, and in the moral

[17] Fr. Marie-Dominique Philippe, O.P., *Follow the Lamb* . . . (Laredo, Tex.: Congregation of St. John, 1991), pp. 179–80.

newness—above all, communion and love—that this belonging
and this certainty engendered, in spite of the sins and weakness
of the Christians. Furthermore, when the texts of the ancient
Church make known to us the attitude with which Christians
viewed the external difficulties of the Church, it is seen that
they did not fear them, generally at least. They were similar to
those that her crucified Lord had had, and they were proclaimed
clearly in the gospel. The Christians thought, rather, that such
difficulties were an occasion for purification and growth of the
Church. The only one they feared was "him who can destroy
both soul and body in hell" (Mt 10:28). In other words, even the
very persecutions did not seem bad to them, but rather seemed
a particular grace that allowed them to give testimony to the
extent to which Christ is, for those who have known him, a
greater good than life itself. The only evil, the true evil, consists
in separating one's self from communion and from the grace of
Christ.

   This simple reflection is enough to place before our eyes
some basic differences between our own consciousness and that
of the ancient Church. To seek the surety of the faith or the
possibility of an authentic missionary proposal whose supports
do not proceed from the faith itself, but rather from a favorable
cultural or social atmosphere, or from the sustenance of the
Church by political powers is, at least, a confession of the
weakness of our faith, and an unequivocal sign that the new
evangelization must begin with ourselves.[18]

While the circumstances are difficult, the greatest difficulty
may be ourselves. We may truly need to be reevangelized ourselves,
to discover the amazing good news of salvation through faith by
grace, of belonging to only the resurrected Christ and sharing in
his inheritance, of being impelled by the Spirit to proclaim him.
   The words of Cardinal Arinze, president of the Pontifical
Council for Inter-Religious Dialogue, are relevant here:

The number of unbaptised people in Europe is growing. In
some countries a growing number of parents do not have their

---

[18] Cardinal Angel Suquia, "The New Evangelization: Some Tasks and
Risks of the Present", *Communio* 2 (Winter 1992): 1.

children baptised. And there are many immigrants who do not yet believe in Christ. Christians in Europe must not starve these people of the "surpassing worth of knowing Christ Jesus" (Phil 3:8). It is a shame for Christians that out of shyness, or fear, or human respect, or a false sense of courtesy and freedom, they do not propose Christ to non-Christians. It is true that we should engage in inter-religious dialogue and collaboration. Such dialogue can promote peace, understanding, mutual growth, greater commitment in response to God and collaboration. But this in no way replaces or opposes the proclamation of the full Gospel of Jesus Christ to other believers, non-believers and the religiously indifferent. . . .

Christians, therefore, should not settle down to becoming an ecclesiastical bourgeoisie. They should not be content with servicing a small Catholic minority, with being a diaspora that never grows. They should launch out into the deep and cast their nets courageously for a big catch, instead of lamenting that they have caught nothing all night. They should help others to open wide their doors to Jesus Christ who will give them life in abundance.[19]

Perhaps, though, it is the words of John Paul II that best sum up what we have been trying to say:

Jesus Christ, the faithful Witness, the Pastor of pastors, is in our midst. . . . With us is the Spirit of the Lord which guides the Church to the fullness of truth and renews her with the revealed word in a new Pentecost. . . . Be faithful to your baptism . . . give new life to the great gift you have received, turn your hearts and gaze to the center and origin, to him who is the basis of all happiness, the fullness of everything! Be open to Christ, welcome the Spirit, so that a new Pentecost may take place in every community! A new humanity, a joyful one, will arise from your midst; you will experience again the saving power of the Lord and "what was spoken to you by the Lord" will be fulfilled. What "was spoken to you", is his love for you, his love for each one, for all your families and peoples . . . today the Lord is passing by. He is calling you. In this moment of grace,

[19] Cardinal Francis Arinze, *The Essence of Evangelisation: The Supreme Value of Knowing Jesus Christ* (Dublin: Veritas, 1990), 4.

he is once again calling you by name and renewing his covenant with you. May you listen to his voice so that you may know true, total joy and enter into his peace (cf. Ps 94:7, 11)![20]

May it be so!

[20] Pope John Paul II, "Address to Bishops of Latin America", *L'Osservatore Romano* (English ed.), October 21, 1992, p. 7, sec. 6.